Anchored to rigorous research and careful evidence-based analysis, Rhiannon Bandiera's assessment of prescription and non-prescription medicines regulation in Australia is as unflinching as it is compelling. Over the course of this book, she shows how and why existing regulatory approaches, built on a neoliberal foundation that is hard-wired to serve the economic self-interest of the pharmaceutical industry, have progressively disempowered both regulators and the public. Bandiera's bold prescription for a radical re-think of how to put health at the centre of pharmaceutical regulation is a vital contribution that could not come at a better time. For scholars and public policy experts across the globe, this book will be an invaluable source of fresh ideas on how to embed the public interest in a broad range of regulatory regimes.

**Jennifer Quaid,** *Associate Professor, Civil Law Section, Faculty of Law, University of Ottawa, Canada*

This book brilliantly exposes how the failure of regulation in Australia's medicines regulatory regime is undeniably bound up with neoliberal obsessions with "risk-based" and "responsive" regulation. The new forms of regulation have not been able to protect the public and rather have led to "regulatory disempowerment" of a regime that enables profit to triumph over people. The regulatory regime that has been consolidated during a period that Rhiannon Bandiera sharply describes as hegemonic governmentality is one in which the public interest might prevail on rare occasions, but only if this does not compromise the interests of the industry.

A familiar story, yes, but one that we need detailed politically nuanced stories to instruct us. And the sophisticated critique of power that we find in this book is urgently needed in this age. If we are living through a period of wild conspiracy theories about Big Pharma, this book provides the antidote; one that presents a reasoned critique of vested interests, but does not hold back on pointing the finger at the state and the pharmaceutical industry. Rejecting the conceptual red herring of neo-liberal versions of 'better regulation' the book powerfully calls for a wider program of social transformation to reduce the harms of both medicines and regulatory failures.

**David Whyte,** *Professor of Climate Justice and Director of the Centre for Climate Crime and Climate Justice, Queen Mary University of London*

Rhiannon Bandiera's book makes an important contribution to the field of state-corporate crime. By examining the intricate dynamics of neoliberalism in the everyday regulation of medicines, readers will no longer be content with solutions based primarily on individual and public empowerment. A highly recommended book for those seeking new solutions.

**Garry C. Gray,** *Associate Professor of Criminology and Sociology, University of Victoria, Canada*

This outstanding achievement significantly develops our understanding of 'neo-liberalism' via an impressively bold theoretical sophistication through which to view regulation, states and corporations. Its empirically rich focus on medicines reminds us that state-corporate power reaches into our bodies and cannot be challenged through law but via socially transformative change.

**Steve Tombs,** *Emeritus Professor of Criminology, The Open University*

We tend to believe that public authorities work in the best interest of the public. Unfortunately, the stream of research on state-corporate crime documents that public authorities create rather than prevent convenient opportunity structures for deviant behaviour, misconduct, and crime. The book by Rhiannon Bandiera is an important contribution to this stream of research.

**Petter Gottschalk,** *Professor, Department of Leadership and Organizational Behavior, BI Norwegian Business School, Oslo, Norway*

# Neoliberalism, State-Corporate Power and Regulatory Failure

Based on over a decade of research, this book examines the social harms of Australian prescription and non-prescription medicine regulation and how these ultimately stem from neoliberalism and its reinforcement of state and corporate power.

Neoliberalism shapes state and corporate power, regulation and the harms resulting from regulatory failure, yet the links between these themes are rarely discussed. Drawing on the concept of hegemonic neoliberal governmentality, this book critically examines Australian medicine regulation and the harms resulting from its failure in areas such as medicine quality, safety and efficacy; direct-to-consumer advertising; and marketing directed at health professionals. It traces these harms through the colonial foundations and evolution of medicine regulation in Australia, exploring both regulatory failure and the attempts at reforming this regulatory system. It argues that neoliberalism is not regulatable and reinforces and sustains itself, empowering the state and corporations while disempowering the public and those representing its interests. Thus, reducing its harms is only achievable through broader, transformative change, rather than by reforming (and thereby continuing to work within) the existing neoliberal capitalist system.

*Neoliberalism, State-Corporate Power and Regulatory Failure* will be of value to practitioners, members of the public and private sector and academics active in the fields of state, corporate and state–corporate crime, social harm and regulation, as well as to those new to the study of medicine-related harms. It will also be of interest to all those concerned about their health and the medicines they use.

**Rhiannon Bandiera** is Lecturer/Assistant Professor in Criminology at the School of Law and Criminology, Maynooth University—National University of Ireland Maynooth, Maynooth, Co Kildare, Ireland. She specialises in state–corporate crime and social harm, regulation, and their transnational dimensions.

**Routledge Studies in Crime and Society**
Edited by Hazel Croall,
*University of Glasgow*

1. Sex Crime (second edition)
   *Terry Thomas*
2. Burglary
   *R. I. Mawby*
3. Armed Robbery
   *Roger Matthews*
4. Car Crime
   *Claire Corbett*
5. Street Crime
   *Simon Hallsworth*
6. Hate Crime
   *Nathan Hall*
7. Fraud
   *Alan Doig*
8. Murder
   *Shani D'Cruze, Sandra Walklate and Samantha Pegg*
9. Safety Crimes
   *Steve Tombs and Dave Whyte*
10. State Crime
    *Alan Doig*
11. State Crime and Resistance
    *Elizabeth Stanley and Jude McCulloch*
12. Neoliberalism, State-Corporate Power and Regulatory Failure
    *Rhiannon Bandiera*

# Neoliberalism, State-Corporate Power and Regulatory Failure

## The Harms of Prescription and Non-Prescription Medicine Regulation in Australia

**Rhiannon Bandiera**

Routledge
Taylor & Francis Group
LONDON AND NEW YORK

First published 2025
by Routledge
4 Park Square, Milton Park, Abingdon, Oxon OX14 4RN

and by Routledge
605 Third Avenue, New York, NY 10158

*Routledge is an imprint of the Taylor & Francis Group, an informa business*



*British Library Cataloguing-in-Publication Data*
A catalogue record for this book is available from the British Library

ISBN: 978-1-032-25943-7 (hbk)
ISBN: 978-1-032-25944-4 (pbk)
ISBN: 978-1-003-28576-2 (ebk)

DOI: 10.4324/9781003285762

Typeset in Sabon
by Apex CoVantage, LLC

# Contents

# Preface and acknowledgements

This book, which examines the state–corporate harms of prescription and non-prescription medicines and their regulation (indeed, the failure of such regulation), and how these are attributable to neoliberalism, was not one I ever intended to write. In fact, this subject matter is quite literally something I stumbled onto when researching another subject. In 2011, the proposal I developed for my MA/PhD thesis (also something I had not intended to do) was on counterfeit medicines—in the simplest sense of the term, 'fake' versions of prescription and non-prescription medicines. These 'fake' medicines contain either the correct or incorrect ingredients or none or an insufficient amount of the active ingredients and are produced by those other than the companies legally authorised to do so. I wrote my undergraduate thesis on medicine counterfeiting, situating the analysis in the context of transnational organised crime. I was particularly interested in the overlap between the illegal and legal markets for and supply of prescription and non-prescription medicines in Australia and globally, and how and why counterfeit medicines end up in legal markets and supply chains, including pharmacies and hospitals (harming patients through their unknowing administration by health professionals). In 2000, under the Liberal government, the *Therapeutic Goods Act 1989* (Cth) was amended to include s. 42E prohibiting the manufacture, import, export and supply of 'counterfeit' therapeutic products, including medicines. By the early 2010s, there had been several convictions for medicine counterfeiting in Australia published in the media involving black market 'counterfeiters'. Thus, the intention of my MA/PhD thesis, as I outlined in my proposal, was to study these convictions, or more specifically, the application of the law in Australia (and thus its deterrent effect on medicine counterfeiting as a form of transnational organised crime). I was accepted into the MA programme (the first step before being able to transfer into a PhD) and received a scholarship on the basis of this proposal from Flinders University, South Australia.

In the first year of my MA, I learned some truths. A number of these prosecutions had in fact been against medicine companies, their executives and employees—essentially, those legally authorised to produce medicines.[1] At the time, I could not wrap my head around how a company legally authorised to produce a medicine could 'counterfeit' it, especially given the strict meaning and use of the term in intellectual property law (as the infringement of the intellectual property rights of the rights holder). Up until this point, I had considered 'counterfeiting' to be a (transnational) organised crime. As someone who is not trained in law, I approached a couple of practising lawyers to explain to me how this worked. I was effectively told that this was logical (and was simply the way in which the law works). Indeed, these lawyers did not appear to be as phased by this issue as I had been.

After doing a bit of research into the history of this amendment to the Therapeutic Goods Act and reading into the debates and speeches on s. 42E in the Australian Parliament, I learned that the Act did not contain sufficient penalties (at least, from the perspective of the politicians legislating this amendment) to prosecute companies for any substandard or unregistered therapeutic goods they produced. In fact, in the 1990s, there had been many known cases of Australian companies exporting these goods to countries in South-East Asia; and this history of corporate harm was in part the reason for the inclusion of s. 42E in the Act. Essentially, the broad definition of a 'counterfeit' therapeutic good in the Act was serving a dual purpose: to prosecute both organised and corporate crimes. (For more on the history of the s. 42E amendment and the 'counterfeiting' prosecutions against companies in Australia, see Bandiera and Marmo 2017.) Naturally, it had me asking why the law was being used in this way; and in seeking the answers, I learned about the range of problems related to regulating prescription and non-prescription medicines in Australia and why s. 42E became necessary (it was really the only provision within the Act that was business-impacting).

I discussed these initial findings in the proposal I presented to my peers at the School of Law (Flinders University) in 2012 for the purposes of being considered for transfer into the PhD programme. The committee presiding over this transfer, comprising my supervisors as well as other academics within the School, gave me a choice: my thesis examines either counterfeit medicines from a transnational organised crime perspective or medicine-related harms from a state-corporate crime perspective. I opted for the latter, which I considered to be the bigger harm. The transformative effect of this (un)learning on my research and its trajectory cannot be underestimated. This book is a representation of that journey of (un)learning and (re)situating of criminological inquiry to focus on where the true harm lies—with prescription and non-prescription medicine companies, as well as states who fail consistently in their regulation of them.

This book would not have been possible without the support of a large number of people. Thanks must go to my former PhD supervisors, Professor Marinella Marmo and Professor Willem de Lint. Your belief in me and the space you provided me with to pursue these ideas have been influential not just in terms of the writing of this book, but also in shaping the trajectory of my research as an early-career academic. This is a testament to your ability as researchers and educators to see the potential in your students, even when they might find this difficult to see for themselves.

I would like to thank my friends and former colleagues in criminology and law at Flinders University, especially Dr Nerida Chazal, Dr Derek Dalton, Dr Diego Domínguez Mejía, Dr Maria Giannacopoulos, Dr Andrew Groves, Dr Sue Jarrad, Dr Wondwossen Kassa, Dr Samantha Kontra, Dr Adam Pocrnic, Dr Jeremy Ryder and Dr Jessica Viven-Wilksch. Thank you also to the wider Flinders University community, namely, the Scholarships Committee; the (former) Faculty of Education, Humanities and Law; and the Office of Graduate Research, for your administrative and financial support of the PhD, including the Flinders University Research Scholarship and Research Higher Degree Project Funding.

Thank you to Professor Paddy Rawlinson (formerly Western Sydney University) and Professor David Whyte (Queen Mary University of London) for your thoughtful and influential feedback on the PhD thesis during the examination. Thanks also to Professor John Braithwaite (Australian National University), Professor David O. Friedrichs (formerly University of Scranton), Professor Fiona Haines (University of Melbourne), Professor Simon Mackenzie (Victoria University of Wellington), Professor Christine Parker (University of Melbourne) and Professor Steve Tombs (The Open University) for generously giving your time to discuss this research in its earlier stages and as a PhD.

Thank you to my friends and colleagues at the School of Law and Criminology, Maynooth University, Ireland. In particular, I am grateful to Dr Bríd Ní Ghráinne and Dr Ciara Bracken-Roche for your generous time and feedback on the draft chapters of this book, and for the financial support of the School in the form of research funding. This book also benefited from the research assistance and placements of Sarah Lindsay Swan and Andrew Newman, to whom I am very grateful.

Thank you to my editor Julia Farrell for your exceptional work in the preparation of this book for publication (especially, your time and patience).

To my wonderful family, Ashleigh, Coralie, Mikaela and Vittorio Bandiera, Anissia, Luisa, Tahlia and Warren Fairlie, and my grandparents Bernardus and Noreen Jansen and Giuseppina and Massimino Bandiera, thank you for your love and support. Also, thank you to all of my incredibly supportive, life-long friends in Adelaide, South Australia.

Finally, thank you to Jarrad Fairlie, who has loved and supported me long before the book was a thesis. Without you, this book would not have been possible.

Any errors contained herein are my own.

## Note

1 In 2013, when I reached out to the Commonwealth Department of Public Prosecutions, they confirmed (in a personal communication, 3 June 2013) that 14 cases had been successfully prosecuted by the Department to date, more than the number published in the media, and that the majority had involved medicine companies and their executives and employees.

# Abbreviations

| | |
|---|---|
| AAT | Administrative Appeals Tribunal |
| ACCC | Australian Competition and Consumer Commission |
| ACCM | Advisory Committee on Complementary Medicines |
| ACM | Advisory Committee on Medicines |
| ACNM | Advisory Committee on Non-prescription Medicines |
| ACPM | Advisory Committee on Prescription Medicines |
| ACSOM | Advisory Committee on the Safety of Medicines |
| ADEC | Australian Drug Evaluation Committee |
| ADHD | Attention-deficit/hyperactivity disorder |
| ADIA | Australian Dental Industry Association |
| ADR | Adverse drug reaction |
| ADRAC | Adverse Drug Reactions Advisory Committee |
| AIDS | Acquired immune deficiency syndrome |
| ANAO | Australian National Audit Office |
| APMA | Australian Pharmaceutical Manufacturers Association |
| APHRA | Australian Health Practitioner Regulation Agency |
| ARTG | Australian Register for Therapeutic Goods |
| ASMI | Australian Self-Medication Industry |
| ATGAC | Australian Therapeutic Goods Advisory Council |
| AusPAR | Australian public assessment record |
| BMA | British Medical Association |
| CDC | Centers for Disease Control and Prevention |
| CHC | Complementary Healthcare Council of Australia |
| CHP | Consumer Healthcare Products Australia |
| CMA | Complementary Medicines Australia |
| CMI | Consumer Medicine Information |
| COVAX | COVID-19 Vaccines Global Access program |
| COVID-19 | Coronavirus disease 2019 |
| CRP | Complaints Resolution Panel |
| CSL | Commonwealth Serum Laboratories |
| DAEN | Database of Adverse Event Notifications |
| DTCA | Direct-to-consumer advertising |
| ELF | Electronic listing facility |

| | |
|---|---|
| EU | European Union |
| EUROPOL | European Union Agency for Law Enforcement Cooperation |
| FDA | Food and Drug Administration |
| GMiA | Generic Medicines Industry Association |
| GMP | Good manufacturing practice |
| HIV | Human immunodeficiency virus |
| INTERPOL | International Criminal Police Organization |
| MA | Medicines Australia |
| MIMS | Monthly Index of Medical Specialists |
| MRA | Mutual Recognition Agreement |
| MSD | Merck Sharpe & Dohme Australia |
| NAA | National Archives of Australia |
| NBSL | National Biological Standards Laboratory |
| NCCTG | National Coordinating Committee on Therapeutic Goods |
| NMP | National Medicines Policy |
| NPS | National Prescribing Service |
| NRAS | National Registration and Accreditation Scheme |
| NSAIDs | Non-steroidal anti-inflammatory drugs |
| NSW | New South Wales |
| NTGC | National Therapeutic Goods Committee |
| OLSS | Office of Laboratories and Scientific Services |
| OTC | Over-the-counter |
| PBS | Pharmaceutical Benefits Scheme |
| PI | Product information |
| PIC/S | Pharmaceutical Inspection Convention and the Pharmaceutical Inspection Cooperation Scheme |
| PMAA | Proprietary Medicines Association of Australia |
| PMP | Promotional Monitoring Panel |
| RACGP | Royal Australian College of General Practitioners |
| RMP | Risk management plan |
| SARA | System for Australian Recall Actions |
| TGA | Therapeutic Goods Administration |
| TGA SMP | TGA Strategic Management Plan 1994–1997 |
| TGC | Therapeutic Goods Committee |
| UK | United Kingdom |
| US | United States |
| VIGOR | Vioxx gastrointestinal outcomes research trial |
| WHO | World Health Organization |

# Figures and tables

## Figures



## Tables

# 1 Introduction

On 30 January 2020, the World Health Organization (WHO) declared coronavirus disease 2019 (COVID-19) to be a public health concern, later declaring it a global pandemic on 11 March 2020. By 30 June 2024, COVID-19 had resulted in more than 7 million deaths globally, with the United States (US) having the higher number than any other country (more than 1.2 million, see WHO 2024). Data reveals the unequal, structural impact of this disease. In the first two years of the pandemic, COVID-19 deaths in the US were up to two times higher for people in the lowest income groups; 2.2 times higher for Black, Hispanic and American Indian and Alaska Native peoples; five times higher for incarcerated people; and 6.5 times higher for the current and former disability pension recipients compared to the rest of the population (Poor People's Campaign 2022; National Academies of Sciences, Engineering, and Medicine 2020; National Organization of Social Security Claimants' Representatives 2024; Weaver 2024). Although the number of deaths directly and indirectly caused by COVID-19 has decreased significantly in the US, it continues to cause thousands of deaths yearly; in 2023, COVID-19 caused the deaths of 76,446 people (an average of 209 people per day) (Ahmad et al. 2024). The reduction in and limited monitoring of the disease (Roknuzzaman et al. 2024; Silk et al. 2023), including its long-term or chronic symptoms (commonly referred to as long COVID, which is still not fully understood), have contributed to the ongoing harms it directly and indirectly causes.

Criminologists are among those who have argued that many of these deaths were preventable and 'due in no small degree to [the] epic failures of numerous governments around the world to respond effectively' (Leighton and Wyatt 2021:1; see also Friedrichs and Vegh Weis 2021; Gordon and Green 2021; Sim and Tombs 2021). In the US, there has been 'continued and relentless defunding' of public health at the federal and state levels by successive US governments over the past two decades, with government public health expenditure in 2019 comprising less than 3% of the total national health expenditure (US Centers for Medicare & Medicaid Services 2024; Simoes and Jackson-Thompson 2023:4). Funding for the Centers for Disease Control and Prevention (CDC), the national authority responsible for

DOI: 10.4324/9781003285762-1

public health and direct coordination with state and local health authorities, was reduced to 2008 levels (Simoes and Jackson-Thompson 2023:4). This resulted in a reduction in the public health workforce across federal, state and local governments, and thereby a reduction in the capacity for developing and conducting laboratory tests and conducting contact tracing and monitoring (Devi 2020; Simoes and Jackson-Thompson 2023). McSwane (2022:46) claims that the funding of the Strategic National Stockpile had also been cut multiple times since 2011, leading to less than 1% of the personal protective equipment required by state and local health authorities being available during the first week of March 2020. After the US Government's slow response to the pandemic, and President Donald Trump minimising the severity of COVID-19, in April 2020, Trump announced that primary responsibility for responding to COVID-19 would be delegated to the states. This delegation, combined with the lack of a centralised federal response, led to extreme variation in state-level responses. By September 2020, for instance, only 33 states in the US had implemented a mandatory mask order (Altman 2020:1). It is estimated that 40% of the more than 500,000 COVID-19 deaths that occurred in the US before February 2021 were preventable (Woolhandler et al. 2021).

Also preventable were the more mundane, harmful effects of 'pandemic profiteering' (Médecins Sans Frontières 2020; Oxfam 2020). In 2021 and 2022, four of the world's largest pharmaceutical and biotechnology companies—Pfizer, BioNTech, Moderna and Sinovac—made an estimated US$90 billion from COVID-19 vaccines and related products, despite many having been in receipt of and developing their vaccines with public funding (de Haan and ten Kate 2023:4). These vaccines were then sold back 'first to the richest countries with the deepest pockets' (Open letter, The People's Vaccine 2023:1). To ensure the equitable distribution of and access to COVID-19 vaccines among countries, in April 2020, the WHO established the COVID-19 Vaccines Global Access (COVAX) programme. However, pre-purchase agreements entered into between companies and states located mostly in the West meant that the latter received their vaccines first (before COVAX recipients). More than 50% of vaccines had already been pre-purchased by Western states in January 2021, including 96% of the Pfizer-BioNTech and 100% of the Moderna vaccines (Vox 2021). Based on the most recent data available, by 31 December 2023, only 56% of people globally had completed their primary vaccination series for COVID-19, the overwhelming majority of whom were located in the West. Vaccine inequity is estimated to have caused at least 295.8 million COVID-19 infections and 1.3 million COVID-19 deaths globally by the end of 2021 (Moore et al. 2022:2418).

Pharmaceutical and biotechnology companies were not the only ones profiting from the pandemic. In March 2020, when President Trump incorrectly promoted the prescription anti-malarial medicine hydroxychloroquine as a potential treatment for COVID-19, there was a marked increase in the sale of hydroxychloroquine globally, including counterfeits (European Union Agency for Law Enforcement Cooperation or EUROPOL 2020). The US-based company that produced hydroxychloroquine, Rise Pharmaceuticals, doubled its sale price in response (Barker 2020). An article, which has since been redacted, initially estimated that hydroxychloroquine use among COVID-19 patients in Belgium, France, Italy, Spain, Turkey and the US caused the premature deaths of 16,990 people (Pradelle et al. 2024).

Other medicines and medical devices were also promoted falsely and misleadingly as being able to prevent or treat COVID-19. Between 3 and 10 March 2020, the International Criminal Police Organization (INTERPOL) and EUROPOL, together with authorities from more than 90 member states, cracked down on the sale of such products by 'criminals' and 'organised crime groups'. They seized €13 million worth of pharmaceuticals (including unauthorised antiviral medicines, including hydroxychloroquine, antibiotics and painkillers, and vitamin C and other similar supplements); 4.4 million units of illicit pharmaceuticals (including 'corona spray' and 'coronavirus medicine'); and up to 34,000 counterfeit surgical masks (EUROPOL 2020:2, 9; INTERPOL 2020). During the operation, INTERPOL, EUROPOL and the participating authorities took down 2,500 links (websites, social media and advertisements in online marketplaces) and made 121 arrests. This response is in stark contrast to the responses to companies marketing medicines and medical devices with fraudulent COVID-19 prevention and treatment claims, which, in the vast majority of cases, involved the issuing of warning letters and a simple request to review and correct the promotional materials. By 13 July 2022, the Food and Drug Administration (FDA), the national food and drug regulatory agency in the US, had issued 220 such letters to US-based companies (published on its website; see FDA 2024).

This book is not about the COVID-19 pandemic. In fact, this introduction is the most the book dedicates to discussing the subject. The harms caused by states and corporations during the pandemic are but the latest symptoms of a more harmful, underlying disease: neoliberalism.

## 1.1 Scope of the book

This book is about neoliberalism, how it shapes regulation, how it shapes the power of (indeed empowers) states and corporations and ultimately how it causes harm, with a focus on prescription and non-prescription medicines. For decades, the themes of neoliberalism, state and corporate power and regulation have dominated debates in the social sciences. Yet, the various ways in which they intersect are rarely discussed. Much of the discussion on neoliberalism has centred on the ill-defined and inherently contradictory nature of the term, particularly in theory compared to practice. In the regulatory literature, scholars debate whether neoliberalism or regulatory capitalism is the better analytical framework for examining the evolving role of the state and regulation. Historically, the orthodoxy has favoured the latter term (see Braithwaite 2005, 2008; Jordana and Levi-Faur 2004; Levi-Faur 2005), which is generally understood as the expansion and pluralisation of regulation, particularly its non-state forms, which is claimed to become progressively stronger over time. Meanwhile, the regulatory, pharmaceutical industry crime (pharma-crime) and medical sociology literature typically discusses the power of states and their regulatory agencies in instrumentalist terms; that they become 'captured' by and 'powerless' to those they seek to regulate (Ayres and Braithwaite 1992:54; Davis and Abraham 2013:12). Although there is a growing body of literature on the crimes of the powerful—which focuses on the crimes and non-criminalised harms committed by states and corporations—and neoliberalism and its effects on this power, regulation is rarely the focus (exceptions include Bittle and Hébert 2020; Tombs 2012, 2016). This book explores all of these themes and expands on these debates. It focuses on state–corporate crime and harm, conceiving the cause of such crime and harm as the 'mutually reinforcing interaction' of the state and corporations (Kramer and Michalowski 2006:20). It argues that medicine-related harms, like those seen during the COVID-19 pandemic, are driven by the state. Not only do states often neglect to regulate prescription and non-prescription medicine companies, thereby facilitating these harms (which, notably, rarely violate criminal law), but neoliberalism itself is a state-led and regulated project. As such, states do not just facilitate or initiate such harms, they also produce the very conditions that enable them to occur in the first place (Bernat and Whyte 2017:77). In this respect, regulation essentially functions as a system or 'regime of permission' (Bernat and Whyte 2017).

The book uses the language of 'social harm' or 'harm' more so than 'crime' for several reasons. While there is no agreed-upon definition of social harm (see Garside 2013; Lasslett 2010a; Raymen 2022), it generally refers to those harmful acts or inactions that may not always violate or be punished by (criminal) law (and therefore, labelled as 'crime'). Many state and corporate (in)actions are not strictly governed by 'law', and even when laws exist, they are not always enforced and penalties are not always applied. It is this inherent inequality within the law and legal system that leads to situations where 'criminals' and 'organised crime groups' involved in selling medicines and medical devices with fraudulent COVID-19 claims have the links to their websites, social media and advertisements forcibly removed and are arrested, while companies are asked to remove the claims and receive warning letters, and politicians' claims are merely 'fact-checked'. (This is not to suggest that such links should not be removed or arrests made, or to equate harms, but rather to highlight the disproportionate response of the law and legal system when it comes to corporations, states and their actions.) This inequality arises for numerous reasons. For one, crime is a legal—and thus social—construction which must be created (through law) to exist. Although harms are very real, crimes are not in the sense that there is nothing inherent about an (in)action that identifies it as being a crime without some sort of external reference (namely, criminal law) (Hillyard and Tombs 2004). This fact is the foundation of critical criminology, one of the lenses adopted in this book, which argues that the definition of crime is asymmetrical and a form of power relation. Because most crimes are defined by the state through the passing of (criminal) law, the state holds a unique position to define what is and is not a crime, including in relation to its own (in)actions. Critical criminology, therefore, focuses on the study of those harms that are rarely criminalised, particularly the harms committed by those in positions of power who shape the law and systems that ultimately govern them.

In the context of the prescription and non-prescription medicines industry, a great deal of conduct is governed by 'regulations', 'standards' and even 'codes of practice' or 'conduct' (sometimes developed by industry itself), and less so 'criminal' or 'civil law'. Further, any related breaches tend to be referred to as 'non-compliance' as opposed to 'crime'. For these reasons, those harmed by medicines or their advertising may not necessarily perceive themselves or be labelled as 'victims'. Establishing causation—the link between the act and its resulting harm—is also challenging. In the context of medicines, determining causation is particularly difficult due to the effects of a medicine on the human body, and therefore, whether a reaction is caused by the medicine itself or another factor intrinsic to a person or their (in) actions. Determining the intent of an advertisement directed to the public or health professionals is just as (if not more) difficult in the absence of information on the decisions made in marketing these medicines.

This book examines the harms linked to both prescription and non-prescription medicines and their quality, safety and efficacy, and advertising to the public (referred to as direct-to-consumer advertising or DTCA) and health professionals (commonly referred to as promotion). In this context, the terms 'quality' and 'safety' are considered self-evident, whereas efficacy refers to the capacity of a medicine to produce a therapeutic effect or benefit for the condition for which it is indicated. Although the harms of prescription medicines are typically studied more so than those of non-prescription medicines (e.g. Abraham 1995; Angell 2004; Braithwaite 1984; Davis and Abraham 2013; Gøtzsche 2013; Law 2006; Lexchin 1984), this does not mean that non-prescription medicines do not cause harm and are therefore less worthy of inquiry. There have been cases where traditional Chinese medicines have been found to contain heavy metals and toxins, and weight loss supplements and protein powders have been linked to deaths and serious injuries (Coghlan et al. 2015; Gilbert et al. 2014; Hansen 2019; Smith et al. 2016). Complementary medicines, such as vitamin, mineral, herbal, traditional, aromatherapy, and homeopathic and naturopathic medicines, with unproven claims have been found to cost consumers hundreds or even thousands of dollars monthly (Hansen 2019; Ahwan 2020).

While this introduction started by situating this discussion in a global and US context, the rest of the book focuses on prescription and non-prescription medicine regulation in Australia, and there are compelling reasons for this. Historically, the literature has focused overwhelmingly on prescription medicine regulation in either the US or European Union (EU). This is because the US and EU pharmaceutical industries are by far the largest. In 2017, pharmaceutical companies contributed an estimated combined total of US$532 billion to the global economy, with companies in the US (24.1%) and EU (21.5%) being the first and second largest contributors, respectively, and Australia (1.7%) just the tenth largest contributor (Ostwald et al. 2020:12). However, this does not mean that the actions of governments and corporations outside the US and EU are any less harmful or less worthy of criminological scrutiny. In fact, between the 2018–2019 and 2022–2023 financial years, the number of advertising complaints reported to Australia's Therapeutic Goods Administration (TGA), the national drug regulatory agency, doubled from 1,468 to 3,064 (TGA 2019d, 2023c). In 2021–2022, as many as one in three complaints concerned COVID-19, references to which are restricted[1] and require the prior approval or permission of the TGA before being used in an advertisement (TGA 2022e:15, 22). The majority of advertising complaints received in that financial year, including those concerning COVID-19, involved products that had not received TGA pre-approval, a legal requirement for sale. The majority of complaints also resulted in either requests to remove the advertisement or the issue of a warning letter, from which '[a] high voluntary compliance rate was achieved' (albeit, retrospectively) (TGA 2022e:18, 22). These harms were exacerbated by the fact that the requirement that any advertisement be approved prior to publication was abolished,[2] taking effect on 30 June 2020. Advertising pre-approval was abolished 'in favour of a more self-regulatory regime', ostensibly so as to be 'consistent with the [Australian] Government's commitment to minimising unnecessary regulatory burden' (Department of Health 2016a:35).

The harms of regulation described here are neither new nor confined to DTCA. Since the 1990s, there has been a 'commercialisation' of medicine regulation in Australia, seeking to increase the efficiency, cost and timeliness of medicines approval (Department of Community Services and Health 1990:19–20). This led to the adoption of a 'risk management' approach and '[s]treamlining' of 'lesser tasks' (*TGA Strategic Management Plan 1994–1997* as cited in Australian National Audit Office (ANAO) 1996:9), including an increased emphasis on self-regulation. Those aspects of medicine regulation that involve less direct intervention by the TGA and rely more on self-regulation tend to experience higher rates of non-compliance among sponsors—companies that import, export, manufacture and supply prescription and non-prescription medicines in Australia. For example, in 2021–2022, 70% of low risk non-prescription medicines (which are practically self-assessed at approval) failed to meet minimum quality, safety and/or efficacy requirements (TGA 2022d). These high levels of non-compliance have been relatively consistent since data was first collected in 2006, so much so that the ANAO (2011:16–17) concluded back in 2011 that their regulation 'has been of limited effectiveness'. Advertising or promotion to health professionals—such as medical practitioners, pharmacists, nurses, dentists, physiotherapists, psychologists, Chinese medicine practitioners, naturopaths, homeopaths and herbalists, among others—is also largely self-regulated and there have been cases involving sponsors actively evading and ignoring promotional requirements, even appealing decisions of the TGA and its complaints bodies. Despite more than a decade of data and cases studies indicating that regulation in these areas is failing to achieve compliance and causing harm, it remains largely unchanged.

It is for these reasons that this book examines the neoliberalisation of medicine regulation in Australia, why it often fails and why it is particularly difficult to disrupt.

## 1.2 Neoliberalism

Before outlining the main arguments and structure of this book, it is necessary to explain what I mean by neoliberalism, because it is a widely used but poorly defined term. Broadly speaking, it emerged out of 19th-century liberalism as part of a wider search for a 'new liberalism' that retained capitalism as its mode of economy. Capitalism is a type of economy that emphasises capital accumulation and growth and has its foundations in colonialism (starting with the Atlantic economy, often referred to as mercantilism, in the 16th century—see Wright 2023; Mignolo 2021). The earliest uses of the term 'neoliberalism' were by European and Western scholars in the late 19th to mid-20th centuries, including the likes of Charles Gide (1898) and Milton Friedman (1951). Its use became more frequent throughout the 1930s and 1940s. 'Neoliberalism' was the preferred term to describe the movement formed at the Colloque Walter Lippmann in Paris in 1938, organised by French philosopher Louis Rougier and attended by German economists Wilhelm Röpke and Alexander Rüstow, Austrian-British economist Friedrich Hayek, Austro-Hungarian economist Ludwig von Mises and French economists Jacques Rueff and Robert Marjolin, among others (Foucault 2008:132–133; Plehwe 2015). Other suggested terms to describe the movement included neo-capitalism (*néo-capitalisme*), positive liberalism (*libéralisme positif*), social liberalism (*libéralisme social*) and left-wing liberalism (*libéralisme de gauche*) (Plehwe 2015:13; Walpen 2004:60). The term is also associated with the Mont Pèlerin Society, established in 1947 in Switzerland by many of those in attendance at the Colloque (Plehwe 2015:13). The term entered into common use in the 1970s, in particular in association with the Pinochet regime in Chile (1973–1990),[3] the Thatcher regime in the United Kingdom (UK) (1979–1990) and the Reagan (1981–1989) regime in the US. Thus, neoliberalism is Euro- and Western-centric in origin. It can be conceived of as one of many harmful varieties of capitalism (hence, neoliberal capitalism) (Pemberton 2015) and therefore a modern/colonial formation.

But as this short overview of its history illustrates, it is not necessarily a singular thought or idea; indeed, it was diverse in its origins and theoretical basis (e.g. it is connected with the Freiburg or Ordo-liberal School, Frankfurt School, Chicago School of Economics, among others). Situating neoliberalism within its entire historical context is crucial, as Garside (2013) argues, to knowing and understanding the 'historical' causes of its 'modern' harms.

Within the criminological literature, neoliberalism is typically understood as either a form of governmentality or hegemony. Therefore, this chapter provides a detailed overview of these two different ways of conceptualising neoliberalism. It also suggests a way of interpreting neoliberalism as a combination of the two, by approaching them from within a critical realist ontological framework, to provide a deeper understanding of neoliberal forms of governance and its reinforcing effect on relations of power.

### *1.2.1 Governmentality*

Neoliberalism is often understood as a form of governmentality. In his lectures from the mid to late 1970s, Foucault (2007) used this term to describe both the act of governing (*gouverner*), which he referred to as a *technique* or *technology*, and the thinking underpinning it (*mentalité*), which he referred to variously as a *rationality*, *mentality* or *art*. For Foucault (1982:790), government meant not only the political apparatus of the state, but also:

> the way in which the conduct of individuals or of groups might be directed . . . [the] modes of action, more or less considered or calculated, which were destined to act upon the possibilities of action of other people. To govern, in this sense, is to structure the possible field of action of others.

As a form of governmentality, neoliberalism takes and applies the ideas of the market broadly to the act of governing (Foucault 2008:131). As such, it seeks to redefine the social sphere as an extension of the economy (Lemke 2001:197).

Foucault argues that neoliberalism is different from classical liberalism in multiple ways. The first difference relates to how it conceptualises the relationship of the state to the economy. Under liberalism, the economy is seen as existing naturally and free from state intervention; the role of the state is simply to ensure that the economy operates fairly and efficiently (see Foucault 2007:118). Because freedom is conditional to rational governance, the state should not act to constrain these freedoms as this undermines its own foundations (Lemke 2001:200). Neoliberalism, however, sees the economy as the 'organizing and regulating principle of the state' (Foucault 2008:116). Like liberalism, neoliberalism sees the economy as functioning only through free and full competition and the state refraining from altering this. However, far from the economy being natural, the state acts in 'direct service to the economy' (Brown 2005:44) and manages, reinforces and protects it through the law, policy and disseminating its norms (41). The rationalities that underpin neoliberal governmentality are therefore premised on a form of economic or market discipline, which sees the state 'under the supervision of' as opposed to overseeing the market (Foucault 2008:116).

Second, liberalism and neoliberalism differ in their conception of freedom. Liberalism is based on the idea of freedom from state intervention, along with other freedoms, such as market freedom, property rights and freedom of expression (Foucault 2008:63). Neoliberalism, however, is based on an 'artificially arranged liberty' whereby it 'endeavours to create a . . . reality that it suggests already exists' (Lemke 2001:200, 203). This artificial reality is not limited to the economy (the 'freedom' of which is the result of state work). Neoliberal rationality constructs the individual as an economically rational being able to calculate the costs and benefits of their actions. This construction rationalises techniques that shift the responsibility of governing from the state onto individuals, a process known as *responsibilisation* (see Burchell 1996:29), and directs individuals to take part in their own governance, a process known as *subjectification* (Foucault 1982). By 'supplying' individuals with the potential to actively participate in the solution to problems that had been the responsibility of the state, the state can govern individuals from a distance, 'without at the same time being responsible for them' (Lemke 2001:201–202). This indirect form of governance aligns with neoliberal rationalities, such as deregulation and individualism. However, having individuals participate in their own governance is also 'a form of power which subjugates and makes subject to' (Foucault 1982:781). It facilitates their transformation into the 'model' neoliberal citizen-subject who strategises among the available options for themselves but does not alter or organise these (Brown 2005:43). According to Brown (2005:43), a fully neoliberalised citizenry is 'the opposite of public-minded' as it 'barely exist[s] as a public'. This is in contrast to the classic liberal conception of *homo œconomicus* ('economic man'), where individual freedom is the precondition for rational governance and the state may not limit this freedom (Lemke 2001:200). Neoliberalism sees *homo œconomicus* as 'behaviouristically manipulable' and a 'correlative' of governmentality (Lemke 2001:200).

Finally, liberalism conceives the economy as distinct from society (i.e. one domain among many), whereas neoliberalism dissolves the distinctions between the economy and society (Lemke 2001:197). Nowhere is this expansion of the economy into every aspect of life more clearly demonstrated than in the phrase 'cost of living', which has normalised the commodification of the value of human life. The same is also true for the 'cost of health' (discussed in Chapter 2). Increasingly, the success (or failure) of state action is rationalised on the basis of its ability to support and foster the economy (Brown 2005:41). This rationality extends beyond the economy to all other state (in)actions, which must meet cost-benefit tests and ensure industry viability (Brown 2005:44). This rationality to which state actions are submitted not only makes 'the health and growth of the economy . . . *the* basis of state legitimacy' but also gives the state entrepreneurial form such that it comes to 'think and behave like a market actor' (Brown 2005:42 [emphasis in original]). The actions of individuals are likewise interpreted through economic criteria, framing them in economic terms and encouraging them to be entrepreneurial (Lemke 2001:198).

Neoliberal governmentality takes a variety of forms. These include direct interventions by the state through state apparatuses (Lemke 2001:201). They also include indirect forms of intervention from above and below. The former, referred to as *technologies of performance*, are forms of governing that shape conduct to optimise the performance of individuals, groups and organisations, such as in the form of a risk management plan or internal audit (Dean 1998:36). The latter, known as *technologies of agency*, are forms of governing that deploy the agency of individuals, groups and organisations (Dean 1998:35–36), such as committee representation or providing a 'voice'. These also include forms of governing that seek to empower individuals and groups through their active and 'democratic' participation—what Cruikshank (1999:67) calls *technologies of citizenship*.

Although governmentality explains *how* governance (and by extension, power) is exercised, as others have previously noted (Jessop 2007; Joseph 2004, 2010, 2014, 2017; Marsden 1999), it cannot on its own explain *why* it is exercised the way it is. This is because, as Foucault (1980:98) explains, power is conceived as 'something which circulates'; '[i]t is never localised here or there, never in anybody's hands, never appropriated as a commodity or a piece of wealth'. Indeed, it 'is exercised rather than possessed' (Foucault 1977:26). Foucault (1980:97) therefore argues that the analysis of power should refrain from posing questions, such as who has power and why do they exercise it (i.e. the intent underlying it). Rather, he argues that power should be studied 'at the point where its intention, if it has one, is completely invested in its real and effective practices' (97). Because power is not located with the state, an organisation or a particular group or individual but, as Foucault (97) argues, 'at the extreme points of its exercise', it is unclear what it is exercised for (indeed, why there may be resistance to its exercise) (Joseph 2004:153). Neoliberal governmentality, then, is a collection of open-ended micro-level techniques and rationalities that lack a general logic (Joseph 2017:13), and the apparatuses of the state merely the 'vehicles' through which it is exercised (Foucault 1980:98).

### *1.2.2 Hegemony*

Neoliberalism is also often understood as a form of hegemony. Hegemony has a 'dual' meaning in Marxist theory: 'domination'; and 'political', 'intellectual and moral leadership' (Gramsci 1971/1992:169, 57). The former conceives hegemony in instrumentalist terms, as a tool of class 'domination', 'force', 'violence', 'dictatorship' and 'coercion' (Gramsci 1971/1992:170,

Gramsci 1965 as cited in Anderson 1976–1977). The latter, however, conceives hegemony as a form of 'direction', 'consent' (Gramsci 1965 as cited in Anderson 1976–1977:21), 'consensus, or mutual agreement' (Anderson 1976–1977:30). For Gramsci, hegemony is a 'synthesis' of these two meanings (i.e. 'consent' and 'coercion'), as well as just a form of 'consent' (i.e. distinct from 'coercion') (Anderson 1976:22). He argues that the dominant class(es) exercises hegemony not only through coercion, but also securing the consent of the less-dominant class(es) and class alliance (or what Gramsci refers to as a hegemonic bloc).

Jessop (1983:100), who builds on Gramsci's concept, defines hegemony as the 'interpellation and organization of different "class-relevant" (but not necessarily class-conscious) forces under the "political, intellectual, and moral leadership" of a particular class (or class fraction)'. The exercise of hegemony requires reconciling the conflicts between class interests and the common interest, which, according to Jessop, can be achieved through the development of a *hegemonic project*. The development of such a project entails 'mobilization of support behind a concrete, national-popular program[4] of action which asserts a general interest in the pursuit of objectives that explicitly or implicitly advance the long-term interests of the hegemonic class (fraction)' (Jessop 1983:100). In mobilising support, the dominant class takes into consideration the interests of the less-dominant class(es); makes compromises in favour of some of these interests while still preserving its own interests, to maintain the support of the less-dominant class(es); and incorporates the interests of the less-dominant class(es) into those of the dominant class by framing them as the common interest. By consenting, the less-dominant class(es) effectively takes part in the implementation of this project. In this way, the hegemonic project disorganises and progressively neutralises opposition to it (i.e. the formation of counter-hegemony and hegemonic projects) (Jessop 1990:42).

Neoliberalism can therefore be understood as a dominant—if not hegemonic—economic, political and social project. According to Jessop (2002:454), neoliberalism is an economic project in the sense that it promotes economic liberalisation and deregulation (within and across borders), the privatisation of state-owned enterprises and the provision of state services, the use of proxies of the market within the public sector, and public welfare as a form of cost. It is a political project seeking to 'roll back' 'normal' and 'exceptional' forms of state intervention that affect capital accumulation and 'roll forward' forms of governing that typically shift responsibility downwards and sideways and are partnership-based—that is, grounded in 'the neoliberal belief in the probability, if not inevitability, of state failure and/or the need to involve relevant stakeholders' (454). It is also a social project seeking to reorganise society and promote 'community' (and thus plural) forms of governance as a way of compensating for state failure (455). The neoliberal hegemonic project is paradoxical in the sense that it generally involves an increase in certain forms of state intervention (454, 464). Jessop stresses that while there may be overlap between hegemonic projects and capital accumulation, the two are not the same. Accumulation strategies become hegemonic through their broad public acceptance, which is driven/shaped by economic leadership (Jessop 1983:92).

#### *1.2.2.1. Strategic-relational approach to the state*

This Gramscian–Jessopian approach to hegemony affects our understanding of the state, regulatory agencies and their power. An instrumentalist approach to hegemony tends to view the state as a neutral and passive tool readily (and equally) seizable by any class. Once a class takes control, the state acts to advance the particular interests of that class. This view aligns with capture theory, which is popular within the 'orthodox' (Lasslett 2010b) state–corporate crime and regulation literature (e.g. see Ayres and Braithwaite 1992; Bernstein 1955; Horwitz 1986). Capture theory argues that states and their regulatory agencies become 'captured' by the interests of those they seek to regulate, therefore regulating in ways that align with their interests. This capture can be as explicit as the 'revolving door' between state and industry, with actors 'revolving out' of and 'in' to the private sector from the public sector and vice versa (see Pons-Hernández 2022).

For the purposes of studying state–corporate crime and harm, instrumentalist and capture theories present a number of problems. First, these theories suggest a lack of agency on the part of the state. They portray states as powerless in their ability to resist capture and as lacking their own interests and a capacity to act on them. In this way, they effectively play into a neoliberal deregulatory rhetoric (see Khoury 2018:182). In the case of capitalist states, minimal intervention by the state in regulation may not be due to capture but rather the alignment of the interests of the capitalist state and class; since the capitalist state does not produce the capital that is indispensable to its power, the exercise of its power relies on maintaining 'healthy' capital accumulation (Offe and Keane 1984:120). In this respect, the power of the capitalist state 'is not external to' but rather 'ever-present in' the processes of capital accumulation (Lasslett 2015:654). Tombs and Whyte (2015:25, 27) similarly argue that the state–corporate relationship is not 'one of *opposition* and *externality*' but is 'symbiotic'. Not only is the corporation a 'legal fiction' created by the state (see Tombs and Whyte 2015:82) but the state also creates and maintains the conditions that enable corporations to produce and accumulate capital, and therefore, to cause crime and harm with minimal or no penalty. Hence, Tombs and Whyte (2015:162) assert that 'the power of one does not decline at the expense of the other . . . [since] the power of the corporation rests upon the power of states, and vice-versa'. Conceiving the state in this way is crucial for understanding the cause of state–corporate crime/harm, and therefore for ensuring that states:

> bear some culpability . . . for their formal legislation of much of this harm, their failures to develop adequate law and regulation which

> might mitigate these, their failures to enforce adequately such laws as do exist, and/or their failures to impose effective sanctions where violations of law are proven.
>
> (Tombs 2016:28)

In the literature on state–corporate crime/harm within the pharmaceutical industry, the relationship between the state and industry is referred to as the 'state–pharma nexus', with the pharmaceutical industry referred to as 'a partner of the state' (see Rawlinson 2017a:89). For Rawlinson (2017a:89), the state–pharma nexus 'operate[s] with greater levels of immunity from accountability and impunity' than is seen in most other industries due to the concentration of knowledge production, and the fact that it is a form of medical (or technical) knowledge. Indeed, it is 'only by being on the inside, which is systematically tied to the interests of the state-pharma nexus, . . . [that] one [can] claim a legitimate voice' (94). In this unique way, the state–pharma nexus is 'sustained by the absence of transparency and critique while demanding loyalty and compliance from the masses' (94).

Second, these theories do not adequately explain why states, on occasion, act against the interests of the dominant class, in spite of being captured by them. Some suggest that capture is 'cyclical', meaning that states and their regulatory agencies cycle or drift in and out of capture (Abraham and Ballinger 2012:1434; Bernstein 1955). However, this account does not explain instances where the state takes action that is contrary, or even detrimental, to the interests of the dominant class while at the same time continuing to act in its interests. This idea of total dominance of the state by a class or coalition of classes receives little support within the literature. For instance, in his study on the US Sentencing Commission's federal organisational sentencing guidelines, Rodriguez (2009:121) found that while successive revisions of the guidelines resulted in a reduction of the overall severity of sanctions against companies, companies regulated by the Commission also favoured the development of an independent commission that could resist legislative interference and create guidelines that bring penalties more into line with those for other offences. Such examples suggest that a more accurate explanation of the role of states and their regulatory agencies is that they 'simultaneously represent and regulate'; they 'represent' the interests of those they regulate while also 'disciplining' them in line with the common interest (Mahon 1979:163, 171). By treating dominance and/or capture as absolute, instrumentalist and capture theories neglect the relative power of states.

It is due to these limitations that Jessop (2010:45) conceives the state as the 'form-determined condensation of the changing balance of [class or social] forces', a theoretical position he calls the strategic-relational approach. Jessop thus views the state and state power as a social relation—that is, the relation between the different forces of power within and outside the state that is institutionally mediated through the state. This relationship includes the 'political and politically-relevant struggle[s]' between forces over the form of the state, and the state apparatus and bases of state power, as well as efforts to influence the balance of forces within and outside the state (45). It is the unequal 'structural' and/or 'strategic selectivity' (Jessop 2008:36, 125) of the state that renders it amenable to and representative of some forces more than others. As such, '[t]he state is not a thing or a rational subject', but rather an 'ensemble' of powers (5). These powers are exercised both individually and collectively through the state's actors (including politicians and political parties) specifically located in the state and its apparatuses. These apparatuses are a 'distinct ensemble' of different organisations, agencies, branches, departments and offices 'whose socially accepted function is to define and enforce collectively binding decisions' in line with the common interest (Jessop 1990:341). Such apparatuses of the state include its regulatory agencies.

Hegemony and the strategic-relational approach have some limitations. As Jessop (2012:5) explains, Marxists generally hold that there is 'no such thing as power in general . . . only particular powers and the sum of particular exercises of power'. Power, then, is thought to be 'contingent on specific actions by specific agents in specific circumstances' (5). Gramsci was no different in his thinking. According to Gramsci (1975/1992:136–137),

> a class is dominant in two ways, namely it is 'leading' and 'dominant.' It leads the allied classes, it dominates the opposing classes. Therefore, a class can (and must) 'lead' even before assuming power; when it is in power it becomes dominant, but it also continues to 'lead'.

A key limitation, then, of concepts like hegemony is that they explain *why* and by *whom* power is exercised, but not *how*—that is, the actual ways in which a class or classes (or social group(s)) exercise power and come to lead and be dominant in the first place. Historically, the literature focuses more on the 'hegemony of production' (i.e. the effects of hegemony) as opposed to a focus on the 'production of hegemony' (Jessop and Sum 2006:161). The strategic-relational approach is also criticised for straying a bit too far from a structural analysis of power, often treating the state as 'no more than a relation of class forces or a condensation of class relations' (Joseph 2003:133).

### *1.2.3 A combined approach*

Both governmentality and hegemony have their limitations, as outlined earlier. Yet many scholars note the affinities between Foucault and Gramsci (Davies 2011; Joseph 2004, 2010, 2014, 2017; Lemke 2007) and between Foucault and Marx (Jessop 2007; Lasslett 2015; Marsden 1999; Paolucci 2003). Generally speaking, Marxist and Foucauldian perspectives explain the *why* and *how* of power, respectively (Marsden 1999:26). For Marsden (1999:135 [emphasis in original]), 'Marx's *explicandum* is a cluster of conclusions in search of a premise . . . [and] Foucault's *explicans* is a cluster of premises in search of a conclusion'. Although Foucault did not directly cite Marx or Gramsci, as Jessop (2007:39) observes, he invoked Marxist or Gramscian concepts such as (but not limited to) 'bourgeois', 'bourgeoisie', 'proletariat', 'proletarian', 'class', 'class struggle', 'domination' and 'hegemony' (Foucault 2000, 2008). In a translated interview, Foucault (1980:52–53) acknowledges that he 'quote[s] Marx without saying so, without quotation marks'. Jessop and Lemke also note that in his later lectures, Foucault became increasingly interested in the form of the state, conceiving it, in Jessop's (2007:39) words, as the site for the 'strategic codification of power relations'. In the English translation of *The Subject and Power*, Foucault (2000:345) explains that power relations are 'governmentalized':

> the state is not simply one of the forms of specific situations of the exercise of power—even if it is the most important—but that, in a certain way, all other forms of power relation must refer to it. But this is not because they are derived from it; rather, it is because power relations have come more and more under state control.

As such, Foucault's 'analytics of government' is still used by state theorists, including Jessop, in conceptualising the state and its power. Foucault's take on Marx and Gramsci can therefore be interpreted in one of two ways: as a critique or as a way of thinking that can be used alongside or supplemental to Marx and Gramsci. Many of those scholars previously cited in this paragraph opt for the latter interpretation.

Of course, this does not mean that we can begin using Foucault together with Gramsci. The challenge in trying to 'Foucauldize Gramsci' or 'Gramscianize Foucault' (Jessop and Sum 2006:165) is in having to reconcile the differences in their ontology—or more simply, understanding—of power. For Foucault, power is relational; he 'rarely concedes that there is an overall structural coherence to social formations apart from the general adoption of specific technologies of power' (Jessop and Sum 2006:164). Although Gramsci has 'a more fluid and interactive understanding' of power than Marx and other Marxists, it is structural nonetheless; '[a] social formation acquires a certain degree of social order [or structure] through the continuing achievement of unstable equilibria of compromise' (Jessop and Sum 2006:164). Therefore, to reconcile these ontological differences and use Foucault and Gramsci together, something more is required. Some scholars suggest that this is only possible by situating both within a critical realist ontological framework (see Joseph 2004, 2010, 2014, 2017; Marsden 1999).

Critical realism is not a theory but a metatheory or social science philosophy (Frauley and Pearce 2007:5) which is considered compatible with both governmentality (Frauley 2007; Joseph 2004) and hegemony (Joseph 2002, 2003). As an ontology, or a way of knowing or understanding reality, critical realism maintains that reality is both objective, in that it 'exists independently of our knowledge of it', and subjective, such that our knowledge of it is 'always mediated' and therefore 'fallible' (Frauley and Pearce 2007:4). It therefore distinguishes between different levels of reality,[5] including 'a deeper reality underpinning what we can see or . . . know' (17, 4). As summed up by Pearce (2007:36), '[r]eality, then, is vertically stratified [that is, structured], and "things" and their powers at any particular level are determined by interactions [relations, actions] between things at another more basic level'. Social structures and relations of power are therefore 'real' and can have material effects despite not necessarily being material themselves (i.e. they can be immaterial or discursive).[6] On this account, social structures pre-exist and structure relations of power. These 'relations of social structure' therefore 'enable us to act, but also determine and limit what we can do' (Joseph 2006:113). Actions, in turn, reproduce social structures, but they also have the potential to change and transform social structures. In this way, social structures are a 'material cause of the events it generates' (Marsden 1999:27). A critical realist ontology can therefore maintain a structural account of power 'without reducing power to some essential basis' (Joseph 2004:159).

For Frauley (2007:259), the concept of governmentality generally fails to consider how action is 'situated activity' that is both 'structurally enabled and constrained', and, in turn, 'reproduce[s] or transform[s]' social structures and their organisation. A critical realist ontology thus provides governmentality with ontological depth. In terms of hegemony, a critical realist ontological framework provides a means of defining hegemony as both a form of social structure (i.e. as something that exists in relation to 'pre-existing and relatively enduring social relations') and a type of 'conscious', 'reflective' and 'intentional' collective action (Joseph 2017:7). Applying a critical realist ontology, Joseph argues that it is possible to use governmentality together with hegemony. 'Hegemonic governmentality', then, occurs when 'certain forms of governmentality become hegemonic' (11). Accordingly, neoliberal governmentality becomes hegemonic when micro-level rationalities and techniques 'are adopted by or coalesce into' a macro-level strategy or hegemonic project (13). When these practices are adopted/coalesce at the macro level, they are 'given the coherence of a neoliberal rationality' which can be 'translated' or 'redirected' to other non-economic, social domains through the ensemble of the state and other 'leading' social groups or forces (13). Hegemonic governmentality therefore attempts to explain the ways in which governmentality comes into being (i.e. its adoption and use by the state or other powerful forces), becomes hegemonic (through forming a hegemonic project), and is therefore reproduced. In so doing, it also attempts to explain that hegemony's 'continued reproduction through social activity is not automatically given' but rather 'socially secured and institutionally embedded' (16).

Approaching neoliberalism as a form of hegemonic governmentality has certain implications (see, e.g. Pearce and Woodiwiss 2001:51–52). Indeed, governmentality and hegemony were only partially developed by Foucault and Gramsci and so these concepts are subject to significant interpretation (even debate) within the literature. The intent of this book, however, is to demonstrate the potential value of the concept of hegemonic (neoliberal) governmentality in furthering our understanding of state–corporate harm and regulation.

## 1.3 Outline of the book

The arguments proposed in this book are that the regulation of medicines in Australia often fails and that the neoliberal rationalities and techniques underpinning the medicine regulatory regime function to limit forms of intervention that constrain capital accumulation. This neoliberal governmentality forms part of a hegemonic project which privileges those rationalities and techniques that are compatible with it (and derogate those that are incompatible with it). As a result, hegemonic neoliberal governmentality shapes the regime and its subjects in ways that effectively align with it, maintaining the established relations of power. In this respect, it continues to empower certain groups (the state, medicines industry and those sympathetic to their interests) while disempowering others (primarily, the public, health professionals and consumer and health professional associations) through disorganising and progressively neutralising opposition. It is therefore a reinforcing project, making it particularly difficult to disrupt (hence, it being hegemonic).

The book begins by examining the historical causes of hegemonic neoliberal governmentality in Australia's medicine regulatory regime and therefore its harms. It examines the history of this regime, starting from the late 18th century when the continent was colonised and Australian settler colonialism/capitalism was established. Chapter 2 traces the shifts in the state project from this period to the early 21st century, specifically through the development of micro-level rationalities and techniques (or governmentality) and formation of a macro-level strategy of governing (or hegemonic project). In so doing, it examines how governmentality became neoliberal, and how neoliberal governmentality, in turn, became hegemonic. The chapter discusses the creation of racial (colonial) difference, and in turn, perceived differences in health (and immunity) across racial groups, which rationalised the development of techniques of governing quarantine (and incidentally, immigration) at ports of entry by the colonial governments and later the Australian Government. Chapter 2 explains how these differences, and therefore the objectification of people, medicine and health, facilitated the subsequent commodification of health (i.e. its attaining a value) and subjectification of individuals (their turning into subjects) in line with neoliberal rationality. The chapter examines the *Quarantine Act 1908* (Cth), a technology of governing both health and race (as it formed part of the White Australia Policy), which led to the creation of the Quarantine Service, the first apparatus of the state for governing health and from which the Australian Department of Health and later the TGA would emerge. The emergence of the modern/colonial system of human rights in the mid-20th century helped to establish hegemonic social liberal (and later, neoliberal) governmentality. This was achieved through the alignment of the discourse of rights—specifically, the 'legitimate' rights of the individual of freedom from and through the state—with (neo)liberal ideas of the real respect for freedom, whereby the state assures but does not infringe upon rights, including the freedoms of private individuals and the economy. The chapter explains how as neoliberal governmentality became hegemonic, it rationalised the decentralisation and deregulation of the medicine regulatory regime, through the delegation of the responsibility of the Department of Health to the TGA and industry associations, and through self-regulation, which increased the responsibility of the public for their own health governance. Finally, Chapter 2 examines the early signs of regulatory failure, with reference to the Pan Pharmaceuticals (Travacalm) and Merck & Co and Merck Sharpe & Dohme Australia (Vioxx) case studies, and how these failures rationalised the implementation of further micro-level (self-) regulatory techniques.

Chapter 3 provides a detailed overview of the TGA and medicine regulatory regime between 2010 and 2014, a period during which it was publicly acknowledged that certain aspects of the regime were failing to achieve compliance, which led to public consultations and reforms. This chapter provides an in-depth overview of the structure of the TGA and the pre- and post-market regulation of prescription and non-prescription medicines. This includes the two-tiered classification scheme the TGA uses to determine, based on risk, the extent to which a medicine is evaluated prior to its approval and regulated post-approval. It also includes an overview of adverse drug reaction (ADR) reporting, manufacturer inspections, laboratory testing, compliance reviews and the pre-approval and complaints reporting processes for advertising to the public (DTCA) and health professionals (promotion). The chapter discusses the TGA's hybrid risk-based and responsive approach to regulation. Drawing on the theoretical framework developed in the previous chapters, Chapter 3 evaluates the strengths and limitations of risk-based and responsive regulation, including their points of incompatibility (and therefore the limitations of combining the theories to form a hybrid approach) and their alignment with neoliberal governmentality. Finally, the chapter identifies the aspects of the regime that have the potential for failure.

Chapters 4 and 5 examine the reasons behind the regulatory regime's failure to achieve compliance from prescription and non-prescription medicines sponsors. Between 2010 and 2014, the Australian Government undertook an unprecedented number of public consultations about reforming the regime, conducting as many as 65 consultations during the period (exceeding the total for the previous 11 years). A qualitative thematic analysis was conducted, using Braun and Clarke's (2006) method, of 451 submissions to 12 of these public consultations, as well as of interview transcripts from semi-structured interviews with 18 participants. These 12 consultations were selected from those listed on the TGA, Department of Health and Australian Parliament websites between 1 January 2010 and 30 June 2014 (as detailed in Appendix 1). They include all three consultations listed on the Department of Health and Australian Parliament websites on the post-market regulation of prescription and non-prescription medicines and 9 of the 65 listed on the TGA website.[7] Of the 12 consultations analysed, 451 (out of a possible 1,658) submissions were published, with most of the unpublished submissions being from a single TGA consultation.[8] Aside from the unpublished submissions and a minority of submissions where the submitter requested that their submission be marked confidential, the majority of submissions were publicly available (details in Appendix 1). Sponsors or industry associations comprised the largest group of submitters to the consultations analysed (173 out of 451, or 38.4%), with professional associations providing the third largest number of submissions (14.6%, or 66 out of 451) (for the complete list of the submissions, see Appendix 3). Given the overrepresentation of industry in the submissions analysed, a qualitative (rather than quantitative) thematic analysis was employed.

The semi-structured, open-ended interviews were conducted between 1 February and 31 July 2013, following ethics approval[9] and five pilot interviews. Participants were sampled from organisations associated with the post-market regulation of prescription and non-prescription medicines. Of the 44 individuals and organisations approached for an interview, 18 consented to participate. Among them, seven were employed by the TGA and one was a former TGA employee. Five participants were from TGA committees: two from the Advisory Committee on the Safety of Medicines (ACSOM), two from the Australian Therapeutic Goods Advisory Council (ATGAC) and one from the Therapeutic Goods Committee (TGC). Of the committee members, two were pharmacists (one practising and one retired); two were medical practitioners (one with a private practice and one from a hospital); and one was a full-time consumer representative. Another two participants were employed by industry associations (Australian Self-Medication Industry and Medicines Australia),[10] two were academics who also identified as consumer advocates and one was a lawyer who represented sponsors in legal cases against the TGA.[11]

The analysis of this data revealed two overarching themes: first, that the TGA is limited in its capacity to intervene in the regulatory regime and the regime itself is limited in generating compliance (which I refer to as *regulatory disempowerment*); and second, the public and those representing the public's interests are limited in their capacity to participate in the regime (referred to as *public disempowerment*). Chapters 4 and 5 delve into each of these themes separately. Chapter 4 examines several aspects of regulatory disempowerment: the limited pre- and post-market evaluation of medicine quality, safety and efficacy, and DTCA and promotion (*limited evaluation*); the limited active enforcement (*limited active/reactive enforcement*); the limited centralisation of regulation (*limited centralisation*); the limited proportionality in responding to non-compliance (*limited proportionality*); limitations in escalating the response to non-compliance (*limited escalation*); and operational constraints on the TGA (*operationally constrained*). The chapter discusses how the approach to risk and cooperativeness of sponsors towards the TGA rationalised limiting the intervention of the TGA in the regime. It also examines how the incompatibility of risk-based and responsive techniques rationalised and therefore further limited the TGA's intervention. It ultimately argues that regulatory failures reinforce hegemonic neoliberal governmentality by rationalising the (re)turn to the use of micro-level (self-) regulatory techniques.

Chapter 5 considers the limits on participation in the regime by the public and representatives of the public interest. This public disempowerment is examined in the form of limited transparency (*limited transparency of information* and *the regulator*) and accountability (*limited accountability*), the public's limited role in the regime (*limited regulatory role of the public*), and the regime's furthering of state–corporate relations (*enhanced state–corporate relations*). The chapter examines how technologies intended to empower participation in the regime by the public and representatives of their interests are shaped by asymmetries of knowledge and power (or knowledge/power as these 'directly imply one another'; see Foucault 1977:27–28), thus disempowering them (and making these technologies of (dis)empowerment). This knowledge/power asymmetry also reinforces hegemonic neoliberal governmentality by rationalising the use of micro-level (self-)regulatory techniques.

Chapter 6 questions whether 'better' or 'more' regulation, and therefore continuing to work within the neoliberal project, is the solution. It examines the reforms to the medicine regulatory regime introduced in the period following data collection up to mid-2024. The thematic analysis identified four recommendations from the submissions and transcripts for 'bettering' regulation: *increasing regulation* (through greater government involvement, centralisation and co-regulation); *increasing penalties* (in severity and range); *increasing resourcing*; and *increasing transparency*, of both the TGA and the regulatory regime. The chapter discusses how these reforms were shaped by (and subordinated to) neoliberal rationalities, such as risk rationality, cost-benefit (economic) rationality and responsibilisation, and how they therefore reinforced the hegemony of neoliberal governmentality.

The conclusion argues that addressing the harms caused by the failures of the regulatory regime will likely require more substantive, socially transformative changes, in place of continuing to reform and work within the neoliberal project. It emphasises the need to rationalise reforms on the basis of health (and not neoliberal rationalities), advocating for the (re)design of not only regulatory but also health systems in ways that oppose the imperatives of neoliberal capitalism. This could involve a form of health communism, or, ideally, decolonising health.

## Notes

1 Restricted representations are implicit or explicit references to a serious disease, condition or other health deficiency generally where diagnosis, treatment,

supervision, interpretation or follow-up is required by a health professional (TGA 2020d).

2 The exception being restricted representations, in which case, an application to the TGA to use the restricted representation in advertising should be made (TGA 2020d). However, this requirement is not necessarily complied with (as demonstrated by the proportion of COVID-19 advertising complaints).

3 Through the so-called Chicago Boys of the Chicago School of Economics and Friedman (see Fischer 2015).

4 Aside from national-popular program/me (both spellings are used by Jessop), the phrasings 'set of interests' (Joseph 2024:251) and 'set of policies or goals' (Jessop 1990:181) are also used interchangeably elsewhere by other scholars, as well as by Jessop.

5 These are the 'empirical' (i.e. what we perceive or experience, directly or indirectly), the 'actual' (what occurs, whether we perceive or experience it or not) and the 'real' (what generates the actual and empirical) (Frauley 2007:266).

6 They generate what actually exists (the 'actual'), together with what we perceive or experience (the 'empirical').

7 Fourteen of the consultations listed on the TGA website were excluded because the consultation theme was outside the scope of this study (i.e. on bloods, tissues, biologics, disinfectants, sterilants, medical and in vitro diagnostic devices, and medicines scheduling and poisons, as well as on the proposed Australia New Zealand Therapeutic Products Authority, which was not established). An additional 21 consultations were excluded because the submissions were unpublished (14) or not published, or the consultation had not closed before 30 June 2014 (7). Therefore, the nine submissions were selected out of a total of 30 consultations (see Appendix 2).

8 Entitled *Regulation Impact Statement: Regulating the Advertising of Therapeutic Goods to the General Public*. The TGA (2014f, para. 2) alleged that most of these unpublished submissions were written by complementary healthcare practitioners who opposed restriction of the term 'healthcare practitioner' to practitioners accredited by the National Registration and Accreditation Scheme (NRAS), which would have seen them excluded. The TGA received criticism for this proposed change—three separate petitions condemning the changes were organised by naturopaths, homoeopaths and herbalists with the support of Blackmores Limited. I made a written request to the TGA to access the remaining submissions, but this was not answered.

9 Obtained from Flinders University's Social and Behavioural Research Ethics Committee (Project Number 5588).

10 A written statement was obtained via phone with consent from a person employed by Complementary Medicines Australia (CMA).

11 A written statement was obtained from the Commonwealth Department of Public Prosecutions in response to a written request to participate in an interview. Although representatives of the Administrative Appeals Tribunal (AAT) were approached with a written request to participate in an interview, a response was not received.

# 2 Historical foundations of the medicine regulatory regime

Historical accounts of medicine regulation typically begin with the development of neoliberalism in the 1970s and 1980s (see, e.g. Davis and Abraham 2013) or of social welfarism in the 1940s and 1950s (see, e.g. Nik-Khah 2014; Löfgren and de Boer 2004). However, this book begins the historical account much earlier, in the foundation of the medicine regulatory regime in Australia. In so doing, it examines the successive shifts in the state project over time, specifically, with reference to micro-level discourses, ideas, rationalities, techniques and technologies of governing (or governmentality) and their coming together or combining to form a macro-level governmental strategy (or hegemonic project). This chapter examines these historical foundations, beginning with the colonisation of the continent and establishment of Australian settler colonialism/capitalism in the late 18th century. From the late 18th to the early 20th centuries, the attempts of the colonial governments and then the Australian Government to secure the population from the threat of foreign disease led to the formation of federal laws aimed at prohibiting the entry of harmful prescription and non-prescription medicines into Australia, and of the Department of Health. The chapter then examines the formation in Australia of 'limited' welfarism (Mendes 1998:66), more accurately described as social liberalism (still a form of capitalism), and the limited success of the Australian Government's attempts to fully socialise medicine from the mid-20th century. The chapter concludes by examining the shift from this social liberal to neoliberal capitalism, the 'commercialisation' (Department of Community Services and Health 1990:19) of health in Australia, and the formation of the TGA, the *Therapeutic Goods Act 1989* (Cth), and a decentralised and deregulated medicine regulatory regime.

The purpose of starting this discussion in the foundation of the medicine regulatory regime in Australia is to demonstrate that hegemonic neoliberal governmentality did not develop in isolation and its harms have historical causes. Its realisation and pervasiveness as a hegemonic project are the result of the convergence of neoliberal thinking with similar ideas. Health and the economy have long been linked—not just in terms of the reproduction and physical health of the population and thereby its capacity to produce but also through the objectification and commodification of health (i.e. attaining a

DOI: 10.4324/9781003285762-2

value, or something to be bought and sold). Relations between the state and the medicines industry are also demonstrated to be long-standing and well established. By examining the transformations to the medicine regulatory regime over time, we can learn how the state project came to be produced and reproduced, how it became neoliberal, and how neoliberal governmentality, in turn, became hegemonic.

## 2.1 The colonial foundations of the Department of Health

The Australian medicine regulatory regime and its neoliberalisation have their beginnings in colonialism and the creation of colonial (racial) difference (i.e. 'the hegemonic conception of the human'—see Mignolo and Walsh 2018:179). The establishment of the British settler colonies, and the 'invasion' of the continent from the perspective of Aboriginal and Torres Strait Islander people (Watson 2017), began in 1788. In the 18th century, neo-European settler colonies, such as those in Australia (its colonial name), functioned as emerging and developing 'settler production regimes' (Lloyd 2012:23) within a Euro-centric (and in time, an increasingly globalist) colonial/capitalist project. In the Australian context, such regimes mostly entailed large inflows of 'free' (convict) labour and outflows of stolen resources (through the annihilation of Aboriginal people and theft and annihilation of Aboriginal land) between England and Australia.

During the early colonisation of the continent and prior to Federation in 1901, there was a lack of inter-colonial quarantine, particularly at ports of entry. Within the earliest (albeit incomplete) records, and oral and traditional knowledges of disease, was the epidemic of smallpox in 1789, which disproportionately 'attacked' Aboriginal people in the south-eastern part of the continent and 'a coloured seaman', but 'no other person amongst the colonists' (Cumpston 1914:1). In the first decade of British colonisation, the rate of mortality among the Aboriginal people from smallpox was estimated to be at least 50% (Dowling 1997). The lack of understanding of the origin of the disease and of the perceived difference in immunity to it led to smallpox being racialised. It was commonly referred to by the colonists as 'native' or 'colonial pox' (Cumpston 1914:4), despite the fact that it was likely introduced by Europeans (and that their immunity was a result of their prior exposure). Foucault (1982:77–78) argues that this form of 'dividing practice', whereby subjects are divided within themselves and from others, is what 'objectizes' them.

The geographical location of the 'healthy' white British settler colonies on a continent within the Asia-Pacific region (construed as 'diseased' and 'not white'—see Bashford 1998:393) bolstered the discourse of racial difference (and a 'self-inflicted fear of difference'—see Mignolo 2021:114). There was particular concern over the 'large . . . influx of Chinese into these colonies' in the second half of the 19th century (Legislative Council of Tasmania 1881:9). Initially, the arrival of people from China in Australia was a result of the need for indentured labour; a reduction in the number of convicts being transported to Australia and therefore in the labour supply in the 1840s led to more than 2,000 Chinese men and boys being imported under indenture as 'cheap labour' from around 1847 to 1853 (Choi 1971:65; Darnell 2004). This preceded Chinese migration and immigration following the discovery of gold in 1851 (see Choi 1971:50–52). According to the colonial governments, Chinese immigration was not only 'highly undesirable' but also to be 'restrict[ed]' (Legislative Council of Tasmania 1881:9). The forming of racial difference in relation to Chinese migrants was said to be:

> not altogether one of prejudice of colour or race, but . . . founded in a *rational* view of the dangers to these British communities which might, in the course of time, flow from a people numbering more than 400,000,000, whose language, laws, religion, and habits of life are alien to those of Her Majesty's subjects in Australasia, and whose geographical position makes the danger more imminent.
>
> (Legislative Council of Tasmania 1881: 18–19, emphasis added)

From the 18th century to the mid-20th century, the 'life' of the population was the 'object' of politics in Australia. This 'biopolitics', as it was referred to by Foucault (2008),[1] can be conceived as a rationality of government, but it is also distinct from governmentality in the sense that it is a form of (bio)power, which rationalises, and therefore shapes and is shaped by, governmentality based on phenomena characteristic of the population (Foucault 2008:317). Such phenomena include health and also race (commonly used as a tool in the defence of the life of the population), both of which are hegemonic constructs.[2] Biopolitics in Australia during this period was therefore concerned primarily with 'guaranteeing health' because it ensured the reproductivity and economic productivity of the population (Foucault 2004:6). It became integral to the development of techniques of immigration control (rationalised under the guise of quarantine and health), and later, the shifting and normalisation of the responsibility for health/healthiness (explained in Sections 2.2 and 2.3).

Unrestricted immigration was considered by the colonial governments to be a threat not just to health but also to 'imperial cleanliness', which John Howard Lidgett Cumpston (1909 as cited in Bashford 1998:393), the would-be first director-general of Australia's Department of Health, famously described as 'colonisation by means of known laws of cleanliness rather than by military force'. People from China in particular were portrayed as 'purveyors of disease', in addition to being 'moral' threats (see Bashford 1998:397). For example, in 1881, the 'most serious' outbreak of smallpox in the colony of New South Wales (NSW) was attributed to migrants who had recently arrived from China and settled in Sydney, despite there being 'absolutely no evidence of the origin' of the outbreak (see Cumpston 1914:11). The NSW

Government proceeded to quarantine vessels arriving from China at ports in NSW, irrespective of whether those on board showed signs of the disease (Curthoys 1973:542). It was this discourse of racial difference in health that was used to rationalise the calls to create a national system (or regime) of quarantine during the 1890s; in 1895, for instance, a quarantine station in Darwin was proposed simply because it was thought to be 'a highway for . . . Chinese brethren to push their way into Australia' (O'Doherty 1895 as cited in Bashford 1998:399).

Although there were multiple attempts to develop a 'uniform' and 'effective' (Cumpston 1913:9) regime of quarantine across the colonies in the 1880s and 1890s, the colonies continued to adopt different approaches. It was only after the continent-wide plague introduced in 1900, which lasted until 1909, that the colonial governments unanimously agreed to establish a regime of quarantine under a national government. Through the Constitution, which came into effect on 1 January 1901, the national government of Australia (herein, Australian Government) was authorised to legislate on quarantine at ports of entry (i.e. to govern *external* populations). The governments of each state of Australia (herein, state governments), however, were authorised to legislate on quarantine within states (i.e. to govern *internal* populations), a power that was retained by the Constitution.

The Australian Government took its first steps in legislating its Constitutional powers in 1906, amid the continent-wide plague. Under the then Prime Minister Alfred Deakin and the Protectionist (Liberal Protectionist) Party, the Australian Government introduced the Quarantine Act, which, together with the *Immigration Restriction Act 1901* (Cth) that took effect shortly after Federation, empowered the government to quarantine and thus enact techniques 'for the exclusion, detention, observation, segregation, isolation, protection, and disinfection of' those persons entering Australia (Quarantine Act, s. 4). These techniques also extended to goods entering the country, such as medicines (along with vessels, animals and plants). The Quarantine Act was significant in that it was a technology of governing both health and race, and it facilitated the introduction of the White Australia Policy (through the segregation of Aboriginal and other non-white populations on the basis of quarantine and health—see Bashford 2004). It was also significant because it led to the establishment of the Quarantine Service, the first apparatus of the state responsible for governing health (and through which the hegemony of the state project would be expressed). The Quarantine Service was situated within the Australian Government's Department of Trade and Customs, but it was operated by the chief health officers of each of the state governments (meaning that these officers governed both external and internal quarantine) (Castles 1988:405). The interference of this arrangement in the responsibilities of chief health officers in governing within their states caused tension between the Australian and state governments, so much so that between 1910 and 1929, most of the state governments ceased cooperating with the Service.

In the period immediately following World War I, the return of Australian Imperial Force personnel and the 1918–1919 global influenza (flu) pandemic were used to justify broadening the powers of the Australian Government (then under the Nationalist Party) in governing health. Cumpston (1910 as cited in Roe 1976:185) was particularly public in his support for the 'nationalisation of medicine'. As the Head of the Quarantine Service, a position he assumed in 1913, he submitted a memorandum to the Conference of Commonwealth and State Ministers in 1919 proposing the establishment of a department of health, among other proposals. According to a later annual report of the Department of Health (1972:11), these proposals were made by Cumpston based on the belief 'that economic benefits were to be gained' from a healthy Australian population. Acting Prime Minister William Watt wrote to each of the premiers following the conference, stating that the Australian Government was prepared to adopt Dr Cumpston's proposal of establishing a national department. The department's role would be restricted to coordinating the public health response at the national level so as not to infringe upon or result in the transfer of state powers (Watt 1919 as cited in Roe 1976:179). Although these proposals received some support, state governments preferred that the Australian Government coordinate (and therefore supervise and subsidise) health governance by each of the states (Department of Health 1972:11). Prime Minister William Hughes was also initially resistant to these proposals, despite the lobbying of the Federal Committee of the British Medical Association (BMA) in Australia and the International Health Board (Department of Health 1972; Roe 1976). It was not until the 1920s when the flu reached pandemic levels in Australia (again, introduced from overseas), that a consensus was achieved, and the prime minister and premiers agreed to the creation of a national department of health (albeit, not the formal conferring of power by the states to the Australian Government) (Roe 1976:179).

The Department of Health emerged institutionally out of the Quarantine Service in 1921 by Order of the Federal Executive Council of the Australian (Nationalist) Government. The Department was charged with administering quarantine through the Quarantine Act, but its powers also included the following: primary coordination of public health measures and education; primary coordination of measures for the prevention and investigation of death and disease, as well as powers to create and control laboratories for these purposes; and control of the Commonwealth Serum Laboratories (CSL), the government body responsible for the production of Australia's vaccines and the commercial distribution of its products (Hughes 1921:1). Cumpston was appointed director-general of the Department, a position he held until 1945.

## 2.2 Limited welfarism and not-so-social medicine

It was during the mid-20th century, at the time of the establishment of the modern/colonial system of human rights, that biopower was gradually expanded with the intent of governing population health for individuals' and less so the state's benefit (Foucault 2004).[3] While the government had managed to bring under control 'classic' diseases (through the quarantining of those external populations entering Australia), previously largely unknown diseases began to emerge, as a result of greater longevity and lifestyle changes among the Australian population (Department of Health 1975:5). Therefore, the idea of the 'healthy individual serving the State' was reversed, and the right to health became the object of state biopolitical intervention (Foucault 2004:6). However, the state's increasing preoccupation with the rights of the population by no means diminished the links established previously between health and the economy (and therefore, the 'appearance of a political economy of health'; Foucault 2004:18). Human rights were highly compatible with social liberal ideas and facilitated the development of social liberal governmentality (and hegemony, in turn).[4] Indeed, it was the discourse of rights and premise of the 'legitimate' rights of the individual (of freedom *from* and *through* the state) that were compatible with the liberal idea 'that freedom, or certain forms of freedom, are really respected', including those freedoms of private individuals and the economy, and that of a centralised (but limited) state (Foucault 2007:353). As Foucault (2007:352–353) argued, the state project shifted to one of respecting, and therefore working with rather than against, 'natural' processes. This meant limiting state intervention, but not limiting it entirely. Thus, the state intervened in health in limited ways to ensure (but not to violate) such rights.

In the post–world war and Great Depression period, the Labor government attempted to nationalise healthcare, starting with the introduction and passing of the *Pharmaceutical Benefits Act 1944* (Cth), which sought to create a scheme for providing prescription medicines free to the public, and thereby increase their accessibility, called the Pharmaceutical Benefits Scheme (PBS or Scheme). However, the Pharmaceutical Benefits Act 1944 was opposed not only by the opposition political parties but also by the medical profession because it was perceived to be a form of rights-violating state intervention that 'seriously jeopardised . . . [and] limit[ed] the freedom of a doctor in prescribing' (Australian Federal Council of the BMA 1943 as cited in Galligan 1987:150). The constitutionality of the Pharmaceutical Benefits Act 1944 was challenged successfully in the High Court of Australia in 1945 by Victoria's then attorney-general Ian Macfarlan (United Australia Party), who brought the case on behalf of the Medical Society of Victoria (Galligan 1987:150). The decision prompted the introduction of the Constitutional Alteration (Social Services) Bill and referendum in 1946. This Bill was designed to alter the Constitution to allow the Australian Government to legislate broadly on 'the provision of maternity allowances, widows' pensions, child endowment, unemployment, pharmaceutical, sickness and hospital benefits, medical and dental services (but not so as to authorize any form of civil conscription), benefits to students and family allowances'. The Bill and referendum received the support of the opposition because of the 'civil conscription' qualification, which was included at the recommendation of Robert Menzies, then leader of the Liberal Party of Australia, and the request of Sir Henry Newland, president of the Federal Council of the BMA in Australia (Goddard 2014; McDonald et al. 2023). The success of the referendum led to the reintroduction of the Scheme by the Labor government through the passing of the *Pharmaceutical Benefits Act 1947* (Cth), but with no provision compelling health practitioners to participate. Because most practitioners chose not to participate in (and instead to boycott) the Scheme after it came into effect in 1948,[5] the government placed those medicines most commonly prescribed in Australia onto the Commonwealth Pharmaceutical Formulary and amended the Act to require practitioners to use the Commonwealth Prescription Form to prescribe them or risk being fined. The 'practical compulsion' of the Scheme led the High Court to again find it unconstitutional, and the practitioner to be 'affected in his [*sic*] freedom of practice . . . whereby he [*sic*] is subject to control as to the form of the treatment and the drugs which he [*sic*] may prescribe', in a case brought by the BMA in Australia in 1949 (*BMA v Commonwealth* 1949 79 CLR 201:256). Before the end of the year, the newly elected Liberal government under Prime Minister Robert Menzies altered the Scheme to limit the number of medicines on the Formulary to 139 (Biggs 2002). The Scheme was further altered under this government to make prescription medicines free to pensioners, their dependants and 'certain members of friendly society dispensaries' (starting with the National Health (Medicines for Pensioners) Regulations 1951), and then to increase the number of medicines on the Scheme and make them available to the wider public but with a fee (or co-payment) in 1960 (under the *National Health Act (No. 72) 1959* (Cth)). The Minister for Health at the time, Sir Earle Page, rationalised the government's approach by stating:

> [t]he great danger in any government-aided health scheme is the tendency to *develop a psychology of dependence and diminished personal and community responsibility*. The fundamental aim of any social security scheme should be to raise the individual to a level at which he [sic] can *help himself* [sic]. Any such scheme should contain elements that encourage *self-reliance* and a sense of *personal responsibility*. Also it should stress the obligation of the individual to make at least a part of *his* [sic] *contribution* directly to the functioning and cost of the Scheme.
> (Australian House of Representatives 1953: 1756–1757, emphasis added)

The cost of the PBS was not only continuously monitored by the Department of Health, given that it was 'the biggest single item' of national health and departmental expenditure (Department of Health 1972:19), but also minimised through the Department's direct negotiations with the pharmaceutical industry to obtain a 'reduction in prices' and 'savings' (Department of Health 1964:16–17). The nationalisation of healthcare in Australia therefore represented a 'limited welfare state' shaped by 'social liberalism' (Mendes 1998:65–66), a form of hegemony combining socialism and liberal, laissez-faire capitalism. As described by Mendes (66), this social liberalism 'provided a safety net' while also fostering some self-reliance.

Concerns that prescription medicines imported and supplied on the PBS were substandard[6] led to the introduction and passing of the *Therapeutic Substances Act 1953* and *1959* (Cth) and the Therapeutic Substances Regulations 1956. These Acts and Regulations were techniques for regulating the unnecessary risks to health posed by therapeutic substances ('substances which have a therapeutic use', including medicines), most of which were imported into Australia. They required those substances imported, exported, subject to interstate trade or commerce, supplied on the PBS and supplied to the government (e.g. by tender)[7] to conform to the British Pharmacopoeia or Pharmaceutical Codex, the quality standard adopted in Australia for manufacturing, labelling and packaging. The importers of these substances were also required to supply a certificate upon import issued by an official appointed by the Director-General of Health to demonstrate the conformity of the substances with Australian laws.[8] Although a process for laboratory testing was in place, testing was carried out by either the laboratories of the Department of Trade and Customs within states (and at the point of import into Australia '[t]o avoid undue delay to importers') or the CSL (Australian Senate 1953; Department of Health 1964:23). In 1958, the National Biological Standards Laboratory (NBSL) was formed within the Department of Health with a remit to test the quality (potency and purity) and safety of those substances subject to the requirements of the Therapeutic Substances Act and Regulations. Prescription medicines to be listed on the PBS were also tested by the NBSL for their efficacy prior to listing and were subject to ongoing testing post-listing; if a sample failed, either the batch would be withdrawn from the market or the medicine would be delisted from the PBS. The NBSL also conducted visits and inspections of manufacturing facilities located overseas and in Australia (in conjunction with state health departments). Historically, the NBSL had 'good relations' with the pharmaceutical industry:

> Officers of the Laboratory have visited a number of pharmaceutical companies to discuss technical problems. In return, the Laboratory has been visited by representatives of the industry. . . . [T]he aim of the Laboratory [was] to maintain a close liaison with industry on technical matters and to encourage manufacturers to co-operate in a joint effort to ensure that high standards of pharmaceutical manufacture are maintained.
>
> (Department of Health 1969:67)

The harms of thalidomide[9] prompted the development of further apparatuses and technologies under the Liberal government to ensure medicine safety and efficacy. The Australian Drug Evaluation Committee (ADEC) was established in 1963 to evaluate and advise on the quality, safety and (later) efficacy of applications for approving and clinical trials for medicines and the extension of indications for already approved medicines referred to it by the Department. In its second meeting, ADEC recommended to the Minister the establishment of an Adverse Drug Reactions Advisory Committee (ADRAC) and a register of ADRs, which came into effect in 1964. The Committee's concerns about the adequacy of (and potential for 'misleading') information being provided to health practitioners by pharmaceutical companies led to the expansion of ADEC's and ADRAC's responsibilities to include the evaluation of the literature provided to practitioners and of the labelling and packaging (including packaging inserts or information) of medicines (Department of Health 1969, 1972, 1973). The *Therapeutic Goods Act 1966* (Cth), which replaced the Therapeutic Substances Acts and Regulations, not only established the general standards for therapeutic goods ('for therapeutic use') but also empowered the Department to compel importers, interstate traders, and suppliers on the PBS or to the government to provide information (such as data) on the composition of goods. A Code of Good Manufacturing Practice (GMP) for the licensing and inspection of pharmaceutical manufacturing facilities, and the recall of medicines from the Australian market, was also developed in 1969 by officers in the federal and state health departments, in consultation with the pharmaceutical industry (Department of Health 1964:51).

The expansion of the Department's responsibility for governing medicines led to the creation of a dedicated Therapeutic Substances Branch in 1964 (later renamed the Therapeutic Division in 1974). It was separate from ADEC[10] and the NBSL but incorporated ADRAC (and therefore, the ADR register) and the pharmaceutical benefits section (later in 1974). Initially, the Branch was responsible for governing those goods subject to the requirements of the Customs (Prohibited Imports) Regulations 1956 and the Therapeutic Goods Act and Regulations. However, its responsibilities were expanded in the 1970s to include governing the advertising of prescription and non-prescription medicines.

Prescription and non-prescription medicine advertising had previously been governed primarily by the states, but due to concerns over 'extravagant' advertising (National Health and Medical Research Council (NHMRC) 1941 as cited in McEwen 2007:15), there had been national-level advertising controls as early as the 1940s. Among the first introduced were controls enshrined in the *Broadcasting Act 1942* (Cth), which required the text for a radio or television advertisement of a therapeutic good to be pre-approved by the Director-General of Health. These advertisements were also required to conform to the 'General Advertising Standards' of the Australian Broadcasting Control Board. The advertising of non-prescription medicines was governed by the Guide for Manufacturers and Advertisers 'Rules Relating to the Advertising of Proprietary Medicines' developed in 1962 by an expert committee appointed by the NHMRC (and 'administered by a Censor appointed by the industries concerned') (World Health Assembly, 21 1968:13).

Between 1971 and 1975, the National Therapeutic Goods Committee (NTGC), comprising representatives from the federal and state health departments, repeatedly expressed concern about the lack of controls covering all aspects of prescription and non-prescription advertising. Chief among these concerns were that advertising directed at medical practitioners often did not contain references to contraindications, side effects, ADRs and interactions, or other precautions (Department of Health 1973:77). In addition, concerns were raised over the advertising of analgesics, vitamins, minerals and other supplements, which were subject to fewer controls than prescription medicines (Department of Health 1973). In 1975, the Minister for Health delegated responsibility to the Therapeutics Division for pre-approving advertisements on radio and television, literature provided to practitioners and (in 1978) packaging inserts. Around the same time, the NTGC established a sub-committee for the purposes of drafting proposals to cover all aspects of prescription and non-prescription advertising. 'To be effective', the then Director-General of Health Sir William Refshauge stressed, the proposals 'need[ed] to be incorporated into appropriate Federal and State legislation' because '[w]ithout such controls the benefits from evaluating and testing therapeutic goods are limited' (Department of Health 1974:35). Instead of legislating these proposals, the Voluntary Code for the Advertising of Goods for Therapeutic Use (later renamed the Therapeutic Goods Advertising Code) was introduced in 1977 and 'reviewed annually . . . by a joint working party comprising industry and Department representatives' (Department of Health 1981:30).[11]

In the same period, there were also concerns (particularly expressed by the NTGC and NBSL) about the lack of consistent standards and controls applicable to all types of therapeutic goods because of the complex mix of national and state legislation and requirements (e.g. see Department of Health 1974–1980). The Therapeutics Division therefore commenced work on the creation of national standards and a national register of therapeutic goods by establishing a working party consisting of representatives from federal and state health departments, industry and the health profession (Department of Health 1978:29).

## 2.3 The 'commercialisation' of health: the neoliberal foundations of the Therapeutic Goods Administration (TGA) and regulatory regime

In the late 20th century, there was a hegemonic shift in the state project from social liberal to neoliberal capitalism. The ideas of the latter—of individualism, deregulation and self-regulation, and an increasingly decentralised (and limited) state—were highly compatible with the ideas of the former, and this convergence of ideas facilitated the formation of neoliberal forms of governmentality (which became hegemonic).

Despite the promises of successive Liberal and Labor governments to reduce their expenditure, the federal budget continued to operate at a deficit throughout the late 1970s and 1980s. These deficits came following the recession in 1974–1975, the first since the Great Depression of the 1930s, and during the recession that occurred shortly thereafter in 1982–1983 (Reserve Bank of Australia 2024; Trading Economics 2024). The manufacturing sector in Australia was most impacted by the first of these recessions, including the pharmaceutical manufacturing sector (Industries Assistance Commission 1978:4). At this time, the Australian pharmaceutical market was composed mostly of imported medicines (both prescription and non-prescription). Further, the Australian pharmaceutical industry was mostly made up of multinational companies whose operations were secondary forms of manufacturing, primarily involving the formulation of imported ingredients and the repackaging of imported medicines to conform with Australian requirements (Industries Assistance Commission 1976, 1986; Industry Commission 1996; Löfgren and de Boer 2004). Australian exports were therefore relatively 'insignificant' and 'almost no R&D was undertaken' (Löfgren and de Boer 2004:2399). In 1976, the Industries Assistance Commission (established in 1973, now the Productivity Commission) found that the lack of profitability had qualified some parts of the pharmaceutical manufacturing sector in Australia to receive a minimal amount of government assistance. Increasingly, the classic social-liberal ideas of a central (but limited) state appeared less suited to addressing these economic failures of the government (Beeson and Firth 1998:215). This crisis of hegemony was not unique to Australia, reflecting similar crises occurring in other states and within the world political-economic order. The neoliberal ideas of the Chicago School of Economics, and the Thatcher and Reagan governments in the UK and US, respectively, were influential in shaping the emergence of a 'New Right' within the Liberal Party of Australia, starting with the backbench in the early 1980s (Mendes 1998). This occurred because these 'new' liberal ideas appealed to and reworked many of the classic liberal ideas of the party (Beeson and Firth 1998). These ideas also influenced the 'repositioning' of the Australian Labor Party, which assumed government between 1983 and 1996, towards the political centre (even to the right), and in turn, that of the Liberal Party further towards the right (to distinguish it from the Labor Party) when it reassumed government in 1996 (Mendes 1998:67). For these reasons, Humphrys (2019) argues that neoliberalism was a state-led and staged hegemonic project from 1973–1983, to 1983–1993 (when it became hegemonic under the Labor government), and 1993–2008 (after which time the current crisis of neoliberalism began to emerge).

Health expenditure had long been a concern of the Australian Government, but in the 1980s, the government recognised that these costs were 'inescapable' and that it could 'no longer devote the [large] share of national resources to health care'; instead, there had to be '*efficient* use of the available resources' (Department of Health 1981:5, emphasis in original). In this regard, expenditure on the PBS increased throughout the 1960s and 1970s (during which time less of a reduction in the prices of medicines was negotiated between the Department and pharmaceutical companies), yet these costs were passed increasingly onto the public by raising the co-payment. In 1960, the co-payment for general patients was 50 cents, and it was increased for the first time to AU$1.00 in 1971. Between 1975 and 1985, however, the co-payment increased from AU$1.50 to AU$5 and was raised further to AU$10, AU$11 and AU$15 in 1986, 1988 and 1990, respectively (PBS 2024).

Health expenditure also shifted from an emphasis on treatment to a focus on prevention. The Department became 'increasingly active in . . . health promotion' (Department of Health 1980:2). Ralph Hunt, the Minister for Health, justified in 1978 that 'health problems' were:

> related to *personal behaviour* and . . . largely preventable by *action at* [the] *individual level*. It would seem appropriate at this time, therefore, to consider an approach to *personal health* which looks beyond the confines of curative medicine and considers the potential of prevention.
> (Department of Health 1985:29, emphasis added)

In 1979, the Department was provided with AU$500,000 in funding from the Liberal government to establish a National Health Promotion Program, which went by the titles of 'Help Yourself' and 'Help Yourself to Better Health', 'to encourage Australians to be more aware of and active in maintaining and improving their health, to assist them to make informed decisions about their personal well-being, and to help them to act on those decisions' (Department of Health 1980:3–4). This shift reflected the hegemony of health evident globally at the time (Owoh 1996:212). The 'Help Yourself' campaigns were influenced by the WHO-UNICEF Conference and the *Alma-Ata Declaration*[12] of 1978, which Australia actively supported (Department of Health 1981:2). Dr Halfdan Mahler, then Director-General of WHO, had promoted 'Health For All', which he rationalised as:

> health [which] begins at home, in schools and in factories. It is there, where people live and work, that health is made or broken. . . . [T]hat people will realise that they themselves have the power to shape their lives and the lives of their families, free from the avoidable burden of disease, aware that ill-health is not inevitable. . . . [T]hat people will use better approaches than they do now for preventing disease and alleviating unavoidable illness and disability, and better ways of growing up, growing old and dying gracefully. . . . [T]hat there will be an even distribution among the population of whatever resources are available. And . . . that essential health care will be accessible to all individuals

> and families, in an acceptable and affordable way, and with their full involvement.
>
> (Department of Health 1981:2)

This shift in hegemonic thinking from social liberalism to neoliberalism and the increasing individualisation of and responsibilisation for health was not big by any means; the mentality was that people simply become 'more free' (O'Malley 2016:111).

The Department of Health (1985:xiii) also became 'leaner' and 'more economical'. The lack of staff (and the high workload it created) had been an ongoing problem within the Department (e.g. see Department of Health 1969, 1973, 1975, 1976, 1979, 1984, 1985). With respect to the NBSL, Director-General Lawrie Willett explained:

> [t]he availability of skilled, highly-qualified staff in Australia is low, presumably as a result of the lack of a research-based segment of the pharmaceutical industry. Generally, it is a much more time-consuming task to recruit good calibre scientists than to recruit similarly capable clerical administrators. The average period taken to recruit a scientist is about twelve months, and usually a further period of training is necessary before an officer's talents can be fully used. Consequently, the laboratories are always under their authorised strength.
>
> (Department of Health 1984:87)

The understaffing and delays this caused to medicines approval were highlighted by the findings of the inquiries conducted by the Industries Assistance Commission (in 1976 and 1986), which considered pharmaceutical regulation to be excessive. Indeed, the pharmaceutical industry was regarded as 'one of the more heavily regulated' industries in Australia (Industries Assistance Commission 1986:41). It was widely believed within the industry that government intervention was 'a major impediment' and that the current regulatory regime (and in particular, the PBS) had an 'adverse impact . . . on industry profitability' (115). In 1985, the Labor government and Prime Minister Bob Hawke announced a wider 'administrative reorganisation' of the government (National Archives of Australia (NAA) 2024). Staff numbers were gradually decreased through transfers out of the Department. In July 1987, the Department was practically 'abolished', with its responsibilities reallocated to a 'new super-ministry', the Department of Community Services and Health (combining the portfolios of community services, health, and housing and construction) (NAA 2024). As part of this reallocation of responsibilities, the Australian Pharmaceutical Manufacturers Association (APMA) was given permission by the Trade Practices Commission (now the Australian Competition and Consumer Commission [ACCC]) to trial self-regulation for prescription medicine promotion between 1987 and 1989 (McEwen 2007:103).

The 1990s saw the 'commercialisation' of health (Department of Community Services and Health 1990:19). Through the passing of the Therapeutic Goods Act, the Labor government created a new national regulatory agency, the TGA—a product of the former NBSL and the Therapeutics Division within the Department of Health (McEwen 2007:51). These former apparatuses of the state were explicitly 'commercialised [through the creation of the TGA] to improve the efficiency, cost and turnaround times for approval of drugs and therapeutic goods for use' (Department of Community Services and Health 1990:20). It was around this time that the language of 'clients', which would include the 'consumers of corporate and other services' (1), entered into use and 'clients' needs and rights' became the object of government (Department of Community Services and Health 1989:8). Charges for approving therapeutic goods were introduced under the Therapeutic Goods Act as a means of increasing the resourcing of the TGA, and thereby decreasing the agency's reliance upon the state (Lexchin 2006:2216). Initially, fees and charges were established to recover just 50% of the TGA's running costs, a feat that would not be achieved until 1996. However, the Liberal government increased cost recovery levels to 75% in the 1997–1998 federal budget, and then to 100% in 1998 (McEwen 2007:44). Cost recovery was rationalised on the basis that it was 'expected to engender greater efficiency and concern of the organisation [the TGA] to meet client [industry] needs' (Department of Community Services and Health 1990:20).

The Therapeutic Goods Act replaced the complex regime of Australian state, territory and Commonwealth legislation, reallocating to the TGA the responsibility for regulating therapeutic goods from the point of supply in the Australian market, rather than at the point of import, as previously occurred. The Therapeutic Goods Act saw the introduction of an Australian Register for Therapeutic Goods (the ARTG or Register) and a two-tiered system for market entry: one for registered (high risk) medicines, another for listed (low risk) medicines (explored in detail in Section 3.3.). Provisions were created within the Act to compel companies to supply certain information with their applications for entry onto the Register; to compel companies to supply information when it was requested by the Secretary of the reorganised Department of Health, Housing and Community Services; and to cancel an entry when companies failed to comply with these provisions (McEwen 2007:57). Provisions were also created to require each manufacturer in Australia and overseas to be licensed (with the licensing fees to be cost recovered by the TGA) and adhere to the Code of GMP (57–58). However, the responsibility for regulating the promotion of prescription medicines to health professionals was formally delegated to APMA. The passing of the Therapeutic Goods Regulations 1990 (Cth) saw responsibility for the approval of advertisements for non-prescription medicines delegated to the Proprietary Medicines Association of Australia (PMAA) for print and electronic media. These technologies of agency were aimed at empowering industry associations and sponsors to become self-regulating so that the overall responsibility of the state in regulating this conduct could be decreased.

Despite these reforms, the TGA, like the Department before it, was criticised for its delays in evaluating and approving prescription medicines; and there were calls, led in part by APMA (e.g. see *Canberra Times* 1991a, 1991b), to 'overhaul' the medicines pre-approval process. Because timelier medicines approval aligned with the need of patients and patient interest groups for ready availability of and early access to medicines, these 'common interests' (through the incorporation of the public interest into the private interest) assisted in 'streamlining techniques' for medicines pre-approval (*TGA Strategic Management Plan 1994–1997* [herein TGA SMP] cited in ANAO 1996:9). For example, persistent calls by industry to speed up medicines' evaluation and approval were 'in line' (*Canberra Times* 1991a:4) with those of the Australian National Council on AIDS, the Australian Federation of AIDS Organisations and other acquired immune deficiency syndrome (AIDS) groups, who had called for greater availability of human immunodeficiency virus (HIV)/AIDS treatments in Australia. This successful alignment and cohesion of interests prompted the Minister for Health, Brian Howe, to act by commissioning an inquiry into the evaluation and pre-approval of prescription medicines in March 1991. During his address at the International Conference on Drug and Device Regulations, the Minister for Aged, Family and Health Services, Peter Staples, rationalised the need for the inquiry on the basis that:

> [p]rotect[ing] the public from unsafe, ineffective and poor quality drugs . . . needs to be balanced against the public's interest in gaining access to new and possibly life-saving medications. . . . Streamlining should be seen as maximising public access to improved drugs in the minimum time.
>
> (Staples 1991 as cited in ANAO 1996:9)

The report that emerged from the inquiry, titled *A Question of Balance: Report on the Future of Drug Evaluation in Australia* (herein the Baume Report), made a total of 164 recommendations, all of which were accepted by the Labor government, aimed at reducing approval times and measuring the TGA's performance (through the development of key performance indicators) (Baume 1991). The Therapeutic Goods Act was amended in December of 1991 to include statutory timeframes; if the TGA failed to complete an evaluation within the period mandated, it would have to forfeit 25% of the application fee (ANAO 1996:9). Between 1990 and 1995, the number of days it took the TGA to approve applications for registered medicines fell from 706 to 106 business days; and this reduction in approval time coincided with a higher number of approvals of applications (and an increase in cost recovery through fees to industry—see Lexchin 2006).

In accepting the recommendations of the Baume Report (Baume 1991), the TGA 'adopt[ed] a risk management approach in the interest of efficiency and in the streamlining of operations to work within available resources' (TGA SMP cited in ANAO 1996:23). To 'lower the workload' when evaluating prescription medicines, the TGA would place more 'trust in, and acceptance of, summary reports and overseas evaluation reports . . . [and] us[e] international standards and harmonization with other regulatory authorities' (9). Electronic technologies would also be used to perform 'lesser tasks' (9). Because 'risk management' was an 'attitude [that] must be adopted across all of TGA' (23), this mentality was also extended to the evaluation of non-prescription medicines. Prior to 1995, applications for listed medicines were evaluated by the TGA in approximately five months; however, this timeframe produced 'unnecessary barriers' and 'impediments' to accessing alternative medicines, especially 'to persons suffering from serious or terminal diseases', as 'their intrinsic safety is not in doubt' (Department of Health and Family Services 1996:1, 3). To reduce processing times, a 'new electronic lodgement facility' (or ELF) for listed medicines applications was therefore established in the mid-1990s. The ELF was 'predicated on self-assessment, rather than the TGA checking every detail to establish whether the medicine meets statutory requirements for listing in the listing process' (Australian Senate 2000:3). By 1997–1998, the ELF had reduced approval times for listed medicines to less than 10 days, and the number of applications for listing submitted to the TGA had more than doubled (TGA 2000:15). '[A] lower level of evidence' and 'increased flexibility in relation to claims' that were accepted were also permitted, based on the recommendations of KMPG's 1997 *Review of the Therapeutic Goods Administration* (KPMG 1997:50, 56). Together, these changes marked a shift in emphasis from pre-market to post-market techniques, and therefore, from social to individual responsibility and risk (in relation to the potential harms of medicines).

The development of the *National Medicines Policy* (NMP) in 1999, premised on a 'partnership approach' to policy development (Department of Health and Aged Care 1999b:6), formalised the alignment of public and private interests in national health policy. The NMP not only emphasised the 'quality use of medicines' and achieving appropriate standards of quality, safety and efficacy for the public's benefit, but also timely access to medicines—'at a cost individuals and the community can afford'—all while 'maintaining a responsible and viable medicines industry' (1). These often-conflicting aims of the NMP contributed to a 'paradox of regulation' (Haines 2011:2) whereby the TGA's regulation of medicines needed to balance the public's interests (of safeguarding them from medicine-related harms) with industry interests (of maintaining its economic viability), despite the framing of these interests (through the NMP) as being in common.

In the first decade of the 21st century, there were several failures of regulation. Two of the most notable, which were integral to shaping and reshaping the regulatory regime, were the TGA's response to Travacalm, manufactured by Pan Pharmaceuticals Limited (Pan); and its response to rofecoxib (Vioxx), sponsored by Merck & Co (Merck) and Merck Sharpe & Dohme Australia (MSD).

### *2.3.1 Pan Pharmaceuticals and Travacalm*

Pan Pharmaceuticals and its Director James Selim had a history of law and regulatory violations dating back to the late 1970s, including instances of the import of unapproved (and contaminated) therapeutic goods, the substitution of ingredients, the improper storage and handling of therapeutic goods, and the supply and export of unapproved therapeutic goods[13] (Dalley 2003:paras. 61–74). Between February 1992 and January 2003, Pan's manufacturing facilities were audited by the TGA on 12 occasions (as stated in court documents—see Commonwealth of Australia & Others 2010:para. 30(a)), the majority of which were announced.[14] According to a former Pan employee, because Pan regularly received advanced notice of an audit by the TGA, this allowed its facilities to be 'cleaned up neat and tidy' to bring them into compliance beforehand (Dalley 2003:para. 46). The TGA's Principal Medical Advisor, John McEwen, justified this approach of regularly announcing audits as necessary to the TGA establishing cooperation with the company:

> [i]f you're going to go through a pharmaceutical plant and ask to observe a production run of tablets, if you want to have access to their computers to get old batch records, you need their cooperation.
>
> (Dalley 2003:para. 56)

In 10 of the 12 audits conducted, deficiencies were found by the TGA. These deficiencies included the alleged manipulation of records to remove references to decisions of a Quality Control or Assurance Manager being overridden by Pan's management and to unauthorised deviations in the manufacturing of therapeutic goods (Commonwealth of Australia & Others 2010:para. 30(c)). Despite the presence of these deficiencies, certificates of compliance were issued to Pan by the TGA following every audit between 1992 and 2001 (para. 30(d)).

In December 2002 and January 2003, multiple reports were received by the TGA of adverse reactions to Travacalm, a registered, non-prescription medicine for travel sickness manufactured by Pan for Key Pharmaceuticals Pty Limited (hereafter Key). Among these were reports of up to 19 people requiring hospitalisation, some in intensive care (Australia, Senate 2005a; Commonwealth of Australia & Others 2010:para. 33(m)). A Class I[15] recall was announced by the TGA, with the approval of Key, on 21 January 2003 for three batches of Travacalm (TGA 2003). On 22 January 2003, laboratory testing by the TGA found the batches of Travacalm to vary between 0 and 700% in strength and that none were claimed to be within specification (Commonwealth of Australia & Others 2010:para. 33(u)). After an unannounced audit of Pan's facilities used in the manufacture of Travacalm was carried out on 30 and 31 January (from which an Audit Report was produced and later provided to Pan on 5 February), the TGA determined that Pan had used an unapproved method for mixing the content that caused the active ingredient to be unevenly distributed. Test results were also claimed to be 'deliberately and systematically manipulated' by Pan employees to conceal the lack of uniformity of the content (Commonwealth of Australia & Others 2010:para. 34(c)). General audits of Pan's facilities were said to have been initiated by the TGA on 24 and 25 February (the February Audit) and then on 7 and 14 April (the April Audit) (Commonwealth of Australia & Others 2010:paras. 40, 49). The TGA alleged that the February Audit was not completed and therefore had to be resumed in April because Selim 'initially refused' and restricted the auditors to an audit of documents rather than an audit of Pan's facilities (Commonwealth of Australia & Others 2010:para. 40(h)). The February and April Audits identified five and nine 'critical deficiencies', respectively.[16] On 28 April 2003, Pan was allegedly provided with the Audit Report outlining these deficiencies alongside written notice of the suspension of its manufacturing licence for six months and of the cancellation of the registration and listing on the ARTG of all of the therapeutic goods it sponsored (Commonwealth of Australia & Others 2010:paras. 63–65). A recall was also initiated of 219 products manufactured and supplied by Pan in Australia and more than 1,600 products exported by Pan, which was regarded at the time as the largest drug recall in Australian (and possibly world) history (Newman and Kellam 2004). Criminal proceedings were brought against Pan and the company was fined AU$10 million—the largest fine in the TGA's history at the time (*R v Pan Pharmaceuticals Pty Ltd* (2008) NSWDC 221:para. 39). Some of Pan's employees were also criminally prosecuted (e.g. see *R v Jain* (Unreported, District Court of New South Wales, Walmsley SC, 2 September 2005)). The suspension of Pan's manufacturing licence, the cancellation of the registration and listing of all of its products from the Register, the recall of all of its products and the court-imposed fine culminated in the company entering voluntary administration in September of 2003.

The TGA was criticised publicly for having 'overreacted', particularly by those companies affected by the recall (e.g. see Fitzsimmons 2003; Nicholas 2003; Robinson 2004; *The Sydney Morning Herald* 2003). The TGA's actions were also questioned in Parliament (e.g. see Australia, Senate 2005b:159–160). Although Prime Minister John Howard and members of the Liberal government publicly stated that they supported the actions taken by the TGA, in October 2003, the government commissioned the ANAO to audit the TGA's post-market regulation of non-prescription medicines. The resultant report, which was not published until December 2004, identified numerous issues. In relation to manufacturer audits, the ANAO (2004:14, 15, 17) found that the TGA did not record manufacturers' level of compliance with GMP, its record keeping was limited and sometimes 'incorrect or out of date', and the documentation of its decisions 'was often incomplete or inadequate'. In relation to Pan, the ANAO (2004:86) concluded that 'the TGA's views that all its decisions in this case were appropriate have not been supported by a thorough and independent assessment'. Following the publication of the ANAO report, the Liberal government made a number of amendments to the Therapeutic Goods Act, including the creation of a 'tiered offence regime' involving civil and administrative penalties (such as infringement notices and enforceable undertakings). In the second reading of the Therapeutic Goods Amendment Bill 2005, Liberal MP Christopher Pyne, then Parliamentary Secretary to the Minister for Health and Ageing, explained that withdrawing and cancelling the medicine or issuing a criminal penalty:

> may not, in some circumstances, be appropriate or achieve the optimal regulatory outcome, given the time and resources taken to prosecute offenders and the possible need to maintain supply of products to the public because of their essential nature or the lack of available substitute products.
>
> (Australian House of Representatives 2005:1)

In 2007, following audits of several other Australian Government regulators, the ANAO published the *Better Practice Guide to Administering Regulation*, seeking 'to improve' the performance of regulators by implementing risk-based and responsive regulatory techniques (see Section 3.2). The document instructed Australian regulatory agencies not only on how to manage risk through 'resourcing efficiency' but also on how to establish 'cooperative', 'client focused' relationships to 'more effectively elicit compliance' (ANAO 2007:26, 27, 36).[17]

In 2008, there were further repercussions arising from the TGA's response to Pan. To justify the immediate suspension of Pan's licence, the cancellation from the ARTG of all Pan's products and the mandatory recall of all products manufactured by Pan, the TGA had to demonstrate that Pan's products posed an imminent risk of death, or serious illness or injury. However, it was alleged (in court) that an expert advisory group assembled by the TGA to advise on the matter found that Pan products did not pose such a risk (Moran 2008:paras. 23–25). Despite this advice, the TGA allegedly pressed forward with the suspension of Pan's licence and the recall of Pan's products (para. 26). Notes taken during the meeting of the expert advisory group were allegedly destroyed by the TGA's Director of the Office of Complementary Medicines (paras. 21–22). Senior TGA staff were alleged to have misrepresented the risks posed by Pan products when seeking approval from the Minister and Prime Minister to close Pan's manufacturing facilities (para. 27). It was also alleged in court documents (Pharm-a-Care Laboratories 2010:paras. 40–41, 45, 47, 49, 52, 70) that the TGA's April Audit Report was illegitimate because its findings were based on two separate audits. Even though this claim was denied by the defence on the grounds that the February Audit was an 'incomplete audit' (see Commonwealth of Australia & Others 2010:para. 40), the February Audit did appear to be problematic insofar as the TGA denied Pan a prior opportunity to respond to and correct those deficiencies identified in February, contrary to its commitment to work cooperatively with industry. Combining the audit findings also appeared to exaggerate the total number of deficiencies identified—it was alleged that at least one of the deficiencies identified in the February Audit had been rectified prior to the April Audit yet remained listed as a deficiency in the April Audit Report (Pharm-a-Care Laboratories 2010:paras. 148(c) to (e)).

Selim brought an AU$200 million case against the Australian Government for negligence and abuse of power. In August 2008, the government agreed to pay AU$55 million to Selim in an out-of-court settlement, but it publicly stated that the settlement 'does not involve the Commonwealth conceding any of the specific allegations in the proceedings' (TGA 2008:para. 3). The Australian Government also agreed to pay a further AU$67.5 million in an out-of-court settlement to the 162 creditors, distributors and retailers financially impacted by the Pan recall (Hall 2011:para. 2). In 2010, the Therapeutic Goods Act was amended to provide the TGA with immunity from civil sanctions. S. 61A of the Act reads:

> No civil action, suit or proceeding lies against: (a) the Commonwealth; or (b) a protected person; in respect of loss, damage or injury of any kind suffered by another person as a result of anything done, or omitted to be done, by a protected person in relation to the performance or purported performance, or in relation to the exercise or purported exercise, of a protected person's functions, duties or powers under this Act or the regulations . . . [this] does not apply to an act or omission in bad faith . . . [or in] reference to a failure to make a decision.

Shirlow and Faunce (2009:767) warned that the level of scrutiny the TGA received in relation to the Pan case could 'increasingly influence' its decisions to the point where public safety concerns will come to be weighed against its financial impact on industry, undermining the TGA's ability to take action in the public health interest.

### *2.3.2 Merck, Merck Sharpe & Dohme Australia and rofecoxib (Vioxx)*

Vioxx, and the extent of harm it caused, also has particular importance in terms of shaping the regulatory regime in Australia. Vioxx was a registered prescription medicine for pain relief produced by Merck and supplied in Australia by its subsidiary MSD. It was first approved in the US by the FDA on 20 May 1999 (and later by the TGA on 23 December 1999) for use in treating the pain associated with osteoarthritis. According to Krumholz et al. (2007), there was evidence to suggest that Merck was aware of but did not communicate the cardiovascular risks associated with Vioxx prior to its approval in the US. The results of a Merck-sponsored study conducted in 1996 and 1997 indicated that Vioxx may increase the propensity for thrombosis (blood clotting). Internal emails from Merck in 1998 evidence that Merck officials requested that the authors of the study change their manuscript to 'soften' their interpretation of the cardiovascular effects of Vioxx, to which the authors largely agreed (Krumholz et al. 2007:120). The nine studies that ultimately formed the basis of Merck's application for approval to the FDA, however, did not collect data on or evaluate the cardiovascular effects of Vioxx. These studies showed that Vioxx had a greater safety benefit compared to other non-steroidal anti-inflammatory drugs (NSAIDs) known to cause gastrointestinal side effects, particularly an increased risk of stomach ulcers and gastric bleeding (Vitry et al. 2007:736). However, the registration data released by the FDA showed that Vioxx did not offer a clinical advantage over existing NSAIDs (736). Moreover, these were small, short-term studies which used participants with a lower risk of cardiovascular disease (Krumholz et al. 2007:120). Vioxx was approved for registration by the TGA with conditions, including the submission of periodic safety updates by MSD.

In 2000, a study conducted by Merck, known as the Vioxx gastrointestinal outcomes research (or VIGOR) trial, found that participants taking high doses of Vioxx (50 mg per day) experienced half the gastrointestinal side effects of participants using Naproxen (a non-selective NSAID) in the comparative sample group, but up to five times the myocardial infarcts (i.e. heart attacks brought on by spasms of the coronary artery) (Faunce et al. 2010:38). MSD first notified the TGA of these results in March 2000 and expressed its intention to communicate information about these cardiovascular effects by amending the product information (PI), a technical document produced and published for health professionals to inform them of the safe and effective use of the medicine, which is written by the pharmaceutical company and approved by the TGA. Both Merck (in the US) and MSD (in Australia) explained this increased risk as the result of the aspirin-like—and therefore, cardioprotective—effect of Naproxen. However, the TGA delegate (presiding over the application for amendment of the PI) believed that this claim was 'not supported' because:

> [t]here are no prospective placebo controlled studies of naproxen that show . . . [it] is effective in decreasing the risk of cardiovascular events [and] [t]he effect size of naproxen in reducing CV thrombotic events relative to rofecoxib in the VIGOR study . . . exceeds the effect size of aspirin compared to placebo in other trials.
>
> (*Peterson v Merck Sharpe & Dohme (Aust) Pty Ltd* (2010) FCR 180:para. 250)

This means that if Naproxen does decrease the risk of cardiovascular events relative to Vioxx, it only provides a small risk reduction, which does not explain the almost 500% increase in events identified in the 2000 study. The TGA delegate recommended that the risk of a cardiovascular-related ADR be included in the PI (*Peterson v Merck Sharpe & Dohme (Aust) Pty Ltd* (2010) FCR 180:para. 250). The PI was amended voluntarily by MSD in the 11 months after the results of VIGOR were released, but Vitry et al. (2007:376) claimed that the revisions 'minimised' the cardiovascular risks.[18] No formal warnings were issued by the TGA until October 2003, when it released an article in the ADRAC bulletin. Like the PI, the article appeared to minimise the cardiovascular risks of Vioxx by concluding that 'evidence for an association between rofecoxib and a risk of cardiovascular events is inconclusive and indirect' (736). The TGA did not insist on MSD conducting any larger safety studies; at the time, McEwen was quoted as saying that 'it's in dispute that we [the TGA] would have the power to force those studies once a drug is on the market' (737).

In the US, Merck invested considerably in the advertising of Vioxx directly to consumers, spending approximately US$160.8 million in 2000—more than PepsiCo spent on advertising Pepsi in the same year (US$125 million) (Vitry et al. 2007:738). Employees of Merck allegedly published articles 'without any disclosure of their interest'[19] and engaged in ghostwriting practices[20] that downplayed, and often neglected to mention, the cardiovascular risks of Vioxx (Faunce et al. 2010:47–48). In Australia, MSD used key opinion leaders and trained its sales team to minimise the cardiovascular risks (e.g. by withholding information about the VIGOR trial) (*Peterson v Merck Sharpe & Dohme (Aust) Pty Ltd* (2010) FCR 180:paras. 274, 281–283). MSD also produced its own 'fake medical journal' to market products, including Vioxx (para. 296). *The Australian Journal of Bone and Joint Medicine* was found to be 'neither peer-reviewed nor independent' and thus 'a highbrow means of promoting some of MSD's products (including Vioxx)' (para. 296). Some members of the journal's editorial board were also not aware of their membership.

It was only after an independent cumulative meta-analysis was carried out, comprising 18 randomised controlled trials and 11 observational studies and published in 2004, that it was concluded decisively that an increased cardiovascular risk was evident from 2000 for patients taking any dose of Vioxx up to 50 mg, and that 'the effect was both substantial and unlikely to be a chance finding' (Jüni et al. 2004:5). The study also concluded that the cardioprotective effects of Naproxen initially detected were 'probably small' and 'not large enough to explain the findings of the VIGOR study' (5). Following the publication of these findings, Merck initiated a voluntary worldwide recall (and MSD a Class II[21] recall). Prior to this recall, the TGA had received 959 ADR reports in relation to Vioxx; 319 were classified as serious and 18 of these were described as heart attacks (Australia, Senate 2005b:160). In the US, it is estimated that Vioxx caused anywhere between 88,000 and 140,000 cardiovascular events (Faunce et al. 2010:47). This is in contrast to the 66 ADR reports and 19 hospitalisations resulting from all of the products manufactured by Pan in the 12 months preceding the recall in February of 2003 (Australia, Senate 2005a:156).

The TGA's response to Vioxx, in contrast to its response in the Travacalm case, raises doubts about the consistency of its risk-management or -based approach. While the Vioxx and Travacalm cases are not directly comparable in the type or severity of the harm caused, comparisons can be drawn on the basis of the cooperativeness of MSD and Pan with the TGA. Pan did not comply with the Code of GMP and the conditions of its manufacturing licence, and the company attempted to prevent the TGA from investigating the ADR associated with the products it manufactured. On the other hand, the application submitted to the TGA by MSD complied with the requirements for registration. MSD complied with the additional conditions imposed by the TGA at registration, and later at the post-approval stage, by informing the TGA of the safety risks associated with Vioxx and revising the PI in light of the identification of these risks. Merck also voluntarily recalled Vioxx when evidence of its risks was published—albeit, only after an independent study was conducted repudiating the conclusions of its own studies. In these ways, MSD and Merck were cooperative with the TGA. The marketing of Vioxx to health professionals, however, did not comply with the Code of Conduct of Medicines Australia (MA, formerly the APMA), and in 2001, MSD was fined AU$10,000 for this non-compliance (Vitry et al. 2007:739). The lack of information available to the TGA on the extent to which Merck and MSD were cooperating with requirements further rationalises the use of cooperative techniques of government—specifically, the regulator refraining from intervening to provide the regulated with the opportunity to cooperate. This cooperative rationality of the TGA, and the benefit of the doubt afforded to those who appear to cooperate, is best demonstrated by the conversation between Jonathan Holmes of the ABC program *Four Corners* and McEwen. When McEwen appeared on the program, he told Holmes that the TGA did not have the data to demonstrate that Naproxen was not protective because it did not exist. This was because 'Merck [had] developed a strategy which was reflected in their dealings with us [the TGA], which was to portray this as being a protective', and 'in order to challenge it we [the TGA] have to have their data and to go through their data' (Holmes 2005:paras. 155–163). The TGA's formal adoption of responsive regulation (see Section 3.2) would rationalise the use of these cooperative techniques, going forward.

## 2.4 Hegemonic neoliberal governmentality

In the later 20th century, neoliberal governmentality came to dominate the government's approach to medicine regulation. It was discourses of health based on racial difference that led to the formation of the first techniques and apparatuses of the state for governing health—the Quarantine Act and Service, and later, the Department of Health. Through techniques restricting the entry of certain persons—and by extension goods, such as medicines—into

Australia, the life of the population came to be a central concern of governance. Ultimately, this objectification facilitated the commodification of health (i.e. its attaining a value) and subjectification of individuals (i.e. their turning into subjects). The centrality of life and later the health of the population to government included the adoption of and preoccupation with rights, starting with the rights to health (i.e. social rights), but in time, also equally private rights and the rights of the economy (i.e. to economic viability), the right to self-govern and ultimately the right for a person to choose (in health terms, 'the right to be sick as one wishes and as is necessary'—see Foucault 2004:6). This shift in the conceptualisation of rights (and therefore, health) was due in part to its compatibility with liberal and in turn neoliberal ideas. Techniques of government that entailed intervention by the state on the basis of the right to health were able to be rationalised not only as violating rights (i.e. in violation of private rights and the rights of the economy) but also as a form of unfreedom (i.e. by relieving the individual of their responsibility for governing their own health and therefore rendering them dependent on the state) (O'Malley 2016:114). Techniques for governing health, including those related to medicines, therefore became freer by limiting state intervention even further and reallocating what were formerly state responsibilities for governing.

Economic rationality was also key to this shift in the state project. Although the government had long been preoccupied with the costs of health, increasingly passing these costs onto the public (and thus individualising responsibility for them) facilitated neoliberal techniques of subjectification. Participation in health by the public became more individualised and active (and therefore less socialised and passive). Through health promotion, indeed, the rationale whereby the public must 'help themselves', the participation (or more accurately, subjection) of the public could be increased, simply by supplying and requiring the public to accumulate the information provided.

As neoliberal governmentality became hegemonic, it further rationalised the decentralisation of the medicine regulatory regime on a cost and 'risk management' basis: first, through the delegation of some of the powers of the Australian Government to the TGA, a specialised apparatus of government empowered to make 'dint' (Lemke 2001:193) interventions in the regime; and second, through the delegation of some of this power to industry associations and sponsors, reflecting technologies of agency that require these associations and sponsors to take primary responsibility for their own governance. In addition, the deregulation of pre-market and post-market prescription and non-prescription medicine regulation increased the responsibility of the public, by having them self-govern, or govern their own health. As the cases of Travacalm and Vioxx demonstrate, ideas of risk and cooperativeness, which have long been a feature of the medicine regulatory regime, have only entrenched neoliberal hegemony by rationalising the implementation of forms of governmentality that are compatible with this project. The severity of the TGA's response to Pan led to the introduction of a suite of governmental techniques designed to be 'proportionate to the risks posed by the non-compliance' (ANAO 2007:64), compatible with risk-based regulation. The TGA's lack of a strong response to Merck and MSD led to the formalisation of cooperative governmental techniques, compatible with responsive regulation. Both risk-based and responsive regulation would come to be adopted formally by the TGA as regulatory techniques (discussed in detail in Chapter 3).

These reforms were largely led and facilitated by the state, but they were also reinforced in part by the alignment of interests of different sets of actors—sponsors, industry associations, health professionals, professional associations, patients and patient interest groups, and the public. The formation of this hegemonic bloc secured broad support for reforms to the regime which, despite appearing to be in the common interest, were ultimately in the best interests of industry.

Chapter 3 builds upon this discussion by detailing the outcomes of this historical process. It provides an overview of the medicine regulatory regime in Australia between 2010 and 2014, the period during which extensive public consultation was conducted to reform the regime and the regime's reform was initiated. The chapter introduces the theories of risk-based and responsive regulation, which underpin the TGA's approach to pre- and post-market regulation of prescription and non-prescription medicines. In so doing, it identifies those areas for potential failure of regulation.

## Notes

1 Meloni (2023:113) has criticised the narrative of the 'birth' of biopolitics as Eurocentric; it situates political concern for the life of populations in modernity (i.e. as beginning in Europe in the 17th and 18th centuries) and therefore neglects earlier forms of biopolitical intervention in colonial encounters and settings. The concept of biopolitics is applied here to explain the highly racialised interventions of the colonial governments to work towards 'disrupting' (Meloni 2023:133) this Eurocentrism.

2 Mignolo (2021:90) argues this insofar as '[t]here are no races out there' and that race must be created (through colonial difference) in order to exist. There are also differences created on the basis of health—as *good* (resulting from correct choices and conduct) or *poor* (such as illness, resulting from incorrect choices) (see Galvin 2002).

3 See Meloni (2023) for a critique on the turn towards socialised medicine.

4 These rights also prioritised the health of the white population. Up until the 1960s, there was a lack of research on Indigenous health and the limited research that was conducted was not aimed at improving the health of Aboriginal people (but rather the health of white Australians). It was also aimed at documenting information about Aboriginal people on the basis that they were perceived as becoming extinct (see Thomas 2004:521).

5 Half of those practitioners were members of the BMA in Australia (see Galligan 1987:155).

6 The Senate of the Australian Parliament was presented with data indicating that 41% (45 out of 110) of products (presumed to be on the PBS) failed to meet official standards (Australian Senate 1953:143).

7 But not those therapeutic substances manufactured and sold within states, as this was within the remit of state governments in the Constitution.
8 The Regulations also led to the development of Australia's first advisory committees that directly advised the Director-General of Health on therapeutic substances (see McEwen 2007:36–37).
9 Thalidomide, an over-the-counter sedative developed and manufactured by the West German company Chemie Grünenthal, was marketed to pregnant women as an anti-nausea medicine, despite the lack of testing of its effects on a foetus in utero. In the late 1950s and early 1960s, doctors reported an increase in rates of phocomelia—a rare birth defect causing infants to be born with deformed or underdeveloped limbs. Despite doctors reporting the link between thalidomide and phocomelia, the company responded by discrediting them (even threatening them with legal action) (Dukes et al. 2014). Evidence of this link was then published by McBride (1961) and Lenz (1962). The Thalidomide Trust (2017) estimates that 10,000 infants were born with thalidomide-induced phocomelia worldwide, but the number of infants affected is likely higher than reported due to the termination of pregnancies, stillbirths, and neonatal and early infant deaths. In Australia, more than 148 people registered with the Australian Government's Thalidomide Survivors Support Program (Albanese 2023).
10 However, it provided the secretariat for ADEC and worked together with the Committee in assessing ADRs.
11 The Code did not become a legislative instrument until 2005.
12 Endorsed at the WHO-UNICEF Conference, the Declaration expressed 'the need for urgent action by all governments . . . and the world community to protect and promote the health of all the people of the world' (WHO Regional Office for Europe 1978:1).
13 This conviction in the NSW District Court in 1996 was later overturned and a retrial was ordered. However, the company, operating under the name Pan Laboratories, went into liquidation before the retrial could take place (Dalley 2003:para. 67).
14 In an interview, the TGA's Principle Medical Advisor stated that they were not aware of the TGA having conducted an unannounced audit of Pan (Dalley 2003:paras. 51–53).
15 Classified as 'potentially life-threatening or could cause a serious risk to health' (TGA 2003).
16 Defined as deficiencies that could lead to or risk a product being harmful to a person (Commonwealth of Australia & Others 2010:paras. 41(b), 146–147).
17 The Guide was influenced by the report entitled *Rethinking Regulation: Report of the Taskforce on Reducing Regulatory Burdens on Business*. Established by the Australian Government in October 2005, the Taskforce was asked 'to identify practical options for alleviating the compliance burden on business'—such as 'non-regulatory options' or 'business self-regulation'—imposed by government regulation, including therapeutic goods regulation (Costello 2005).
18 The maximum dose prescribed in Australia was 25 mg (per day), which was half of the dose used in the VIGOR trial. The lack of evidence of an increased cardiovascular risk at the dosage prescribed in Australia may have had the effect of lessening the relative risk of harm; indeed, the risk at a 50 mg dose relative to a 25 mg dose was discussed at length in *Peterson v Merck Sharpe & Dohme (Aust) Pty Ltd* (2010) FCR 180.
19 For example, the article 'Cardiovascular Thrombotic Events in Controlled, Clinical Trials of Rofecoxib', published in the journal *Circulation*, was written entirely by Merck employees but did not disclose the authors' interests (Faunce et al. 2010:47).

20 Jeffrey Lisse, who was listed as the lead author on an article published in the *Annals of Internal Medicine*, stated that the trial was designed, paid for and administered by Merck, and that Merck wrote the initial paper which they sent to Lisse 'for editing' (Berenson 2005 as cited in Faunce et al. 2010:47).

21 Classified as 'defects [which] could cause illness or mistreatment, but are not Class I' (TGA 2003).

# 3 Overview of the medicine regulatory regime

In the period prior to the commencement of the public consultations and the regime's reform, there was mounting evidence to suggest that medicine regulation was failing, particularly the regulation of listed, non-prescription medicines. Desktop audits (known as compliance reviews) conducted by the TGA revealed consistently high rates of non-compliance among the sponsors of listed medicines. In 2006, 75% (178 out of 237) of listed medicines that underwent a random compliance review were found to be non-compliant in relation to labelling, product specification and evidence requirements (ANAO 2011:107). Similarly, over the ten-month period between July 2008 and April 2009, 70% of listed medicines that underwent compliance reviews were found to be non-compliant, mostly for inappropriate claims and violations of the Therapeutic Goods Advertising Code (ANAO 2011:109). Over the nine-month period between July 2009 and March 2010, approximately 90% (98 out of 110) of listed complementary medicines were found to be non-compliant. These rates were relatively consistent for both random and targeted compliance reviews and the TGA regarded a substantial proportion of these non-conformities, which were wide-ranging in terms of their type, either 'moderate' or 'significant' in severity (ANAO 2011:17, 109–110). Not only did this evidence indicate that 'a high level of non-compliance has endured for some years', but in a landmark audit report published in August 2011, the ANAO concluded that listed medicine regulation 'has been of limited effectiveness' (ANAO 2011:16–17). Months later, in December 2011, the Parliamentary Secretary for Health and Ageing, Catherine King, conceded that recent public consultations had 'highlighted a number of issues of concern' and that there was a need for medicine regulation to be 'more effective and transparent' (Department of Health and Ageing 2011). The ANAO's findings and recommendations and the Australian Government's concession provided a major impetus for the public consultations that led to proposals to reform medicine regulation (for both listed and registered medicines), which began in 2010 and increased significantly in number from December 2011 following the production of the document *TGA Reforms: A Blueprint for TGA's Future* (herein referred to as the Blueprint Reforms).

DOI: 10.4324/9781003285762-3

This chapter provides a detailed overview of the TGA and medicine regulatory regime from 2010 to 2014, the period in which it was publicly acknowledged that aspects of the regime were not achieving compliance, and public consultations and reforms were initiated. This overview of the regime is organised into four parts. It begins with a brief outline of the structure of the TGA and its various committees at the time. The second part of the overview details the hybrid risk-based and responsive regulatory approach underpinning the regime adopted by the TGA. In so doing, it draws on the theoretical framework developed in the previous chapters to explore the strengths and criticisms of the theories of risk-based and responsive regulation, including their points of incompatibility (and therefore, the limitations of combining the theories to form a hybrid approach) and congruence with neoliberal governmentality. Part three of the overview details the process of pre-approval for medicines, including the two-tiered medicine classification scheme used to determine, on a risk basis, the extent to which a medicine is evaluated at the point of application for approval. It also details the processes involved in the licensing of Australian and overseas manufacturers prior to the approval of medicines for the Australian market. Finally, the overview details the post-market regulation of medicines following their approval. This part includes an overview of ADR reporting, manufacturer inspections, laboratory testing, compliance reviews and pre-approval and complaints procedures related to DTCA and promotion. The chapter concludes by identifying those areas of the regime where there is potential for failure.

## 3.1 Structure of the TGA

Prior to 2014, the TGA comprised three internal units: the Market Authorisation Group, the Monitoring and Compliance Group and the Regulatory Support Group (incorporating the TGA's legal, financial, information technology, communications, parliamentary and human resource services) (TGA 2014i:3).[1] These units reported to the executive branch of the TGA, which consists of the Head of each group, Chief Operating Officer, Principal Medical and Legal Adviser and National Manager. The TGA's National Manager reports directly to the Secretary of the Department of Health (and the Secretary reports to the Minister for Health). A visual representation of the structure of the TGA is provided in the TGA's business plan (TGA 2012g:17).

The TGA also had several committees that advised and made recommendations to the Market Authorisation Group and Monitoring and Compliance Group. These committees were an extension of the TGA apparatus, functioning as technologies of citizenship, or 'instruments of "voice" and "representation"' (Dean 2010:196) through which interest groups can participate in regulation and the TGA's decision-making. These committees included the Advisory Committee on Prescription Medicines (ACPM) (formerly the ADEC); Advisory Committee on Non-prescription Medicines (ACNM); Advisory Committee on Complementary Medicines (ACCM); ACSOM (formerly the ADRAC); TGC and ATGAC. All of these committees, excluding the ATGAC, were statutory committees. The ACPM, ACNM and ACCM made recommendations on the approval of prescription, non-prescription and complementary medicines, respectively, and were composed of health professionals (e.g. in medicine, pharmacy and nursing) and academics. Of the three remaining committees, ACSOM was responsible for making recommendations to the TGA on the safety of a given medicine, and its risk assessment and management, and comprised a consumer representative, as well as health professionals and academics. The TGC provided advice to the Minister for Health on standards for therapeutic goods. Unlike the TGA's other statutory committees, the TGC included representation from industry associations and the sponsors of prescription and non-prescription medicines. The ATGAC was a stakeholder committee established to 'improve' and 'provide broad strategic advice to the TGA' (TGA 2015a).[2]

## 3.2 Hybrid risk-based and responsive regulatory framework

The TGA regulates medicines using a combination of risk-based and responsive regulation—two theories that underpin the 'regulatory orthodoxy' or dominant school of thought within the literature on regulation (also sometimes referred to as the compliance school) (Pearce and Tombs 1990, 1997; Tombs 2016).

### *3.2.1 Risk-based regulation*

As a form of governmentality, risk-based regulation prioritises regulatory techniques on the basis (i.e. rationalisation) of risk.[3] Risk is therefore not an object of risk-based regulation, but a tool through which particular types and levels of harm are rationalised (indeed, accepted) (Paul 2017:68). In theory, risk-based regulation consists of a set of objectives (a rationalisation of the types of risks the regulator is concerned with); a risk threshold (a rationalisation of the types of risks to be tolerated and the level to which they will be tolerated by the regulator); a risk assessment (a rationalisation of the likelihood and impact of risks); a classification of risk (based on the risk assessment) and a means of allocating resources based on these risk classifications (Black and Baldwin 2010:184–185). In practice, however, how risk-based regulation operates—'as an intervention strategy distinct from a mechanism for allocating resources' (Gunningham 2011:189)—is not clear.

Risk-based regulation is subject to criticism. Because it sees resources prioritised towards those regulatory sites of highest risk, regulators tend to 'pull back' on resources at lower-risk sites (comprising the bulk of sites) (Black and Baldwin 2012:2). This lack of resources can impede regulators in responding to risks and cause some risks 'to fall out of the regulatory net altogether' (Black and Baldwin 2012:8). Threats to the regulator's legitimacy, or political risks, may result in resources being prioritised towards those sites that are most politically sensitive, irrespective of the actuarial risk (Black and Baldwin 2012; Haines 2011). Regulated entities classified as lower risk are likely to have less contact with the regulator, which may result in the regulator obtaining less information relevant to assessing risk (see, e.g. Tombs 2016:176–178). The prioritisation of risk can trump and render meaningless all other criteria used to determine the regulator's response (Gunningham 2011:193–194). The construction of risk can also be harmful because it is a 'construction'; '[l]ow risk' means, in practice, 'low priority' and is therefore indicative of its 'relative significance' to the regulator (Black and Baldwin 2012:4).

The TGA regulates on the basis of two types of risk: product risk, or the risk inherent to the medicine; and compliance risk, or the risk of non-compliance by the sponsor (TGA 2012h:6–9). Medicines are classified as either high risk (registered) or low risk (listed). This classification, or rationalisation, of product risk determines the extent to which a medicine is regulated pre- and post-market: high risk (registered) medicines are regulated by the TGA more so than low risk (listed) medicines. The TGA's classification of compliance risks is less clear, but it appears to be based on the sponsor's internal compliance system (or internal controls) and its compliance orientation (i.e. attitude towards and history of compliance) (see, e.g. TGA 2012h). Although the TGA and medicine regulatory regime have placed emphasis on regulating product risks since the early 1990s, the language of 'risk-based regulation' did not come into prominence until the early 2000s (e.g. see TGA Expert Committee on Complementary Medicines in the Health System 2003 and TGA 2004). The language of 'compliance risk' did not appear until much later (e.g. see TGA 2012h:6, 8).

### *3.2.2 Responsive regulation*

Responsive regulation, as a form of governmentality, involves the use of graduated techniques of increasing or decreasing severity based on the cooperativeness of the regulated. According to Ayres and Braithwaite (1992:50), the authors of this theory, deterrence-based techniques should be used as a last resort, after compliance-based techniques have failed to compel the regulated to comply. It is the threat of punishment, rather than the punishment itself, according to Ayres and Braithwaite, that compels the regulated to comply voluntarily. Through the use of compliance-based techniques, regulated entities that are motivated to comply are provided with the opportunity 'to put their cooperative self forward' (prior to the regulator penalising them) (Ayres and Braithwaite 1992:33). The regulator can shift from compliance- to deterrence-based techniques if the regulated exploits this cooperativeness, and the regulator can then resume the use of compliance-based techniques when the cooperation of the regulated is (re)attained.

This hierarchical relationship between compliance- and deterrence-based techniques is envisaged in the *enforcement pyramid* (see *Figure 3.1*).

Self-regulation, which represents the greatest amount of regulatory activity, is located at the pyramid's base. Intervention by the regulator should occur and become increasingly severe as the severity of non-compliance by the regulated increases and dialogue fails. Regulators should first use lower-level, persuasive tactics, such as written warnings, to compel compliance from the regulated, and then higher-level, punitive tactics, such as civil and criminal penalties and licence suspension and revocation, to punish non-compliance if it continues. The greater the height to which the regulator can escalate its response, the more effective the regulator is said to be at securing compliance from the regulated, and the less likely it is that the regulator will have to resort to punitiveness (Ayres and Braithwaite 1992:6). This is because the height (or level) of its response should maximise the difference between compliance (the *cooperation payoff*) and non-compliance (the *punishment payoff*), and make cooperation appear the more rational choice (Ayres and Braithwaite 1992:26). Regulatees that cooperate are rewarded by being able to continue self-regulating without much intervention by the regulator. The regulator's 'scare regulatory resources' can then be directed away from compliant companies and towards those companies that 'play fast and loose' (Ayres and Braithwaite 1992:129). In this way, responsive regulation has some overlap with risk-based regulation (even if the authors did not articulate responsive regulation as risk-based).

Because responsive regulation encourages cooperation between the regulator and regulated, it also runs the risk of 'regulatory capture' (Ayres and Braithwaite 1992:54). According to Ayres and Braithwaite, the potential for capture can be mitigated through *tripartism*—the empowerment of a third player, such as a public interest group. A third player, they argue, immediately impacts upon the ability of the regulated to capture the regulator because it must capture this third player in order to do so. The empowerment of a third player also places them in a position to punish the regulated directly and indirectly (the latter by punishing and thus pressuring the regulator for failing to act on non-compliance). To better empower the public, Ayres and Braithwaite (1992:57–58) argue that public interest groups must be provided with:

> access to all the information that is available to the regulator . . . a seat at the negotiating table with the firm and the agency when deals are done . . . [and] the same standing to sue or prosecute under the regulatory statute as the regulator.

This theory can be critiqued for several reasons. To foster cooperation, responsive regulation requires regular, tit-for-tat interaction between the regulator and regulated, but in reality such interaction is rare. Despite the authors' intention that responsive regulation apply to the regulation of 'a small number of firms in a single industry' so that 'the chances of repeated regular encounters are greater' (Ayres and Braithwaite 1992:55), it is often applied in regulating large numbers of companies operating in multiple, highly diverse industries (e.g. see Ivec et al. 2015). Such complexity means that regulator–regulatee interaction is likely to be reduced by virtue of there being too many regulated entities for the regulator to contact (Gunningham 2011:188). Interaction is also likely to be between a number of individuals (representing the regulator and regulated entities) and therefore to be less intense and direct (i.e. 'one-to-many' and 'many-to-many' forms of interaction) (Ford 2013:19). This in turn can increase the potential for miscommunication (e.g. by way of information inconsistency, misinformation or confusion) (Baldwin and Black 2008:63). As such, 'continuing responsiveness . . . is more a normative ideal of how parties should interact . . . than an actual empirical phenomenon' (Nielsen and Parker 2009:389).

In a few of the studies where regular, tit-for-tat interactions were observed and had a measurable impact on the actions of both the regulator and the regulated, the latter's lack of cooperation with the regulator was also often observed (Makkai and Braithwaite 1994; Mascini and Van Wijk 2009; Nielsen and Parker 2009; Parker 2006). Parker (2006:603), for instance, found that companies engaging in cartel and other anti-competitive behaviour 'criticised and openly expressed their resentment' towards the ACCC when it switched from using cooperative- to deterrence-based techniques. There was also evidence of companies 'complaining to government ministers, including the Prime Minister, both openly and secretly, about particular ACCC decisions, enforcement strategies, and investigations and about ACCC commissioners, particularly the chair' in an attempt to influence the ACCC and the exercise of its statutory authority (Parker 2006:612). Regulators may be unwilling or unable to escalate their action on non-compliance because of its potential to threaten regulator–regulatee cooperation—what Parker (2006) calls the compliance trap. Because deterrence is considered to be a barrier to cooperation, regulators may find themselves trapped whereby their actions lack either deterrent effect (because they refrain from punitiveness to maintain the regulatee's cooperation) or legitimacy (because the regulated interpret punitiveness as unjust and therefore choose not to cooperate, or regulators do not receive the backing of the state) (Parker 2006:593). Responsive regulation also raises concerns in relation to proportionality because punishment is based on the extent of cooperation by the regulated (and not the severity of the offence). As such, severe forms of non-compliance may be treated more leniently because of the full cooperation of the regulatee with the regulator, whereas less severe non-compliance could be treated more punitively (Yeung 2004:168).

Tripartism has also been subject to some criticism in the literature. Schwarcz (2014) argues that third players are no less susceptible to capture than the regulator; and although it is possible to have different public interest groups compete for the privilege of being the third player, this requires having multiple groups to choose from, and in some regulatory regimes, this is simply not possible. Tripartism also draws on democratic and empowerment theories that have been criticised for their neglect of power inequalities—they incorrectly assume that the public can be effective third players or regulators and complement state or corporate regulation and correct its failures simply by, for example, becoming informed (Gray and van Rooij 2021:801).

The TGA assumes that 'the majority of regulated entities intend to comply' (TGA 2012h:8), and so it first encourages compliance from sponsors on a voluntary basis using cooperative techniques. When this encouragement fails, the TGA claims to resort to more punitive techniques, such as 'restrictions or warnings, suspensions or sanctions and cancellations . . . [and] criminal or civil court action' (TGA 2017a:59). This hierarchy of techniques is depicted in the TGA's enforcement pyramid (see *Figure 3.1*), which is comparatively smaller to and has less levels than the Ayres and Braithwaite enforcement pyramid. Although the TGA has adopted a hierarchy of regulatory techniques since the mid-2000s, their representation in a pyramid and the language of 'responsive regulation' did not appear until 2012 (see TGA 2012h:8).

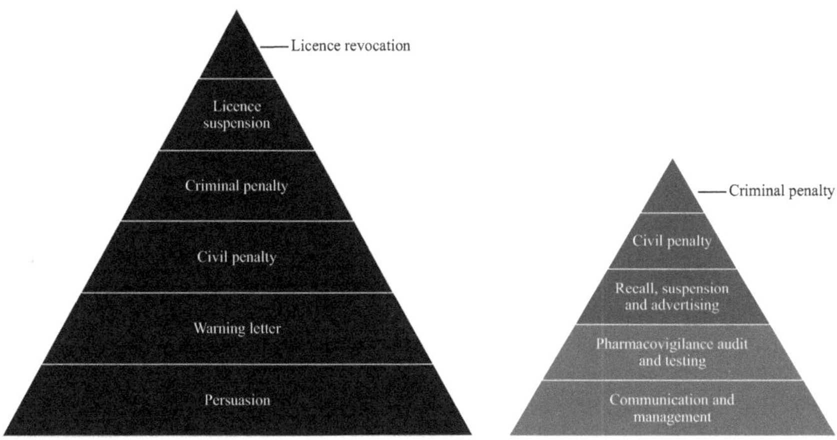


*Figure 3.1* The Ayres and Braithwaite enforcement pyramid (left) compared to the TGA enforcement pyramid in 2012 (right)

*Source*: Adapted from Ayres and Braithwaite (1992:35) and TGA (2012h:8 [originally green and red in colour]).

### 3.2.3 *Incompatibility of risk-based and responsive regulation and their congruence with neoliberalism*

Combining risk-based and responsive regulation to form a hybrid regulatory approach has implications due to the limited complementarity of the two approaches. As Gunningham (2011:194) explains, risk-based regulation calls for a strong response by the regulator when the risks are higher, whereas in responsive regulation, the regulator bases its response on the assumed cooperativeness of the regulatee, not the level of risk. Responsive regulation is therefore based on good will and not utilitarianism (like risk-based regulation). Consequently, regulators must give consideration to how risk-based and responsive regulation will be used in concert when combining the two approaches; but such consideration, Gunningham notes, rarely occurs.

Both risk-based and responsive regulation are congruent with neoliberal governmentality. Risk is a means 'of ordering reality' and 'rendering it into a calculable form' (Dean 2010:206). When risk rationalities are tethered to governmental techniques (forming a risk governmentality), it shapes conduct towards specific ends, often with relatively final but unanticipated effects (Dean 2010:207). Through the construction of risk, it is possible to rationalise the reallocation of some of the responsibilities for governing. For example, the classification of risks as 'low' rationalises the use of micro-level techniques (such as decentred and deregulated forms of governing), in line with the neoliberal idea of limited state intervention. By constructing risks as too big and complex for the state or other sets of actors (such as industry) to take responsibility for but nevertheless (and rather paradoxically) as something that individuals as well as collectives like public interest groups can assume responsibility for (through being 'empowered'), and by having the state (and industry) only foster this capacity ('empower' them), the use of micro-level governmental techniques (i.e. responsibilisation and self-governance) is rationalised. In public health, this (re)allocation of responsibility from the state onto the public occurs by shifting social 'risks' into the domain of the individual, constructing them as risks to the individual's health that result from their choices (such as eating well, exercising or visiting the doctor) and 'self-care' (Lemke 2001:201). Individuals thus come to be responsibilised and therefore participate in their health governance through health literacy, which the Australian Commission on Safety and Quality in Health Care (2014:2) generally defines as the way in which health and healthcare information is understood and applied and used by people when making decisions about and acting on their health. Health education and promotion, which attempts to 'communicate' information to the public on health, fosters not only an awareness of health risks among the public but also their internalisation of and acting on the information provided to them (Aykan and Güvenç-Salgırlı 2015:88). In this way, health literacy is a disciplinary technique of government (and the health-literate individual is the ideal neoliberal citizen-subject).

Since it is the individual who comes to be responsible for managing their own risks, they bear the full responsibility regardless of the constraints on their action (Brown 2005:42–43). The inability to navigate these risks, or engagement in risky behaviour, allows these risks to be constructed as a failure of the individual—that is, 'a failure of the self to take care of itself' (Greco 1993 as cited in Petersen 1997:198)—rather than a form of regulatory failure or the failure of state and corporate regulation. This rationalisation of risk 'ignores the social origins of illness' (Galvin 2002:117, 127), socialising the harms of states and corporations as 'inevitable risks' (Rawlinson 2017b:215).

It also 'redefines health as a "duty" rather than a "right"' (Galvin 2002:117, 127). Ultimately, this rationalisation of risk places the individual in an 'untenable position' where they are blamed for becoming ill, an inevitability of life and unmitigatable risk (Galvin 2002:120).

'[S]uperficial similarities' (Haines 2016:234) also exist between responsive regulation and neoliberal ideas. In practice, responsive regulation is often reduced to its enforcement pyramid (see Mascini 2013:55) and is thus severed from the tenets underlying the theory. The adaption of the pyramid, which was encouraged by the authors to suit the regulatory context in which it is being applied, has also led to the pyramid becoming 'broken, incomplete or outside the control of instrumentally orientated agencies' (Scott 2004:158). The failure to implement the pyramid in full renders it unable to deliver the punishment payoff necessary to channel regulatee behaviour towards the pyramid's base. This limitation is apparent in the TGA's enforcement pyramid (see *Figure 3.1*), which only goes so high as criminal penalties for non-compliance (and does not threaten the revocation or loss of a licence, as per the Ayres and Braithwaite enforcement pyramid). The difference in the 'punishment threat' between the Ayres and Braithwaite and TGA enforcement pyramids (and therefore, their capacity to compel compliance) is illustrated in the difference in their height and number of levels in *Figure 3.1*. In addition, through the treatment of punishment as something that compromises cooperation, it comes to be viewed as the 'notional opposite' of cooperation (Tombs and Whyte 2015:51). Although Ayres and Braithwaite (1992:17, 158) explicitly state that they are not 'sympathetic to the libertarian view that the state should be kept weak', and that they are staunch advocates of a 'regulatory delegation that is underwritten by escalating (and increasingly undelegated) forms of government intervention', the congruence of responsive regulation with light-touch neoliberal regulatory techniques has helped rationalise limiting forms of intervention by the state.

Like risk, cooperation and (regulatory) failure are used not only to legitimate the turn to but also to reinforce micro-level techniques (and even forms of 'governing through failure'—see Joseph 2016, 2018). Techniques that emphasise self-regulation—and therefore that the regulated must rectify their own non-compliance without incitement by the regulator—reinforce the mentality that the regulated are compliant (or cooperative). This belief (mentality) that regulatees are cooperative arises for two principal reasons. The first is that because the state has reallocated the responsibility for regulating onto the regulated, the regulator is less able to identify and act on non-compliance. In turn, the regulator lacks the information necessary to assess compliance risk (or uncooperativeness). The second reason is that when regulatees are non-compliant but rectify their non-compliance (with or without incitement from the regulator), they appear to be cooperative. In this way, and to the regulator, the regulated always appear cooperative. This is a key feature of neoliberal governmentality, which attempts to create and reproduce a reality that it already assumes to exist (Lemke 2001:203); it 'create[s] a discursive field' or 'knowledge' (Lemke 2002:55) or 'regime of truth' (Foucault 1977) whereby the exercise of a particular type of governance is rationalised. Market freedom is another example of a reality contrived by neoliberal governmentality; it is the product of state work, specifically, market deregulation and the implementation of laws and policies by governments to maximise competition (through tax exemptions, free trade agreements and so on).

Technologies of citizenship, like tripartism, also have both an enabling and constraining (and therefore disciplinary) effect (Cruikshank 1999). Information and its transparency are necessary to tripartism and 'rest upon a fundamental assertion that the information disclosed is "true", as only if that information is "true" can it be used to hold governments to account and effectively participate [in the regime]' (Adams 2020:26). But information transparency is a form of power; transparency is performed by those who create the information and therefore have the power to control what information can be known, how and when it can be known (or disclosed), and to an extent how it can be received (Adams 2020:3, 25). Foucault (1977:27–28) referred to this relationship as power/knowledge (and knowledge/power), whose interplay can facilitate the development of techniques of subjectification.[4] Information, and its transparency, is neither neutral nor value free; the mentality that 'the information which could be disclosed . . . already existed prior to any intention to disclose it, and that its disclosure involves merely an opening up of the authoring institution', is an 'illusion' and in fact 'conceals' that it is frequently produced 'for the direct objective of disclosing it' (Adams 2018:10–11).

The medicine regulatory regime comprises a range of 'players'; roughly grouped, they include the TGA, industry associations, sponsors, the public, public interest groups and health professionals and professional associations. It is their overall position within the regime's structure (or the regime's structuration) that renders some groups more powerful than others (and therefore the regime more representative of their interests). Tripartite participation by the public and health professionals and their professional associations (such as in the form of participation on TGA committees evaluating applications for listing or registration) relies not only in large part on the TGA making the necessary information available but also on the form and extent to which this information is made available. The TGA, in turn, relies on the information made available to it by the sponsor in the application. Even if all the information made available were to be conceived as 'truth' (and therefore as being made available neutrally), its availability, nonetheless, takes place asymmetrically in that it requires the participation (indeed, 'empowerment') of its recipient. In this way, technologies of citizenship and information transparency have a disciplining effect that shape the relations (and therefore, structuration) of power within the regime. These criticisms or risk-based and responsive techniques and their congruence with neoliberal governmentality are explored in further detail in the analysis in Chapters 4 to 6. The sections that follow detail how prescription and non-prescription medicines are evaluated prior to their approval, and the post-market regulation of these medicines.

## 3.3 Pre-market regulation

Medicines[5] imported, exported, manufactured and/or supplied in Australia must be pre-approved and registered or listed on the ARTG. Registered medicines contain scheduled substances[6] and are identifiable by an 'AUST R' number on their packaging. Registered medicines include prescription medicines (high risk registered medicines) and some non-prescription medicines (low risk registered medicines) like over-the-counter (OTC) medicines (such as analgesics and cough and cold medicines) and complementary medicines containing scheduled substances.[7] Listed medicines do not contain scheduled substances or substances otherwise restricted in Schedule 4 of the Therapeutic Goods Regulations 1990 (Cth) and are identifiable by an 'AUST L' number. The classification of a medicine as registered or listed 'depends on the level of risk posed by the medicine' (TGA 2011d:14), and therefore, product risk.

### *3.3.1 Registration*

Prior to approval, registered medicines are evaluated by the TGA for quality, safety and efficacy. Applications for registered medicines, submitted online via the TGA's eBusiness Services (eBS) portal, consist of data (to evidence the quality, safety and efficacy of the medicine), completed forms and the payment of fees. The type of data that is evaluated by the TGA includes quality data (on composition, batch consistency, stability, sterility and impurity), nonclinical data (pharmacological and toxicological) and clinical data (from clinical studies or trials) (TGA 2020b).[8] This data is evaluated by technical staff within and outside the TGA and compiled into separate reports, each of which is examined by the TGA delegate[9] for final approval. The delegate can seek advice and a review of this data from one of the TGA's committees (prior to 2014, these were the ACPM, ACNM, ACCM or ACSOM). The sponsor is provided with copies of the evaluation reports for comment and asked to address any issues that may have arisen during the evaluation and may require the submission of further data (TGA 2011d:15). When the application is approved by the TGA delegate, sponsors receive a Certificate of Registration and an 'AUST R' identification number to be displayed on the product packaging. As a condition of registration, sponsors are required to adhere to the MA Code of Conduct.

The specific risks posed by the medicine may warrant conditions being imposed on the sponsor by the TGA at the time of approval. For example, the TGA may declare that the medicine can only be supplied under certain conditions (e.g. for hospital use or specific indications only), or that it be manufactured in certain conditions (such as by particular manufacturers only) (TGA 2011d:16). A summary of the conditions of registration is provided in the Australian Public Assessment Record (AusPAR), a document that is produced and published (on the ARTG) by the TGA summarising its evaluation of and decision to approve the medicine (TGA 2010a). The TGA can also prescribe that certain information, such as safety warnings, be displayed on medicine labels and on PI or Consumer Medicine Information (CMI) to communicate the particular product risks to the public and health professionals. The CMI, like PI, is produced and published by the sponsor, but for the patient, and although initially approved by the TGA, it is not subject to further monitoring (TGA 2013b). Applications for new medicines or indications for existing medicines[10] also require the sponsor to develop and adhere to a risk management plan (RMP), a technology of performance intended to manage the safety risks of the medicine post-approval. The RMP typically consists of an overview of the safety profile of the medicine, and a risk minimisation and pharmacovigilance (or adverse reactions response) plan (TGA 2012f). The TGA may also stipulate that the RMP include additional post-market clinical studies or educational programs to inform health professionals (TGA 2017c:11). While RMPs are evaluated by the TGA prior to approval and sponsors must submit RMP updates (as per the timeline specified in the RMP), the sponsor's adherence to those activities stipulated in the RMP is not proactively monitored by the TGA (TGA 2017c:11, 2019c). 'Relevant details from RMPs' are often provided in the AusPAR (TGA 2010a, 2017c:11).

If the TGA rejects an application for registration, sponsors can appeal the decision. Appeals are first handled internally by the TGA, whereby it reconsiders the application and determines whether the initial decision should be overturned. If the application is rejected a second time, the sponsor can then appeal the decision with the Secretary of the Department of Health or the Administrative Appeals Tribunal (AAT)—another apparatus of the state which independently reviews decisions made by Australian Government departments and agencies.

In the 2014 financial year, registering a new chemical entity cost sponsors a minimum of AU$221,400 as well as an annual fee—AU$6,585 for biological medicines and AU$3,955 for non-biologics (TGA 2014g:5–6). To register a non-prescription medicine in the same period required an application and evaluation fee of AU$3,525 and an annual fee of AU$1,350 (TGA 2014g:7).

### *3.3.2 Listing*

Unlike registered medicines, listed medicines are 'not subject to pre-market evaluation' by the TGA (TGA 2011d:17). Instead, sponsors self-assess the eligibility of a medicine for listing (and are thus responsibilised) by submitting an application for listing via the TGA's ELF on the eBS. The ELF is a software program that determines (electronically) whether a therapeutic good fits the prescribed parameters for listing. The electronic application form requires the sponsor to provide the name of the medicine and its manufacturer(s) and steps of manufacture, route of administration, dosage, ingredients, indications and warnings (TGA 2016a:57–58). The form also requires the sponsor to select from a list of ingredients pre-approved by the TGA. It allows the sponsor to either select indications from a standard list or enter indications of their own using the free text field (TGA 2016a:44). The TGA does not assess the efficacy of each indication proposed in the application, and therefore whether there is 'any evidence to show that the ingredient in the listed medicine is effective in the way claimed by the sponsor' (TGA 2013d:2). Moreover, 'the type and level of evidence required is not specified in the law', meaning that the sponsor can base the indication 'on whatever evidence they believe appropriate' (ANAO 2011:51–52), including evidence of its traditional or historical use. The ELF, however, can scan the form for restricted and prohibited terms.[11] Upon the submission of the form, the sponsor is directed to complete a Statutory Declaration, requiring them to agree to several conditions, including that they 'hold' evidence to support each indication listed in the application (TGA 2016a:58).[12] The application is then forwarded to the TGA's Business Management Unit and the sponsor is required to pay an application fee (which takes less than two days to process) (TGA 2016a:56). When the payment is finalised, the sponsor receives a Certificate of Listing and an 'AUST L' number to be displayed on the product packaging. The speed of listing a medicine on the ARTG means that there is little opportunity for the TGA to verify the information provided (ANAO 2011:71).

In 2014, a medicine could be listed on the ARTG for AU$760 in application fees and AU$965 in annual fees (TGA 2014g). Failure to list *or* register a medicine could attract a maximum penalty of up to 4,000 penalty units[13] or five years' imprisonment for criminal offences, and up to 50,000 penalty units for civil offences (under s. 19B(1) to (4) and 19D(1) of the Therapeutic Goods Act). Under the Therapeutic Goods Act, the Secretary can also suspend (s. 29d) or cancel (s. 30) the registration or listing of a medicine, or recall a medicine (s. 30EA).

### *3.3.3 Licensing of manufacturers*

The manufacturer nominated by the sponsor at the time of registration or listing must be licensed by the TGA. Carrying out a step of manufacture without a licence attracts a maximum criminal penalty of 4,000 penalty units or up to five years' imprisonment, or a civil penalty of 50,000 penalty units (under s. 35 and 35A of the Therapeutic Goods Act). In Australia, manufacturers are required to adhere to principles of GMP which are modelled on the Guide to GMP operating under the international Pharmaceutical Inspection Convention and the Pharmaceutical Inspection Cooperation Scheme (known jointly as PIC/S).

To obtain a licence, Australian-based manufacturers are audited through a site inspection by an inspector or group of inspectors from the TGA. The application for licensing requires the payment of an application fee (AU$940) and inspection fee (AU$615 per hour) (TGA 2013c, 2014g). The inspection report that is produced identifies whether any practices are inconsistent with the Code of GMP, and if so, the manufacturer must undertake specified corrective action. The TGA will then carry out a follow-up inspection before the manufacturer can be issued with a certificate of compliance (TGA 2013c).

Overseas-based manufacturers obtain their licence through a mutual recognition agreement (MRA), compliance verification or a TGA audit (TGA 2011d). A licence under an MRA is automatically granted to manufacturers based in Europe, Canada and Singapore, as well as member countries of the European Free Trade Association (because they are recognised as having near-identical standards of GMP to those in Australia) (TGA 2011d). Under an MRA, all post-licensing authorisations, inspections and certifications are carried out by the national regulatory authority of the country in which the manufacturer is based (European Agency for the Evaluation of Medicinal Products 2003). A licence issued under a compliance verification requires the TGA to assess the GMP certificates and inspection reports supplied by the manufacturer as part of the initial application to determine whether they were issued in line with Australian standards (TGA 2011d). Put simply, a compliance verification involves a desktop audit. This type of clearance is automatically extended to those manufacturers based in countries that endorse PIC/S, as well as manufacturers based in New Zealand. The TGA audits (i.e. conducts a site inspection of) manufacturers in those countries not recognised by the TGA as having compatible GMP standards. These types of audit are usually only conducted as a last resort, in circumstances where an MRA or compliance verification cannot be granted (TGA 2011d).

## 3.4 Post-market regulation

Medicine quality, safety and efficacy are regulated post-approval through ADR reporting, manufacturer inspections, laboratory testing and compliance reviews (and using risk-based and responsive techniques).

### *3.4.1 Adverse drug reaction (ADR) reporting*

ADRs are reported either online via the TGA website or through the Adverse Medicine Events telephone hotline run by the National Prescribing Service (NPS).[14] These reports are then entered into the Australian Adverse Drug Reaction Reporting System, a TGA-run database used by its staff to identify safety 'signals' (risks) associated with medicines listed and registered on the ARTG (TGA 2016f). ADRs are 'risk assessed'. No further action is taken by the TGA for an 'expected' ADR (known to be associated with the medicine's use); but for an 'unexpected' ADR, the TGA will undertake a 'detailed evaluation' to establish the possible cause (TGA 2016f, 2017d). From here, the TGA can act by requiring the sponsor to carry out further post-market studies; requiring changes or the addition of warnings to the labelling, PI or CMI; informing health professionals and the public through alerts and in publications (such as via Medicines Safety Updates); placing restrictions on the medicine's use; or cancelling the listing or registration of or recalling the medicine (TGA 2016f).

As part of their pharmacovigilance requirements, the sponsors of registered and listed medicines are legally required to report a 'serious' ADR—one that results in death, inpatient or prolonged hospitalisation, persistent or significant disability/incapacity, or congenital anomaly or birth defect, or that is otherwise life-threatening or medically important—to the TGA within 15 days of receipt of this information (TGA 2014a:17–18, 2017d:8, 11–14). 'Significant safety issues' (such as the withdrawal or suspension of a medicine by an overseas regulatory agency) are required to be reported in less than 72 hours (TGA 2014a:17–18, 2017d:11–14). However, prior to the introduction of its pharmacovigilance inspection programme in 2017, the TGA did not assess sponsors' compliance with pharmacovigilance requirements as pharmacovigilance was 'not a legislative requirement' (TGA 2014a:9; TGA 2017d); thus it relied on sponsors being responsible. A sponsor's failure to comply with a condition of registration or listing (under s. 21A(5) to (8) and 21B(2)) and notify the Secretary of an ADR (s. 29A(1) and 29AA(1)) can attract a maximum penalty of up to 4,000 penalty units and/or up to five years' imprisonment for criminal offences, and up to 50,000 penalty units for civil offences under the Therapeutic Goods Act. There are no mandatory reporting requirements for other stakeholder groups under the Act.

In 2015, up to 54% of all ADR reports received by the TGA came from sponsors (TGA 2016d:5). Of the remaining ADR reports, 15% originated from state and territory health departments, 14% from hospitals and hospital pharmacies, 6% from community pharmacies, 4% from general practitioners and 4% from consumers (TGA 2016d:5).

### *3.4.2 Manufacturer inspections*

In accordance with GMP, manufacturers are required to document all processes and activities relating to the manufacture of therapeutic goods (PIC/S 2009). Failure to document these activities constitutes a breach of a manufacturing licence and attracts a maximum penalty of up to 4,000 penalty units and/or five years' imprisonment for criminal offences, and 50,000 penalty units for civil offences under s. 35B(1) to (4) and 35C of the Therapeutic Goods Act. In addition, manufacturers are required to implement a system of quality management and self-inspection, quality controls and regular and periodic quality reviews, among other requirements (PIC/S 2009).

In addition to this self-regulation by the manufacturer, the TGA can conduct site inspections of the manufacturer's facilities to ensure its compliance with the Code of GMP. Inspection frequency is determined by the product and compliance risk of the manufacturer (the latter being based on

*Table 3.1* TGA inspection frequency matrix for medicines (in months)

| *Risk category* | *Re-inspection period (in months)* | | | | | |
|---|---|---|---|---|---|---|
| | *Compliance rating* | | | | | |
| | *Acceptable* | | | | | *Unacceptable* |
| | *3 × A1*[a] | *2 × A1*[b] | *A1* | *A2* | *A3* | |
| **Registered medicines** | | | | | | |
| High | 36+ | 36 | 24 | 18 | 12 | Determined by Review Panel |
| Medium | 36+ | 36 | 30 | 20 | 12 | Determined by Review Panel |
| Low | 36+ | 36 | 36 | 24 | 12 | Determined by Review Panel |
| **Listed medicines**[c] | | | | | | |
| Low | 48+ | 48 | 42 | 30 | 18 | Determined by Review Panel |

*Source*: Adapted from TGA (2013e, 2016c).

*Notes.*

a Third consecutive A1 rating received on an inspection.

b Second consecutive A1 rating.

c A different inspection frequency was established for listed medicines in 2016.

the previous compliance ratings it received on inspections). Those manufacturers that have lower risk of non-compliance and produce high risk medicines are inspected by the TGA at a higher frequency than those with higher risk of non-compliance and lower risk medicines. Inspection frequency can also be based on other information, such as changes to the corporate structure, approved product changes or warnings issued by a national regulatory agency, ADR reports, product recalls, random or targeted laboratory testing results and tip-offs (from informants) (TGA 2011d:32–33). This information is also used to determine whether an audit will be announced or unannounced (TGA 2011d:34). A guide to the frequency of TGA site inspections is depicted in *Table 3.1*. Australian-based manufacturers and overseas-based manufacturers that are unable to obtain a licence through an MRA or compliance verification are subject to this auditing scheme.

Inspections are carried out by either an individual inspector or a group of inspectors and are often announced; the manufacturer is notified by phone and then by formal letter before the inspection is due to commence (the amount of notice manufacturers are given is not specified by the TGA—see TGA 2013c:15). Inspections begin with a meeting between the TGA inspector(s) and the manufacturer's management team (TGA 2013c:16). The inspector(s) will then collate the information on the manufacturing facility that they gather from interviews with the facility's personnel, observing manufacturing processes and procedures, and reviewing company files and computerised systems (TGA 2013c:16–17). At the end of the inspection, the findings are presented in hard copy to the manufacturer at a closing meeting. The TGA inspector(s) outline any conformity issues that were identified during the inspection and the types of consequences the manufacturer could expect if these nonconformities are not rectified—namely, the suspension or revocation of their licence, or civil or criminal penalties (TGA 2013c:11, 17–18). At the closing meeting, the manufacturer is provided with the opportunity to discuss the conformity issues directly with inspectors to resolve or clarify the issues identified (TGA 2013c:18), consistent with a cooperative (responsive) technique of government.

Following the inspection, the manufacturer is sent a formal Inspection Report by email. The report provides the manufacturer with an overall compliance rating (either an acceptable A1, A2 or A3, or an unacceptable rating), which is used to determine the frequency of future inspections. The conformity issues identified in the Inspection Report are classified as a critical, major or other deficiency. Critical deficiencies either cause or may potentially cause physical harm or constitute a form of fraud (such as the misrepresentation or falsification of quality control data) (TGA 2013c:19–20). Major deficiencies do not conform with marketing authorisation or conditions of licensing and constitute a major deviation from GMP. These deficiencies are noncritical in the sense that they are unlikely to cause physical harm or constitute a criminal offence under the law. Other deficiencies are those that cannot be classified as either critical or major but demonstrate a departure from GMP. Multiple deficiencies can be grouped together and classified as a major deficiency even if each individual deficiency does not constitute a major deficiency on its own (TGA 2013c:20). If a manufacturer breaches a condition of their manufacturing licence, criminal or civil penalties can be applied (s. 35B and 35C of the Therapeutic Goods Act) or their licence can be suspended or revoked (s. 41 of the Therapeutic Goods Act).

According to an ANAO (2014:69) audit report, 59% of inspections conducted at prescription medicine manufacturing sites between 2008 and 2013 identified at least one major deficiency. Only 1.1% of inspections identified more than one critical deficiency (see *Table 3.2*). Audit data for other types of sites (for manufacturers of OTC and complementary medicines) has been made available to the public since 2014 but is only expressed as a combined total for all manufacturers.

*Table 3.2* Deficiencies identified by the TGA at sites manufacturing prescription medicines between 2008 and 2013

| *Classification* | *No. of deficiencies* | *% of inspections with this deficiency* | *Total* |
|---|---|---|---|
| Critical | More than 1 | 1.1% | 1.1% |
| Major | More than 10 | 3.6% | |
| | 6–10 | 8.4% | |
| | 1–5 | 46.8% | 58.8% |
| Other | More than 10 | 44.8% | |
| | 1–10 | 51.3% | 96.1% |

*Source*: Adapted from ANAO (2014:69).

In 2014–2015, 198 domestic and 133 overseas inspections were conducted by the TGA for manufacturers of medicines and blood, tissue and cellular therapies (TGA 2016e:44–45). As of 30 June 2015, there were a total of 404 domestic and 419 overseas manufacturing sites for medicines and blood, tissue and cellular therapies within the TGA's scope of inspection (TGA 2015b:43–44).

### *3.4.3 Laboratory testing*

The TGA's Office of Laboratories and Scientific Services (OLSS) conducts both targeted and random laboratory testing on samples of listed and registered medicines. These tests are conducted in addition to the self-regulation (quality controls and reviews) by manufacturers as part of their GMP requirements. The frequency with which products are tested by the OLSS is determined on both a product and compliance risk basis: registered medicines and those medicines subject to an ADR report or complaint are prioritised over other types of medicine. Prior to 2014, failure rates for listed and registered medicines during laboratory testing were not published consistently by the TGA. Since 2015, however, the TGA has increased its reporting of its laboratory test results and tests a higher proportion of complementary medicines (which have a higher risk of non-compliance) compared to OTC medicines. As shown in *Table 3.3*, those medicines which are pre-approved and most likely to undergo laboratory testing demonstrate the lowest failure rates.

*Table 3.3* Product samples that failed OLSS laboratory testing in 2015–2016

| *Product type* | *No. tested* | *% Fail* |
|---|---|---|
| Prescription medicines | 941 | 0.5% |
| OTC medicines | 47 | 19.1% |
| Complementary medicines | 108 | 20.4% |
| Unregistered products[a] | 467 | 76.2% |

*Source*: Adapted from TGA (2016e:49).

Note.

[a] Unregistered products include all products that fit the definition of therapeutic good under the Therapeutic Goods Act but are not registered or listed on the ARTG. This includes unregistered (produced by authorised manufacturers) and counterfeit (produced by unauthorised manufacturers) complementary medicines (TGA 2016e:49). The rate of failure for complementary medicines overall is therefore likely to be higher than is reported in this table.

### *3.4.4 Compliance reviews*

Because the TGA (2018e) 'cannot review' all listed medicines prior to their approval, it adopts a 'risk management approach' to prioritise compliance reviews for listed medicines post-approval. A compliance review involves an

*Table 3.4* Compliance issues identified in compliance reviews of listed medicines completed in 2014

| *Compliance issue* | *No. reviewed* | *% Fail* |
|---|---|---|
| Information provided in ARTG entry | 7 | 3.7% |
| Manufacturing, quality and/or formation | 14 | 7.4% |
| Labelling and/or advertising | 83 | 43.9% |
| Evidence | 39 | 20.6% |
| Safety | 0 | 0% |
| Other | 46 | 24.3% |
| **Total** | **189** | **100%** |

*Source*: Adapted from TGA (2015b:21).

audit of the documents held by the sponsor that were not supplied at the point of listing. Compliance reviews are either conducted randomly (determined by the software at the time of listing) or targeted (because of a complaint, a referral from within the TGA or by another regulatory agency, information published in the ARTG, or the prior compliance history of the sponsor) (TGA 2016e:21). Sponsors of newly listed medicines receive an automatic notification at the time of listing when their medicine is selected for a random review (ANAO 2011). The TGA aims to conduct reviews for 24% (or 688 out of 2,800) of all new ARTG listings each year (TGA 2011d:34), although annual and half-yearly report data indicates that this number is much less.[15] In 2011, 10,000 complementary medicines were said to have an active listing on the ARTG (ANAO 2011:13). In 2014, 75% (123 out of 164) of the listed medicines that underwent a random or targeted compliance review were found to be non-compliant (TGA 2015b:19). *Table 3.4* shows that a large proportion of these cases involved a failure to comply with labelling, DTCA and evidence requirements.

Compliance rates for those reviews described in *Table 3.4* exclude listed medicines that were cancelled by the sponsor upon the TGA's request for documentation and prior to the commencement of the review.[16] When the sponsor voluntarily cancels a medicine, the TGA ceases its investigation into it (ANAO 2011:110). Non-compliance rates could therefore be higher than those reported.

Of those reviews that are completed and where non-compliance is found, the TGA most commonly responds by issuing the sponsor with a notice proposing to cancel the listing (a cancellation notice) (TGA 2015b:22, 2016e:25)—a cooperative technique intended to provide sponsors with the opportunity to act on the non-compliance before the regulator escalates the severity of its response. Should the notice fail to generate compliance from the sponsor, the TGA can either suspend or cancel the medicine's listing or recall the medicine (TGA 2015b, 2016e).[17] In 2015, 63.8% of all compliance actions against listed medicine sponsors following a post-market compliance review resulted in the issue of a cancellation notice (TGA 2015b:22). The remaining 34.5% and 1.7% of actions resulted in the sponsor addressing the non-compliance identified by the TGA and the TGA concluding the review without taking further action or the direct cancellation of the medicine by the TGA without notice (TGA 2015b:22). Of those products that received a cancellation notice, 56.8% were rectified voluntarily by the sponsor, 27% were cancelled voluntarily by the sponsor and 16.2% were cancelled by the TGA (TGA 2015b:22). Although the TGA half-yearly performance report from which these figures are drawn did not specify the time it took for sponsors to comply with the cancellation notice, data from the ANAO (2011:106) indicates that it took sponsors an average of 200 days to cancel the listing 'voluntarily'.

### *3.4.5 DTCA and promotion pre-approval and complaints*

Advertising to the public (DTCA) and health professionals (promotion) is largely self-regulated. Due to the 'information asymmetry between industry and consumers', and the fact that consumers are not expected to be able to evaluate advertising claims (Toogoolawa Consulting 2002:35–36), DTCA of prescription medicines is prohibited (under s. 42DL(1)(f) of the Therapeutic Goods Act). Even so, DTCA complaints for prescription medicines are usually handled in the first instance by the industry association, MA, under its Code of Conduct. DTCA of non-prescription medicines is both co- and self-regulated, with the pre-approval and complaints functions split between government (the Complaints Resolution Panel, or CRP) and industry associations (Australian Self-Medication Industry or ASMI, formerly PMAA, and Complementary Medicines Australia or CMA).

The promotion of prescription and non-prescription medicines to health professionals is permitted on the basis that this 'information asymmetry . . . is less stark' (Doran and Löfgren 2013:20). Prescription and non-prescription medicines' promotion is largely self-regulated, with little to no intervention by the TGA *except* in exceptional circumstances, such as when a complaint concerns a non-association member (in which case, the complaint may be forwarded to the TGA).[18] Promotional materials must, however, conform to the requirements of the Therapeutic Goods Act,[19] the *Competition and Consumer Act 2010* (Cth)[20] and the applicable industry code of practice.

#### *3.4.5.1. Advertising pre-approval*

Only certain forms of DTCA require prior approval. DTCA of non-prescription medicines published in *specified media*, which includes broadcast media (such as television and radio), print media (such as newspapers, magazines and academic journals), outdoor advertisements (such as billboards, bus shelters, taxi displays and the sides and interiors of buses) or cinema advertisements, are pre-approved by ASMI (for OTC medicines) or CMA (for complementary medicines) (TGA 2011a:3). Under this self-regulatory arrangement, sponsors are required to submit all proposed broadcast media advertisements to ASMI and print, outdoor and cinema advertisements to ASMI (for OTC medicines) or CMA (for complementary medicines). These advertisements are reviewed against the Therapeutic Goods Act, Therapeutic Goods Regulations 1990 (Cth) and Therapeutic Goods Advertising Code 2015 (Cth), and they must not contain prohibited[21] or restricted[22] representations. When approved, the advertisement receives an approval number which must be published on all print media (TGA 2011a:8). When an advertisement fails to receive approval, the sponsor can appeal the decision with the Minister for Health (TGA 2011a:8–9). Pre-approval fees are outlined in items 17 and 17A under Schedule 9 of the Therapeutic Goods Regulations and range from AU$120 to AU$1,115, depending on the medium. A further AU$205 per hour is charged by ASMI and CMA for every additional hour of processing outside the allotted time.

There is no formal requirement for non-prescription medicine DTCA appearing in *other media* (such as leaflets, flyers, brochures, catalogues and letterbox drops) or in promotional materials directed at health professionals to obtain prior approval; sponsors are ultimately responsible for ensuring that all claims about a medicine conform with legislation and industry codes of conduct. However, according to ASMI's website, it is a condition of membership that all advertisements appearing in 'not specified media' and directed at health professionals be reviewed by its Promotional Monitoring Panel (PMP) which meets four times per year. The PMP advises ASMI members on the extent to which an advertisement complies with the Therapeutic Goods Advertising Code but does not provide a formal endorsement for an advertisement (ASMI 2016:para. 1). Promotional materials for prescription medicines also do not require formal approval prior to publication (Wong 2001:21).

### *3.4.5.2. Direct-to-consumer advertising (DTCA) complaints*

The complaints process for DTCA of non-prescription medicines contains facets of co-regulation and self-regulation. The TGA's CRP handles complaints related to DTCA published in *specified media* (i.e. advertisements requiring prior approval). The panel consists of representatives from ASMI, Australian Traditional Medicines Society, CHOICE, CMA, Consumers Health Forum, the Pharmacy Guild of Australia, Pharmaceutical Society of Australia, Royal Australian College of General Practitioners (RACGP) and the Medical Technology Association of Australia, as well as a representative from the TGA. Complaints are submitted to the CRP in writing along with a copy of the advertisement (CRP 2020a). When a complaint is received, the CRP asks the advertiser—usually the non-prescription medicine's sponsor—to respond to the complaint in the form of a written submission (CRP 2020b). A copy of the response is sent to the complainant, who can then challenge the response in a separate written submission (CRP 2020b). The CRP then presides over the investigation into the initial complaint and submissions by the sponsor and complainant to determine whether the complaint has merit (CRP 2020b). Should the CRP find for the complainant, it can request that the sponsor withdraw the advertisement, publish a retraction, publish a correction and/or withdraw the offending claim(s) and provide the CRP with a written undertaking that they will not reuse the claim(s) in future advertisements (s. 42ZCAI, Therapeutic Goods Regulations 1990).

The majority of complaints received by the CRP in the 2014–2015 financial year concerned complementary medicines (40.1%) and devices (42.2%) (CRP 2014–2015:1), and were often the result of a lack of evidence to support claims of efficacy (79.8%) or misleading claims (86.6%) (CRP 2014–2015:3).[23] The highest proportion of complaints received concerned advertisements on the internet (81%) and in print (11.6%) and *other media* (6.4%) (CRP 2014–2015:1). Although the CRP does not publish data on the proportion of complaints received for pre-approved advertisements (versus those that have not been pre-approved), O'Reilly (2016) claims that fewer than 0.05% of pre-approved advertisements are subject to a successful complaint. Most CRP determinations request that the advertiser withdraw either an advertisement (97.5%) or a representation (97.5%) (CRP 2014–2015:2). Few determinations result in a retraction (16.8%) (CRP 2014–2015:2).

Should a sponsor fail to comply with the CRP's determination—which occurred in at least 20% of all determinations (TGA 2013a:24)—the CRP can then refer the complaint to the Monitoring and Compliance Branch of the TGA. In these circumstances, the TGA can issue warning letters of various strength or a Regulation 9 Order (i.e. a formal order to withdraw and/or publish a retraction or rectify an advertisement) (ANAO 2011:121). Should either of these cooperative techniques fail, the TGA can escalate the severity of its response by cancelling a product's listing or referring the case to the Commonwealth Director of Public Prosecutions (ANAO 2011:127). The CRP can also go to the Secretary of the Department of Health directly to recover any advertisement in circulation and order its destruction (under s. 9(1) of the Therapeutic Goods Regulations). Should a sponsor wish to appeal a CRP determination, they can make a written request to the Minister for Health within 90 days of the determination (under s. 48(2) of the Therapeutic Goods Regulations). Sponsors can also make an application to the AAT should the Minister fail to overturn the decision (under s. 48(5) and (6) of the Therapeutic Goods Regulations).

Data from 2011 indicates that the CRP takes an average of 149 days, or five months, to issue a determination following the initial receipt of a complaint (ANAO 2011:141).[24] Sponsors take an average of 183 days, or six months, to rectify non-compliant and misleading advertising claims following the issue of a warning letter or multiple warning letters by the TGA (ANAO 2011:127). It takes the TGA an average of eight and a half weeks to issue a sponsor with a Regulation 9 Order at the recommendation of the CRP (ANAO 2011:130). The TGA also waits an additional three weeks to contact those sponsors who do not respond to the initial Regulation 9 Order (to allow sponsors sufficient time to cooperate with the TGA voluntarily) (ANAO 2011:130). Prior to 2011, there were no records of the TGA having cancelled a medicine's listing after a sponsor failed to comply with a Regulation 9 Order (ANAO 2011:130). Legal action was also limited '[d]ue to the very low financial penalties currently available' (ANAO 2011:130). Historically, it was 'not cost-effective for the TGA to initiate a formal investigation of an advertising breach with a view of preparing a brief of evidence for consideration of prosecution by the Director of Prosecutions' (ANAO 2011:130–131).

The self-regulatory aspects of the non-prescription medicines DTCA regime include voluntary codes of conduct and built-in complaint-handling processes. ASMI and CMA handle complaints about DTCA published in *other media* (i.e. for all advertisements that do not require prior approval) for OTC and complementary medicines, respectively, using separate industry codes of conduct (the ASMI Code of Practice and the CMA's Marketing & Supply Code of Practice), distinct complaints committees (ASMI's Marketing & Ethics Subcommittee and the CMA's Complaints Resolution & Monitoring Committee[25]) and internal appeals processes. ASMI and CMA also have mechanisms to proactively and randomly monitor advertisements that are not subject to pre-approval. Unlike the TGA and CRP, industry associations can issue monetary penalties in addition to demanding retractions, corrections and enforceable undertakings to discontinue advertising. Prior to the reform of the regime, ASMI (2015:45) and CMA (2015:31) issued fines of up to AU$50,000 for repeat breaches of their Codes. Additional sanctions included the termination of industry association membership and, for industry-generated complaints to ASMI's Marketing & Ethics Subcommittee, the reimbursement of out-of-pocket expenses to the successful party (ASMI 2015; CMA 2015). Historically, there has been inconsistent and minimal reporting of complaints outcomes by ASMI and CMA.[26] While ASMI and CMA would hear complaints regarding non-association members in *other media*, these complaints were more commonly dealt with and referred to the TGA (TGA 2011a).

The TGA can investigate advertising breaches for non-prescription medicines directly, irrespective of whether they are first subject to a complaint (ANAO 2011). The TGA accepts and investigates complaints regarding non-members of industry associations, retailers, distributors and health professionals, as well as those complaints forwarded to it from the CRP, ASMI or CMA (ANAO 2011). Most of the complaints dealt with by the TGA are those referred to it from the CRP—approximately one-third of CRP determinations on complaints are referred to the TGA due to the advertiser's failure to comply with a determination (TGA 2012a:29). Yet how these complaints are handled by the TGA is unclear due to the lack of transparency from the TGA in this area. Much like the CRP, the TGA can take up to several months to complete a complaint investigation. Complaints made to the TGA directly between 2008 and 2010 took an average of 182 days, or six months, to resolve (ANAO 2011:141).

Complaints concerning DTCA of prescription medicines are handled by the MA. Although DTCA of prescription medicines is prohibited under law, the MA does permit DTCA in some forms. For example, an advertisement of a medical condition that does not publish the name of a medicine but publishes a company name and/or logo (also known as a de-facto advertisement) is permissible under the MA Code of Conduct provided that the name or generic name of the medicine is not used in the advertisement (s. 9.4 and 9.5.2) and that the advertisement is primarily educational in nature (s. 9.5) (MA 2006). MA publishes a summary of each complaint determination (for both DTCA and promotional complaints) in its annual reports. Under the Therapeutic Goods Act, DTCA of prescription medicines can attract a fine of up to 60 penalty units (AU$10,800). Under the MA Code of Conduct, DTCA attracts fines of up to AU$300,000.

#### *3.4.5.3. Promotion-related complaints*

Complaints about promotion to health professionals are predominantly self-regulated. Complaints concerning the promotion of non-prescription medicines are handled by ASMI's Marketing & Ethics Subcommittee and the CMA's Complaints Resolution & Monitoring Committee in the same manner as DTCA advertising complaints. While ASMI and CMA can hear complaints regarding non-association members, complaints can also be referred to the TGA (ANAO 2011; TGA 2011a).

The MA is charged with handling complaints for promotional materials concerning prescription medicines. However, unlike sponsors of non-prescription medicines, all sponsors of prescription medicines are legally required, as a condition of their registration on the ARTG, to comply with the MA Code of Conduct (TGA 2011a:2). The MA Code of Conduct has a more extensive range of rules governing the interactions between industry and health professionals than the ASMI and CMA Codes; for example, the MA Code prohibits the giving of gifts and offers to health professionals (MA 2015). The MA can require from the sponsor the withdrawal and/or cessation of the promotion, the publication of correctional notice or the distribution of corrective letters to health professionals; issue fines of up to AU$300,000; and suspend or terminate the sponsor's MA membership (MA 2015). As with ASMI and CMA, if a sponsor subject to a complaint is not a member of the MA or refuses to abide by an MA determination, the complaint can be forwarded to the TGA for further action (ANAO 2011; TGA 2011a). Yet, again, how these complaints are handled by the TGA is not clear.

## 3.5 The potential for failure

The TGA claims to regulate sponsors of registered and listed medicines using a combination of risk-based and responsive regulatory techniques. The TGA first claims to regulate on a product and compliance risk basis, through assessment of the risks inherent to the product and the sponsor's risk of non-compliance. Product risk forms the basis of the regime's two-tiered registered and listed medicine classification scheme, and the extent of pre- and post-market regulation of registered and listed medicines. The TGA claims to use graduated techniques in responding to these risks; it begins by using lower-level cooperative techniques before escalating to higher-level punitive techniques when initial techniques fail to compel compliance. While the TGA is the principal regulator of this regime, regulation is also carried out by the industry associations the MA, ASMI and CMA in the areas of DTCA and promotion. In the advertising space, pre-approval is said to occur for all specified media through the industry associations ASMI and CMA. Complaints handling is said to be split across government (the CRP) and industry associations (ASMI and CMA) based on media type (specified or other) and industry association membership (non-member or member). DTCA of prescription medicines is within the domain of the state; however, the MA is usually the first point for the receipt of DTCA complaints. Promotion is regulated by the MA, ASMI and CMA, usually with little intervention by the TGA. Sponsors are also responsibilised in some aspects of the regime where regulation by the TGA is otherwise lacking. Because this self-regulation deploys the agency of industry associations and sponsors, it constitutes a form of technology of agency. The public, public interest groups, health professionals and professional associations are responsibilised insofar as they must ensure that both the TGA and industry carry out this regulation through various technologies of citizenship and agency (the latter through both regulatory and health literacy).

Although the TGA appears to prioritise risk-based techniques (and product risk) in the pre-market regulation of registered and listed medicines, and responsive (and cooperative) techniques during post-market regulation (in response to compliance risk), the prioritisation of the former can come into conflict with and occur at the expense of the latter. In particular, this prioritisation could affect cooperation between the regulator and regulated. Risk-based and responsive regulation, with their emphasis on prioritising regulation on the basis of risk, self-regulation, intervention as a last resort and cooperation in place of punishment (and punishment as a last resort), are also compatible with the neoliberal rationale of limited intervention by the state. These theories could therefore provide 'unintended' (Mascini 2013:56) justification for the use of neoliberal techniques.

The following chapters, Chapters 4 and 5, critically examine the extent to which this regime actually achieves compliance from sponsors and allows its third players—the public, public interest groups, health professionals and professional associations—to participate meaningfully as regulators in the regime. Using a thematic analysis of submissions to public consultations and interview transcripts, Chapters 4 and 5 examine participants' perceptions of the TGA and medicine regulatory regime, and those aspects of the regime that they perceive to fail to compel compliance from sponsors.

## Notes

1 In 2024, these units were restructured and renamed to the Medicines Regulation Division, Medical Devices and Product Quality Division, Regulatory Practice and Support Division and Regulatory Legal Services.
2 All these committees, excluding the ACCM, have been disbanded. In 2017, the ACPM, ACNM and ACSOM were replaced by a new committee called the Advisory Committee on Medicines (ACM).
3 'Risk' has a variety of meanings. For instance, in the UK, risks are regulated 'comprehensively' in 'all aspects' of regulatory regimes (the Hampton Review or Hampton 2005:1, 28) and therefore extend beyond the risk of non-compliance by the regulated.
4 Joseph (2004:145) argues that it is possible to use concepts like knowledge/power while adopting a critical realist ontological framework by conceiving knowledge as both transitive and intransitive, meaning that it develops not merely as a result of our attempts to understand the world, but also according to 'the dynamics of its practical, institutional and discursive context'.
5 Excluding those subject to exemptions under the Therapeutic Goods Act.
6 Classified in the Poisons Standard 2013 (Cth) as therapeutic goods that are either pharmacy (Schedule 2), pharmacist-only (Schedule 3), prescription-only (Schedule 4) or controlled (Schedule 8), or contain cautions (Schedule 5), poisons (Schedule 6), dangerous poisons (Schedule 7) or prohibited substances (Schedule 9) or substances whose danger warrants the prohibition of their supply and use (Schedule 10).
7 High risk registered medicines are typically classified as being Schedule 4, 8 or 9 and low risk registered medicines as Schedule 2 and 3 in the Poisons Standard.
8 Sponsors of generic registered medicines need only provide evidence that establishes a medicine's therapeutic equivalence to an existing registered medicine (TGA 2015c:10).
9 A representative appointed by the Secretary of the Department for Health.
10 Referred to by the TGA as new chemical entities.
11 While the ELF can scan for restricted and prohibited terms, the free text fields still allow the sponsor to make unsubstantiated claims of efficacy. The TGA has indicated that some sponsors do 'game' the system intentionally by entering information into the form on the ELF to identify which terms will prohibit an application from being accepted (ANAO 2011:80).
12 Sponsors must also certify that the medicine is being manufactured by a licensed manufacturer in accordance with the Code of GMP and that it only contains ingredients (substances) that are pre-approved by the TGA (ANAO 2011:70).
13 In 2014, a penalty unit was equivalent to AU$170.
14 The NPS is a not-for-profit organisation funded by the Department of Health, providing medicine information and resources to the public and healthcare professionals (Low et al. 2010:22).
15 The TGA completed random or targeted reviews for 11% (or 222 out of 1,992) of all new listings in 2014 (TGA 2015b:17, 19). Even if we were to include all reviews initiated by the TGA during this period (a total of 103), this would still equate to just 16% (325 out of 1,992) of all new listings (TGA 2015b:17, 19).
16 In 2014 alone, 62.1% of the compliance reviews initiated and subsequently abandoned by the TGA were terminated on the basis that the product was cancelled from the ARTG by the sponsor prior to the commencement of the review (TGA 2015b:19). The remaining 37.9% of reviews were abandoned on the basis that the medicine subject to the review had not yet been manufactured (2015b:19).
17 Listings can also be cancelled by the TGA without prior notice in cases where the product could cause imminent death or harm, contains prohibited ingredients or

substances, has been manufactured by an unlicensed person or company or when a sponsor fails to respond to requests for information within 20 working days of the request (TGA 2016a:53).

18 When a complaint involving a non-member is received by an industry association, that association will invite the non-member to have the complaint adjudicated by the association. If the non-member declines, the association can, if it chooses to, forward the complaint to the TGA for adjudication (TGA 2011a). The specific details of how these complaints are handled and the sanctions (if any) that apply have not been stated publicly.

19 For prescription medicines, this means only advertising a medicine within the indications approved on the ARTG (s. 22(5)). For non-prescription medicines, this means advertisements that do not contain prohibited or restricted representations, or statements that suggest or imply that the good has the recommended approval (endorsement) of the Australian Government (s. 42DL).

20 Which includes the prohibition of advertisements containing false or misleading representations (s. 29, 151).

21 Prohibited representations include references to abortifacient action or the treatment, prevention or cure of disease such as neoplastic disease, sexually transmitted diseases, HIV/AIDS, or mental illness (under Schedule 2 of the Therapeutic Goods Regulations 1990).

22 Restricted representations include references to any of the following: cardiovascular disease; dental and periodontal disease; diseases of the joint, bone or collagen and rheumatic disease; diseases of the eye or ear that lead to blindness or deafness; diseases of the liver, biliary system or pancreas; endocrine disease and conditions including diabetes and prostatic disease; gastrointestinal disease or disorder; haematological disease; infectious disease; immunological disease; mental disturbance; metabolic disorder; musculoskeletal disease; nervous system diseases; poisoning, or venomous bites and stings; renal disease; respiratory diseases; skin diseases; substance dependence or urogenital diseases and conditions (s. 5(2) of the Therapeutic Goods Advertising Code). Unlike prohibited representations, which are outlawed entirely, a restricted representation could be made with the expressed approval of the Secretary of the Department of Health and with the endorsement of the Therapeutic Goods Advertising Code Council (the government body charged with maintaining the Therapeutic Goods Advertising Code).

23 These percentages were calculated according to the total number of violations against certain aspects of the Therapeutic Goods Advertising Code in the 2014–2015 financial year. For lack of evidence to support efficacy, scores were calculated on the basis of the number of s. 4(1)(b) violations. For misleading claims, scores were calculated based on the number of s. 4(2)(c) violations.

24 Data from 2014–2015 indicates that this average increased to 268 days (CRP 2014–2015:3).

25 The membership of ASMI's Marketing & Ethics Subcommittee includes a lawyer with trade practices experience, a consumer, representatives from the RACGP and Pharmaceutical Society of Australia, up to three association members and a TGA representative-observer (ASMI 2015:38). CMA's Complaints Resolution & Monitoring Committee is comprised of a complementary health professional, a consumer, up to six association members, the CMA's Chief Executive Officer and a TGA representative-observer (CMA 2015).

26 ASMI has an inconsistent history of publishing complaints outcomes in its annual reports. In the 2012–2013 Annual Report, 29.2% (82 out of 281) of the complaints received concerned a breach of the ASMI Code of Practice and TGAC (ASMI 2012–2013:15). Of those products found in breach, 63% were due to the failure to include mandatory statements, or that the mandatory statements were incorrect or not prominently displayed; 11% contained misleading information;

9% implied that the product was recommended by a health professional; 6% did not include reference to an approved indication; 3% contained inappropriately presented scientific information; and 2% referred to a serious condition (ASMI 2012–2013:15). There is no mention of complaint determinations in ASMI's annual reports in the 2018–2019, 2019–2020 and 2020–2021 financial years. This could be due to no complaints being heard or determined during this period, but unlike in previous reports (e.g. see ASMI 2016–2017:16), this was not explicitly stated. In total, 26 determinations are published on ASMI's website for both DTCA and promotional complaints (see Consumer Health Products Australia 2024). CMA only appears to publish data on the number of complaints received, finalised, forwarded to the TGA or referred on to the CRP in its annual report. A large proportion of the complaints received by CMA in 2013–2014 concerned non-members (CMA 2013–2014).

# 4 Regulatory disempowerment

Between 2010 and 2014, the Australian Government undertook an extensive period of public consultation seeking comment on potential reform to the regulation of listed and registered medicines. According to the TGA archive of consultations and reviews, available through Trove at the National Library of Australia, no fewer than 65 public consultations and reviews were completed during this four-year period. This number exceeded the annual rate of public consultations and reviews completed between the years 1998 and 2009, which amounted to 63 over the 11-year period (for a complete list, see Appendix 2). Initial consultations conducted between 2010 and 2014, such as *Improving Advertising Arrangements for Therapeutic Goods*, completed in 2010, and *Review to Improve the Transparency of the TGA* (also referred to as the Transparency Review), completed in 2011, contributed to the production of the Blueprint Reforms document and, in turn, shaped the reform of the regulation of listed and registered medicines. The Blueprint Reforms made multiple recommendations to 'enhance' the pre- and post-market regulation of listed medicines, and DTCA and promotion, and recommendations to increase the transparency of the TGA (as part of a wider Australian Government commitment to 'open government') (TGA 2011c:2).

The number of consultations completed and the release of the Blueprint Reforms document during this four-year period reinforce the argument made in the previous chapters that rates of non-compliance were—or at least were perceived to be—high in relation to certain aspects of the Australian medicine regulatory regime; so much so, that a major reform of the regime was warranted. The purpose of this book, and therefore its value to the literature, lies not in a deductive analysis of how regulation compels (or fails to compel) compliance, but in an abductive analysis of *why* regulation failed, or was perceived to have failed, to compel compliance.

To identify the source of regulatory failure, a qualitative thematic analysis was conducted using 451 submissions to 12 of these public consultations and interview transcripts from semi-structured interviews with 18 participants. A complete list of the submissions can be found in Appendix 3, with the citations in-text numbered from one to 451 (authors are de-identified in-text,

DOI: 10.4324/9781003285762-4

consistent with the interviews). The interviews are cited as numbers one to 11 and TGA 1 to TGA 7 (for the TGA staff). From the analysis of this data, two overarching themes were identified: that the TGA and regulatory regime were limited in their capacity to act on non-compliance (which I refer to as *regulatory disempowerment*); and that the public and those representing the public interest were limited in their capacity to participate in regulation (referred to as *public disempowerment*). This chapter focuses on the former theme (and Chapter 5 on the latter). In those areas of the regime where non-compliance was greatest, the capacity of the TGA and regulatory regime to act on this non-compliance was reduced due to the following factors: the limited pre- and post-market evaluation of medicine quality, safety and efficacy, and DTCA and promotion (*limited evaluation*); the limited active enforcement (*limited active/reactive enforcement*); the limited centralisation, particularly in the regulation of DTCA and promotion (*limited centralisation*); the limited proportionality in responding to non-compliance (*limited proportionality*); limitations in escalating the response to non-compliance (*limited escalation*); and constraints on the TGA's operations (*operationally constrained*). Each of these sub-themes is discussed in detail in this chapter. It is argued that risk-based and responsive regulation conveniently rationalised limiting, and therefore disempowering, the TGA and regulatory regime in ways that aligned with neoliberal governmentality. However, this failure of regulation, in turn—in fact—rationalises a (re)turn to neoliberal governmentality, through a greater use of micro-level self-regulatory techniques.

## 4.1 Limited evaluation

In several areas of the regime, the TGA's capacity to evaluate medicine quality, safety and efficacy and DTCA and promotion, both pre- and post-market, was found to be limited.

Most of the submissions and interviewees referred to the TGA's limited pre- and post-market regulation of listed medicines. Pre-market listed medicines were assessed by the TGA to the extent that some of the information included in their application for listing required prior approval,[1] and the TGA's ELF scanned this application for the use of restricted and prohibited terms; but otherwise, listed medicines were approved electronically without much further assessment. Because listed medicines were also less likely to undergo a post-market assessment (such as laboratory testing or a compliance review) by the TGA, the likelihood that non-compliance would be detected was low. Even if a listed medicine was subject to post-market assessment, the likelihood that the sponsor would be penalised was low if the medicine was non-compliant.

Limited pre-market assessment of listed medicines rendered the regime largely reliant on reporting by the public or health professionals (or spontaneous reporting), such as reports of ADRs and complaints. Not only were the public's and health professionals' knowledge of and engagement in spontaneous reporting found to be limited (see Section 5.1), but for the CRP in particular, the limited pre-market assessment increased the number of listed medicines subject to (and therefore, delayed the remediation of) complaints.

Registered medicines were regulated for quality, safety and efficacy to a greater extent than listed medicines, but within limits. Because the TGA placed greater emphasis on the pre-market than the post-market regulation of registered medicines' safety, fewer resources were dedicated to assessing sponsors' post-market adherence to safety requirements. For example, the TGA did not regulate every clinical trial, nor did it always regulate trials end to end (Gill 2014; Skerritt 2019; TGA 2006, 2021b). The TGA approved clinical trials for medicines not yet registered on the ARTG (i.e. unapproved medicines) and for registered medicines for use(s) beyond the conditions of their original approval (i.e. medicines unapproved for a particular use) (TGA 2006, 2021b). It was otherwise the responsibility of the sponsor of the trial to monitor and manage the trial, evaluate ADRs and report them to the TGA as they arose, and notify the TGA of the trial's completion (TGA 2006, 2021b:21, 25).[2] Clinical trials for registered (approved) medicines, more commonly referred to as post-market studies, were criticised in submissions and by interviewees for being of a lower standard and quality compared with trials conducted prior to market. Interviewee 7 (13–14) stated:

> post-marketing collection of information is very loose . . . when you read those study proposals, they're absolutely shockingly bad. . . . [Prior to market] in order to get the drug tested you go through very intensive protocols. Like, you know, for example, you'd have to write a grant application and you'd have to go through a committee member, you know lots of people, be peer reviewed and then you do the testing—phase one, phase two, phase three—and then the randomised control trials. It's a huge undertaking and every single adverse event is recorded, and it's a very rigorous protocol for trials now. But once a drug has been approved, the system is hopeless. . . . [T]hese studies that they [the sponsor] were proposing were based on electronic databases in the US and Europe, and there's no way you're going to get any useful information out of that. They were trying to compare the instance of a particular side effect based on all these other drugs and it was totally unclear. That would be rejected by any grant committee, so it would not have passed at all. . . . Why do we have these differences in standards post-marketing versus prior to the drug being approved? . . . [T]hat's actually the most important part of the drug development because that's when you've got these untoward effects that may be captured.

In research conducted in the US and Europe, data collected on companies' compliance with post-market study requirements indicated that delays in the completion of or failure to complete post-market studies were commonplace.[3] Although the TGA requires sponsors to implement a pharmacovigilance plan and provide it with updates, a consumer association (280:2) reaffirmed that the TGA does not monitor sponsors' compliance with these plans, stating that it 'has no power to monitor whether companies are complying with requirements to report serious or unusual adverse events, maintain records of all adverse event reports received and inform the TGA if any patterns emerge'. In the US, where the reporting of ADRs by companies is monitored, one study found that 10% of companies failed to report serious ADRs within the mandated timeframe (Ma et al. 2015:1565–1566).[4] ADR reports by companies were also more likely to contain incomplete information (and were therefore less useful for assessing and ongoing monitoring of a medicine's safety).[5]

Registered medicines were also regulated for efficacy prior to approval, but not necessarily for comparative efficacy—that is, as having greater efficacy compared with medicines already on the market. In general terms, sponsors registering a medicine needed only establish that the medicine was more effective than a placebo.[6] The limitations posed by the lack of comparative efficacy assessment were best summarised by Interviewee 2 (3) when discussing the musculoskeletal condition intermittent claudication (pain in the lower extremities induced by exercise):

> The end point that the regulators require for that condition is a six-minute walk test, which means they put people on the treadmill and they walk them for six minutes, with the drug and without the drug. They look at the increase that they walk on the treadmill in six minutes. So, a drug I recently saw, the incremental increase in distance walked within six minutes on a treadmill was 30 metres. So, the company says, 'this drug works for intermittent claudication'. Who says that it works? They walked 30 metres more in six minutes on a treadmill. . . . Does that equate to people being able to walk around to do their activities of daily living? The answer is no.

Although sponsors were required to conduct post-market comparative efficacy studies to obtain a listing on the PBS, they needed only establish non-inferiority for the purposes of the application. This means that '[a] drug that is less effective and/or more toxic than a drug already listed for the same indications might be considered for listing' provided that it 'decrease[d] the overall costs of therapy' or was 'restricted to a subsequent line of therapy after the more effective or less toxic therapy' (Department of Health 2008:6).

Certain types of listed and registered medicine advertisements (such as those appearing in *other media*, on the internet and paid TV) and promotion directed at health professionals were not pre-approved by the TGA. Not only did this lack of prior approval render the regime reliant upon post-market spontaneous (complaints) reporting to identify non-compliance (which contributed to the delays in the CRP hearing complaints), but it also provided sponsors with less incentive to comply because 'any breaches and penalties would be administered after the profits had been garnered' (Multiple authors,

385:9). This was best demonstrated by the high proportion of complaints the CRP received for advertisements that had not been pre-approved (see Section 3.4.5.2).

The aforementioned issues around evaluation are the result of a product risk rationality. Medicines are classified on the basis of product risk (as high or low risk), that is, on risks that have to do with the medicine itself. It is this risk classification that determines how regulatory techniques are prioritised. Because of the predominance of this type of risk rationality, techniques for regulating all other risks not inherent to the medicine, such as the risk of non-compliance by the sponsor or compliance risk, are deprioritised. As a result of this prioritisation, the focus of regulation shifts towards the medicines (and away from the sponsors). This mentality of regulating product (and not compliance) risk was apparent in statements by the TGA:

> TGA adopts a risk-based approach to *product* regulation. This risk-based approach identifies *the risks posed by therapeutic goods* and regulates *products* based on this degree of risk. . . . [A] *high risk product* (such as a new chemical substance) receives more in-depth analysis than a *lower risk product* with extensive safety data. . . . [T]he TGA applies a system of oversight for identifying, analysing and evaluating *the risks associated with the product itself*, as well as the manufacturing process to ensure *products* available in Australia meet community expectations.
> (TGA 7:5, emphasis added)

The focus on product risk prioritises the regulation of registered (not listed) medicines; as listed medicines are classified as low risk, their regulation by the TGA is deprioritised irrespective of the risk of non-compliance by the sponsor. This relation between product and compliance risk was noted in both the submissions and by the interviewees:

> The risks of being non-compliant are much greater for your business in those high risk products . . . part of the reason why there is an emphasis on [reforming] complementary medicines and on devices is because the prescription medicines sector is so highly regulated that it doesn't have a record of high non-compliance . . . therefore it wasn't the focus.
> (Interviewee 11:9)

Emphasising product risk also rationalises the prioritisation of pre-market (over post-market) techniques of regulation, as well as those techniques that have to do with the medicine itself (such as laboratory testing), as opposed to compliance reviews, DTCA and promotional complaints, and so on.

But product risk rationality not only prioritises certain regulatory techniques; it is also a means to limit such techniques to levels commensurate with the category of risk (Bandiera 2021:185). Product risk thus categorises risk as one of only two types (and therefore oversimplifies risk). Risks that do not fit these prescribed categories have to be 'reinterpreted in ways that assimilate them' (Simon 2010:5). We see this in the regulation of listed medicines: although the compliance risk of sponsors was high, the level of regulation listed medicines received continued to align with their product risk, which was categorised as low. The simplification and therefore lumping together of risks into categories also limits the identification of risks (Weick and Sutcliffe 2007 as cited in Simon 2010:5). Because the focus on product risk prioritises the risks posed by the medicine itself, differentiating between the risks of comparable medicines is limited. In the case of Vioxx, the deprioritisation of clinical trials that would require the comparative efficacy and safety of Vioxx to be evaluated against existing treatments[7] limited the capacity of regulators to identify its safety risks. In this way, product risk rationality limits regulator intervention. This is by no means intended to suggest that regulation should not be proportionate to product risk; only that it should not be at the expense of other types of risk.

## 4.2 Limited active/reactive enforcement

The TGA was often perceived as being 'reactive' and not 'proactive' (Academic 145:6) in its response to non-compliance. This was due in part to the perception that the TGA engages in a relatively small number of post-market regulatory activities each year (laboratory testing of medicine samples, manufacturer inspections, random and targeted compliance reviews and so on). The TGA was thus thought to rely primarily on spontaneous reporting:

> apart from that, there isn't anything else. As far as I know, it's up to the prescriber or the pharmaceutical industry dealing with that new drug to report that then.
>
> (Interviewee 7:15)

Regulation was also believed to be something that was largely sponsor- rather than TGA-initiated, as the extracts below indicate:

> When TGA was contacted to ask why some products were still listed [on the ARTG] as being TGA registered . . . the response was that the TGA rely on the sponsoring drug company to notify them that the drug has been removed from the Australian market . . . if the drug has been withdrawn from the Australian market due to safety concerns, it would seem sensible to remove the drug from the ARTG (e.g. sibutramine[8] and sitaxentan[9] still have an active listing status).
>
> (Non-governmental organisation, 112:3)

> [Our organisation] formally approached [name redacted] with details of inaccuracies in the CMI for allopurinol[10] . . . The below was received from [name redacted] . . . *the Clinical Evaluation Unit has written to*

> *all sponsors of allopurinol pointing out the inconsistencies in CMI and PI information . . . The TGA does not approve the CMI information but is in a position to request that sponsors amend their PI documents as the Secretary approves PI's and there is also a requirement in our legislation that CMI is consistent with the approved PI. We have also raised with the innovator product a separate issue that the PI in MIMS* [Monthly Index of Medical Specialties] *is incorrect and doesn't reflect the approved PI* . . . It is more than nine months since the fundamental errors in the CMI and MIMS were raised. Many thousands of patients and allied health professionals may have read the inaccurate information on dosing; . . . patients may have had their healthcare adversely affected by this advice.
>
> (Professional association, 24:1, emphasis in original)

There was acknowledgement, too, that spontaneous reports were made mostly by sponsors:

> if you don't complain nothing will happen. So it means that you rely on people like me . . . to do the job. . . . So most of the complaints are, I think that the majority come from drug companies complaining against others, but if they have all the same interests they would not have complaints against each other. Even if the promotion is misleading.
>
> (Interviewee 5:10)

Prioritising product risk rationalises the responsibilisation of sponsors by having them take on more responsibility for governing risks, including their own risk of non-compliance (thereby reducing the TGA's responsibility for them). Responsibilisation is not only a technique through which to limit intervention by the regulator, but it also reinforces itself, in that it manifests the reality that the regulated are responsibilised (or capable of self-regulating). The TGA is limited in its capacity to regulate post-market (because product risk rationality deprioritises post-market regulatory techniques) and is therefore reliant on sponsors to self-regulate. Sponsors acting on risks, irrespective of whether it was voluntary or at the direction of the TGA, are viewed as responsibilised (indeed cooperative, as per a responsive rationality of governance). Because responsive rationality insists not only that sponsors acting cooperatively should continue to self-regulate but also that penalties should not apply even if non-compliance occurs (Yeung 2004 as cited in Morgan and Yeung 2007), responsibilisation is further reinforced. This mentality was evident in a statement made by TGA 1 (5–6), who claimed that the TGA was inclined to act on sponsors who intentionally withheld information that a medicine was substandard (i.e. who were non-compliant with standards of quality, safety or efficacy) rather than those sponsors who reported it to the TGA, 'as the company have done the right thing by reporting it'. In this way, responsibilisation creates and reproduces a reality that it assumes already exists.

## 4.3 Limited centralisation

There was limited centralisation in regulation, particularly in relation to DTCA and promotion. The decentralisation of pre-approval for advertising and for complaints for listed medicines had the potential to lead to (and in some cases did lead to) inconsistencies in decisions made by the TGA, the CRP and industry associations. For instance, inconsistencies arose by virtue of a listed medicine being subject to a complaint or TGA enforcement action after it had received advertising pre-approval because it was later found to have insufficient efficacy:

> There have been instances where a TGA Delegate exercising a different power under the Act to that which CHC [Complementary Healthcare Council, now the CMA] has used to approve an advertisement, (i.e. Paragraph 30(2)(ba)), has decided to propose the cancellation of the product from the Register partly because the advertising approved by the CHC does not comply with the Advertising Code. This raises serious issues for the industry . . . a company will often in good faith embark on a costly advertising campaign in reliance on the CHC approval processes.
>
> (Industry consultant 98:7–8)

> [Advertising] pre-approvals officers do not review the evidence to support therapeutic indications that are listed on the Australian Register of Therapeutic Goods (ARTG) (such as 'temporary relief of pain'). They will only assess whether such claims are in fact listed on the ARTG, and also review extrapolations on these claims (such as 'clinically tested to provide temporary relief of pain in 15 minutes'). The complaints process, on the other hand, will review the evidence to support claims. As such, the two systems review the same advertisements based on different parameters.
>
> (Sponsor 380:2)

Because the CRP and industry associations would only hear complaints about advertising appearing in certain mediums, there was potential for the same non-compliant advertisement that appeared in two different mediums to be adjudicated by two separate bodies, which could therefore result in two different decisions:

> The split delegation [for pre-approval] means that the ASMI delegate will review a therapeutic claim for a complementary medicine in television or radio while a CHC delegate will review the same claim in

print. . . . The notion that the same claim may be acceptable in a print advertisement but not a television advertisement is unacceptable.

(Sponsor 380:3)

Complaints about print media, radio, television and internet advertisements for non-prescription medicines and medical devices may be made to the TGA's Complaints Resolution Panel (CRP), but complaints about other advertisements (for example, in-store promotions) must be made to either the CHC (for complementary medicines) or to ASMI (for non-complementary over the counter medicines) . . . a complaint about the same advertisement in two different media (for example, in a newspaper and an in-store brochure) must be made to two different complaints bodies, 'even if the substance of the advertisement and the complaint is the same'. The separation of these functions creates confusion and inconsistency.

(Consumer association 132:3)

Discrepancies were also noted in the application of penalties by the bodies that adjudicated complaints. Penalties were not only inconsistent due to differences in their type and severity (e.g. not all bodies applied fines for DTCA or promotional non-compliance and only one body issued fines beyond a maximum of AU$50,000, per offence) but also because advertisements published in a less prominent medium (*other media*) being adjudicated by an industry association could receive a penalty that was more severe than that applied for advertisements appearing in a more prominent medium (*specified media*) adjudicated by the CRP (see Section 4.4).

Not all sponsors were compelled to be members of industry associations,[11] and so they could opt out of self-regulation. This was best demonstrated in a submission by an academic (259:4) that referred to the case of Ranbaxy Australia. In 2012, Ranbaxy offered pharmacists AU$14,648 worth of free samples and a 90% discount on subsequent orders for its generic cholesterol-lowering medicine Trovas. This promotion violated both the MA and the Generic Medicines Industry Association (GMiA) codes of conduct. However, when a complaint was lodged with the GMiA, Ranbaxy declined to participate in hearing the complaint on the grounds that it was not a member of either association (Academic 259:4). Although the ASMI, CMA and GMiA had mechanisms to allow sponsors of listed medicines to voluntarily subscribe to a code of conduct without having to become a member of an association, few associations have reported an uptake of such offers:

We have procedures in place to allow non-members to agree to be subject to our Code. But no one has taken us up on that offer as far as I can tell . . . there is no means to compel non-members if they don't agree to be bound.

(Interviewee 6:5)

In this way, decentralisation gave rise to perceptions of inequalities in regulatory enforcement among sponsors, as the extract below demonstrates:

> members are held to higher standards of conduct and bound to remediate all advertising that is found in breach of the relevant code, whilst non-members may disregard codes of conduct as well as any orders to remediate advertising. This failure to comply with industry mandates carries no consequences for non-members and there is no authority that member advertisers can appeal to in such cases. Further, non-members may presently lodge complaints against member organisations . . . with the full knowledge that they, themselves are not held to the same standards of compliance. Industry members are also frequently at a disadvantage with respect to non-members. . . . [M]ember companies are required to provide the data substantiating a claim being made to any consumer or competitor company that requests it. Often this data is commercial-in-confidence, yet it is still provided as it is a requirement of membership. In contrast, competitor companies that are non-members are under no obligation to provide data to substantiate any claims being made.
>
> (Sponsor 144:16–17)

Decentralisation also diffused responsibility, particularly when there was overlap between regulation by the TGA and regulation by industry associations. In this regard, multiple submissions and an interviewee alleged that sponsors of registered medicines had been using de-facto advertising to advertise prescription medicines directly to the public, which is prohibited by the Therapeutic Goods Act. Pfizer was a specific example provided by a consumer association (132). In 2009, Pfizer allegedly published a print advertisement[12] directed at people who took multiple medications for their blood pressure and cholesterol. This advertisement, which featured a large red heart and tear-off slips, encouraged the public to talk to their doctor about combination treatments for heart conditions. The advertisement coincided with another full-page advertisement published by Pfizer in medical magazines and journals for its two-in-one combination medicine for heart conditions called Caduet. These publications were regularly accessed by (and therefore, directed at) health professionals. In addition to detailed information about Caduet, the advertisements contained the statement that 'patients will soon be asking about their suitability for combination heart medications' (Consumer association 132:3). Although industry may argue that these advertisements increase awareness of the medical condition and the availability of different treatments, research suggests that they only lead to an increase in sales for certain types of treatments (usually those produced by the advertiser) (Leonardo Alves et al. 2014; W't Jong et al. 2004). According to the MA, these advertisements did not constitute DTCA as no specific medicine was advertised and the information they contained was construed as educational in nature (MA 2010:5–6). Although the consumer association (132:4) believed there was scope to challenge this interpretation of DTCA under the Therapeutic Goods Act (because the provisions on DTCA in the Act are not as specific as those in the MA Code of Conduct), they claimed that complaints to the TGA regarding the alleged de-facto advertising of Caduet by Pfizer went unanswered.

The decentralisation of these aspects of the regime was a result of a product risk rationality that sought to shift some of the responsibility for regulating away from the TGA. Decentralisation has led to a flattening of regulatory techniques and less of a hierarchy. The TGA, the CRP and industry associations acted rather independently of and therefore did not necessarily complement each other. The CRP and industry associations also acted largely in place of the TGA. This lack of centralisation and hierarchy has led to differences in the techniques used by all of these organisations. In addition, it has made the regulatory techniques employed less prescriptive, and more flexible, and therefore less applicable to those sponsors that choose not to comply (in turn, giving rise to perceptions of differences in treatment among sponsors). This flexibility limited the responsibility of both the TGA and industry associations for the resultant risks, because the onus of responsibility for regulation (and failure thereof) was diffused and shifted onto others. It also allowed industry associations to (re)interpret the rules (e.g. by categorising a wider range of acts within the scope of compliant advertising).

## 4.4 Limited proportionality

There was a lack of criminal or civil penalties for certain types of non-compliance, meaning that the penalty was not always proportionate to the harm caused. Civil and criminal penalties did not apply to cases where listed medicines were found to be non-compliant by a random or targeted compliance review; in such cases, the TGA could only issue a cancellation notice, suspend or cancel a medicine's listing, or issue a product recall (although the third option had never been done by the TGA before). The ease and low cost of listing a medicine on the ARTG, and the lack of civil and criminal penalties for the type of non-compliance mentioned earlier, meant that sponsors could avoid taking remedial action and being penalised by cancelling the medicine and relisting it under a different name on the ARTG. Because the TGA was generally not able to complete the compliance review prior to the medicine's cancellation (and therefore determine its non-compliance), and the medicine was no longer listed (at least, not under the same name), the TGA would have to terminate the review into the medicine. Notable examples of such provided in the submissions and by the interviewees included Swisse Appetite Suppressant and Undoit. The TGA cancelled Swisse Appetite Suppressant on the grounds that there was insufficient evidence to support the claim that it suppressed appetite (Earl and Smith 2013). Swisse Wellness (Swisse) relisted the product as Swisse Hunger Control and replaced the claim that it suppressed appetite with the following statement: 'Traditionally used in India to help reduce hunger levels'. Swisse sent a letter to its distributors shortly after its (re)listing to affirm that Swisse Hunger Control was 'not a new line of Swisse product, rather a new name for the same product' (Earl and Smith 2013). Unlike Swisse Appetite Suppressant, Undoit, a diet pill that claimed to prevent fat and carbohydrate absorption, was subject to a complaint at the CRP in 2012 (Hobday 2012). The inefficacious claims also prompted a concurrent compliance review by the TGA (Hobday 2012). Four months following the submission of the complaint to the CRP, Undoit.com.au Pty Ltd cancelled the listing for Undoit and relisted it as Undoit Plus. The director of Undoit.com.au Pty Ltd, Michael Romm, claimed that the timing of the cancellation was 'not a coincidence'; '[w]hen the TGA was looking into our advertising claims . . . they noticed at the same time that we'd changed the formulation but left the name the same and because they were looking at it at that time, they asked us . . . to change the name as well' (Hobday 2012:para. 14). The initial complaint and review were discontinued by the CRP and TGA (TGA 2012d), despite the complainant maintaining that the claims for Undoit Plus were identical to those made for Undoit (Hobday 2012). Undoit Plus was cancelled by the TGA in late 2012 (TGA 2024k).

Few civil and criminal penalties applied for the non-compliant promotion of listed and registered medicines. Except in a select number of circumstances—for example, where a listed or registered medicine is promoted in violation of a condition of its approval, such as for an unapproved indication (punishable under s. 21A, 21B and 22(5) of the Therapeutic Goods Act)—promotion to health professionals is otherwise excluded from the Therapeutic Goods Act (see s. 42AA).

For advertising non-compliance, the CRP was only empowered to request that sponsors withdraw an advertisement, issue a retraction or correction, or commit to an enforceable undertaking (such as not to reproduce the offending claim for a defined period). Due to these limited powers, the CRP was unable to apply further sanctions when sponsors failed to comply with determinations. As sponsors were required to do no more than rectify the initial advertisement and issue a correctional notice (which can incur a cost depending on the advertising medium), they had less incentive to comply with CRP determinations. Multiple examples were provided in submissions and by an interviewee of sponsors ignoring the CRP determination and continuing to advertise false and misleading claims. Such examples included Reckitt Benckiser and the advertising of pain-specific Nurofen products that claimed to provide 'targeted' relief from specific types of pain; Reckitt Benckiser ignored the initial determinations of the CRP (2011, 2013), as well as requests from the TGA (2012e, 2014e) to comply with these determinations. When determinations fail to compel compliance, the CRP can refer these cases to the TGA or Secretary of the Department of Health, both of whom are able to issue a warning letter or Regulation 9 Order, but few graduated responses exist when the TGA or Secretary requests fail. Such referrals contributed further to the delays in the remediation of complaints, decreasing their deterrent effect. For example, one submission referenced four cases where a complaint was referred to the TGA by the CRP and the TGA took more than 15 months to issue the sponsor with an Order (Industry association 328:4–5).

The issue of a determination by the CRP in and of itself was thus unlikely to have a material and reputational effect on sponsors. Sponsors could continue to sell a product while it was subject to a CRP investigation. The CRP also allowed sponsors to sell all remaining product after a determination had been issued in relation to false and misleading claims. These problems were conveyed by Interviewee 9 (15) in relation to a successful complaint they had made against a falsely advertised product:

*Interviewee:* eventually the TGA delisted it. I was still upset that it was continued to be sold, often of course with the TGA they are likely to be sold off—

*Researcher:* —Until the stock runs out?

*Interviewee:* —Until the stock's run out without any sort of warning label or whether that this product has been delisted for lack of efficacy. . . . [W]hat's the point of delisting if it's still in the pharmacies without any warning label?

When sponsors were directed to publish a correctional notice, these notices were often published in a medium different from that in which the initial advertisement was placed, such as on the sponsor's website, because the advertisement was no longer in circulation (in part, due to delays in the hearing of complaints). However, retractions are unlikely to have a reputational impact for reasons other than that they appear in a different medium from the original. In particular, false and misleading information is difficult to retract and correct. Instead of evaluating information as it is received, people often rely on cognitive biases and filters, and this affects their decision-making. For instance, a person is more likely to accept information that aligns with existing information they believe to be true, appears coherent, and originates from sources they believe to be credible (Lewandowsky et al. 2012). Even when misinformation is corrected and a person acknowledges its correction, research shows that 'retractions rarely, if ever, have the intended effect of eliminating . . . misinformation' (Lewandowsky et al. 2012:114). Corrections that are incoherent or create gaps in coherence can lead people to continue relying on retracted information simply because it aligns with what they know or seems more comprehensive. Moreover, when corrections are complex or numerous, a person may reject them in favour of a simpler explanation, as this requires less cognitive effort. Paradoxically, the repetition of misinformation can increase its acceptance (through its familiarity) (see Lewandowsky et al. 2012). A request to retract and correct an advertisement is therefore 'a reflective measure' that 'occurs after an offending advertisement has been exposed to the public and [has] most likely made some impact on consumers' (Professional association 147:1).

Delays in the hearing and remediation of complaints by the CRP also limited their deterrent effect. In fact, some of the submissions and interviewees believed that these delays were exploited by sponsors to increase the immediacy of benefits (i.e. profits from the false or misleading claim) and decrease the immediacy of penalties (i.e. the CRP's determination or TGA's warning or Order). Interviewee 9 (9) believed this to be the case with Reckitt Benckiser's advertising of pain-specific Nurofen, arguing that Reckitt Benckiser relied on 'continued appeals' and 'delays in the system to just keep on promoting'. In the case of Sensaslim, the sponsor went so far as to take the complainant to court as legislation prohibits the CRP from investigating a complaint when the product is subject to court action (Dowden 2012:38).[13]

For DTCA and promotion non-compliance, industry associations could apply financial penalties of between AU$10,000 and AU$300,000 for code violations. However, the submissions and interviewees believed these fines have little financial impact on sponsors relative to the profit the advertisement and promotional material generated:

> if the fines are not high enough they'll continue to do things. That's still much less than all the profits [they receive] . . . they will do whatever they can to maximise their profits.
>
> (Interviewee 5:11)

> They just write this shit off. They don't care . . . sanctions have to matter and it doesn't feel to me as though they have sufficient effect.
>
> (Interviewee 3:11)

> $50,000 is not going to actually stop the activity. That's a big part of the problem.
>
> (Interviewee 4:2)

> the maximum fines imposed by MA for Code breaches ($300,000) are relatively modest and unlikely to be a significant deterrent.
>
> (Academic 134:2)

For example, in 2009, a misleading advertisement by Bayer implying that age-related testosterone loss in men was a medical condition requiring treatment with testosterone therapy[14] attracted an AU$10,000 fine from MA—less than half the cost of placing the initial advertisement (Mackee 2012:para. 14). Fines in Australia appeared to be lower than those issued in some overseas jurisdictions. For example, in 2009, an academic (134:2) claimed the US Justice Department fined Pfizer the equivalent of AU$2.7 billion for off-label prescribing. The same type of offence attracts a fine of AU$300,000 under the MA Code (and just AU$10,200 per offence under s. 22(5) of the Therapeutic

Goods Act). Although the MA did not receive any complaints against Pfizer concerning off-label prescribing at this time, Pfizer had received a total of 16 convictions under the MA Code for unethical promotional activities between 2005 and 2009, the fines for which averaged AU$55,000 (Academic 134:2). Other companies that had advertised products for off-label uses in 2009 received fines of no more than AU$100,000 (MA 2009:30–31).

In cases where penalties could be applied by the TGA, their selective use gave rise to perceptions of targeting among those it regulated. Interviewee 8 provided two such examples. In the first, a sponsor was selling several unlisted goods. According to Interviewee 8 (8), the sponsor was aware of the legal requirements for listing, having previously listed goods on the ARTG, but had acted on incorrect advice provided to them by a regulatory consultant. The TGA responded by quarantining and seizing the non-compliant goods, filing a case in court and prosecuting them. The sponsor, who was aware of other sponsors selling identical goods that were not listed, wrote to the TGA about these other sponsors but received no response. Interviewee 8 alleged that the sponsor wrote multiple letters to the Head of the TGA and the Minister of Health providing them with the details of these sponsors' non-compliance; but these, too, went unanswered and the goods continued to be sold. As a result, Interviewee 8 (8) believed that the TGA simply 'knocked off the biggest player in the field because they were the largest distributor . . . [and] made an example of them'. The second example concerned Pan Pharmaceuticals (see Section 2.3.1). Interviewee 8 (5–6) alleged that the TGA conducted two separate audits prior to suspending Pan's licence and initiating a recall: the February and April Audit. The TGA claimed (in court) that the February and April Audits had not been two separate audits, but part of the same audit conducted in two distinct parts.[15] Interviewee 8 argued that if the TGA had determined in February that Pan had been operating on a basis of five critical deficiencies, it should have acted on these deficiencies immediately because of the potential harms they posed to the public (Interviewee 8:6). Further, Interviewee 8 (5–6) alleged that the TGA chose not to act on these deficiencies (or alert Pan to them), and instead conducted another audit (the April Audit) with the intent of building a stronger case against Pan. This mentality was evident, according to the Interviewee (8:5), by the fact that one of the nine critical deficiencies identified in the April Audit Report, which had been one of the original five critical deficiencies identified in the February Audit, was allegedly rectified by Pan between the February and April Audits, and prior to Pan being provided with the April Audit Report. In another submission, a regulatory consultant (98:6) raised concern about the potential for reprisal if a sponsor were to challenge a decision of the TGA:

> industry has generally been fearful of offending the TGA in case this prejudices their relationship with the regulator and adversely impacts on new products coming down the research and development stream. This fear is genuine as it is based on specific experiences. . . . [I]n many cases,

particularly where procedural fairness has been lacking, companies will seriously weigh up whether it is best to challenge the adverse decision or risk the TGA behaving negatively towards future applications.

The lack of techniques for penalising non-compliance limits the deterrent capacity of the regime, as the TGA, the CRP and industry associations must generally resort to less punitive, cooperative techniques (see Section 4.5). The lack of punitive techniques is in part a result of rationalising risk primarily in terms of product risk. Risk-based regulatory techniques prioritise punitiveness based on the level of perceived risk. The categorisation of listed medicines as low risk, in conjunction with the deprioritising of regulation in those areas of the regime that have less to do with product risk (such as DTCA and promotion), has led to the predominance of regulatory techniques commensurate (in their severity) with this categorisation of risk. However, these techniques are also due in part to a responsive rationality that aims to compel sponsors to cooperate voluntarily and thereby to avoid punitiveness. Together, these risk and responsive rationalities support the development of techniques that limits intervention (and is congruent with neoliberal rationality).

A sponsor cancelling and relisting a formerly non-compliant medicine voluntarily may represent a form of responsibilisation, but it may also reflect the exploitation of the TGA's cooperativeness (and the sponsor's economic rationality). The lack of intervention by the TGA in post-market regulation reinforces the rationality that sponsors are responsibilised. When a sponsor cancels a medicine before the TGA can complete a compliance review, the TGA's non-detection of non-compliance is not only a regulatory failure, but it also reinforces the sponsor's appearance as cooperative and the mentality that it is responsibilised, as non-compliance was not detected. Where reviews are completed, sponsors who voluntarily cancel or correct non-compliance appear cooperative, again reinforcing the idea that they are responsibilised. However, the reality is that this responsibilisation is manufactured; these cancellations and corrections are only made after the TGA notifies the sponsor that it is initiating a compliance review or issues the sponsor with a cancellation notice following completion of a review. In this way, responsibilisation creates a reality that it suggests exists already (and rationalises its ongoing exercise). The mentality that TGA intervention should be limited is reinforced in each case (Bandiera 2021:186).

Perceptions of targeting by the TGA among sponsors stem from a governmentality that combines risk-based and responsive regulation. In the case of the TGA, product risks are prioritised (more so than compliance risks). Because of the prioritisation of this type of risk, it is not always feasible for the TGA to use graduated techniques, especially if there is a risk harm to the public. In this way, risk rationality is incongruent with responsive rationality because the latter appeals to the better nature of the regulatee and therefore emphasises cooperativeness (irrespective of the level of risk). The use of punitiveness in the first instance may potentially undermine the cooperation of the regulated and lead them to evade regulation. This in turn may lead to punitiveness being perceived as a barrier to cooperation, and therefore to the regulator increasingly refraining from using punitive techniques.

## 4.5 Limited escalation

The lack of civil or criminal penalties for some types of non-compliance limited the ability of the TGA to escalate the severity of its response. For example, when sponsors failed to comply with administrative requests and Orders, the TGA (and Secretary) was unable to apply civil or criminal penalties simply because they did not exist under the Act. In the case of Nurofen, when repeated requests by the TGA failed to persuade Reckitt Benckiser to comply with the CRP's determinations, Australia's competition and consumer protection regulator, the ACCC, took the company to the Federal Court of Australia. Reckitt Benckiser was subsequently fined AU$6 million under s. 33 of the *Australian Consumer Law* (Schedule 2 to the Competition and Consumer Act) for having made a misleading representation (*Australian Competition and Consumer Commission v Reckitt Benckiser (Australia) Pty Ltd (No 7)* (2016) FCA 424; *Australian Competition and Consumer Commission v Reckitt Benckiser (Australia) Pty Ltd* (2016) FCAFC 181). But given the 'breadth' of its role and that it 'must prioritise . . . regulatory interventions' (ACCC 2017:3), the ACCC is not always able to intervene (and its intervention in the case of Reckitt Benckiser was a rare example). Moreover, it is 'not a substitute for a specialist regulator such as the TGA . . . [because] medicines and medical devices, whether low or high risk, require expertise and ongoing risk assessments that the ACCC is not able to provide' (ACCC 2017:4).

Even when civil and criminal penalties were available to the TGA, they were rarely used. The submissions and interviewees noted that this was particularly the case in relation to advertisements that did not comply with the Therapeutic Goods Advertising Code (and therefore violated s. 42DM of the Therapeutic Goods Act). This lack of action on the part of the TGA was attributed in part to cost—specifically, the cost of compiling a case and taking it to court relative to the size of the fine that might be subsequently applied (a problem noted by the ANAO—see Section 3.4.5.2). However, it was also attributed to the difficulties of establishing liability. For example, an academic (246:2) observed that proving the intent of an advertisement for the purposes of establishing criminal liability would be difficult when an advertisement can be construed as a form of education for the public/consumer.

TGA decisions have been appealed and overturned, as evidenced in a small number of judgements (see *Aspen Pharmacare Australia Pty Ltd and Minister for Health and Ageing* (2012) AATA 362, 376; *Aspen Pharmacare Australia Pty Ltd and Minister for Health and Ageing* (2013) AATA 197, 649;

*Ego Pharmaceuticals Pty Ltd and Minister for Health and Ageing* (2012) AATA 210; *Health World Limited and Minister for Health and Ageing* (2013) AATA 388). Because TGA enforcement is not standardised (a limitation of responsive techniques) and is sometimes motivated by the risk posed by the medicine rather than the cooperativeness of the regulatee (a limitation resulting from a governmentality that combines risk-based and responsive regulation), sponsors did not always perceive TGA decisions as judicious. This can lead to sponsors retaliating by appealing the TGA's decisions. When the TGA cancelled Di-Gesic and Doloxene, two painkillers containing dextropropoxyphene (an opioid), from the ARTG in 2011, Aspen Pharmacare successfully appealed the decision with the AAT, allowing it to continue to sell these products with updated safety warnings and PI and CMI documents, and by writing letters to prescribers. The TGA cancelled the medicines, which had been 'grandfathered' onto the ARTG, due to their safety risk; they were found to 'affect the electrical activity of the heart, increasing the risk of serious arrhythmias (disturbances in the normal rhythm of the heart-beat)', which 'can cause sudden death' (TGA 2011b, 2014b). These medicines were thought to be 'fatal' in 'a small overdose' (TGA 2014b), and they therefore presented a suicide risk. The medicines also provided 'only limited pain relief' compared to existing medicines on the ARTG (TGA 2011b). Medicines containing dextropropoxyphene had been cancelled by regulators in Canada, the EU, India, New Zealand, Singapore, South Africa, the US and the UK, making the TGA one of 'the last of the world's leading drug regulatory agencies to do so' (Buckley and Faunce 2013:259). Aspen appealed the initial decision on the basis that there were some patients for whom there was no alternative to dextropropoxyphene for mild to moderate pain. Interviewee 10 (12–13) argued that such decisions were susceptible to being overturned because legal courts do not evaluate quality, safety and efficacy to the same extent as the TGA:

> [a registered medicine] goes through several months of scrutiny by a number of experts. . . . if the company doesn't like the decision, it can go to the AAT with one judge and two experts. . . . You've got two people [experts], who by definition cannot be qualified in all . . . the areas the TGA have looked at [quality, safety and efficacy] . . . you can't have two people who are qualified in all of those.

Buckley and Faunce (2013:258) have noted that there is no case law that defines 'safety' or 'efficacy',[16] and nor was Aspen Pharmacare required to provide clinical trial data in this case.

The lack of punitive regulatory techniques limits the TGA to employing cooperative techniques only, decreasing the overall deterrent capacity of the regime. According to the theory of responsive regulation, punitiveness is necessary to elicit the cooperation of the regulated; the greater the extent to which the regulator can escalate techniques, the more likely it will compel the regulated to comply (without necessarily having to use said techniques). The inability of the TGA to escalate beyond lower-level cooperative techniques therefore decreases its capacity to deter sponsors from not complying. The irregularity (and rarity) of ACCC intervention further diminishes the response to non-compliance (and therefore, escalation).

In addition, the successful appeal of decisions limits their deterrent effect. In the case of Health World Limited's product Urinary Tract Support, for instance, the AAT overturned the decision of the CRP to require Health World Limited to publish a retraction on the grounds that the advertisement and labelling containing the misleading claims were no longer in circulation—they had been replaced by a new advertisement and labelling containing a different statement (*Health World Limited and Minister for Health and Ageing* (2013) AATA 388:para. 84). The appeal of its decisions may result in the TGA refraining from punitiveness, not only because sponsors perceive punitiveness as unjust (which affects their cooperation) but also because the TGA perceives that its decisions will not have backing (by the state, judiciary or public). Evidence of this refrain was present in the comments of a former member of TGA staff:

> [we] often used to talk about the *Canberra Times* test: 'if we do this and it goes wrong, what's it going to look like in *The Canberra Times*?' . . . 'if we make this decision and it goes to appeal, how are the courts going to look at it?' You're trying to sort of pre-empt the courts without really making your own decisions.
>
> (Interviewee 10:12)

This 'compliance trap' (Parker 2006) may limit the TGA to using lower-level cooperative techniques.

## 4.6 Operationally constrained

The submissions and interviewees believed the TGA to be under-resourced and therefore limited in its capacity to act on non-compliance. The lack of resourcing was attributed, in part, to the Australian Government's policy of prioritising full cost recovery, which restricted the TGA to undertaking only those types of activities for which the costs were directly recoverable. This includes activities directed at the public. For example, Interviewee 11 (10) argued that:

> it constrains the TGA from doing some of the public health activities that it should be doing . . . that can't come from direct cost recovery. By being directly cost recovered, you . . . [are] paying for the services . . . and there are some public health messages around education, awareness . . . information and safety that are part of the regulator's remit . . . [that] can't be cost recovered.

But the TGA's lack of resourcing was also attributed to staffing. By way of an example, some submissions and interviewees contrasted the ratio of staff to workload at the TGA with that of the US FDA:

> the FDA have significantly more resources to run a therapeutic goods list comparable to Australia's ARTG with 17,000 staff to TGA's 500.
>
> (Consumer association 43:5)

> [the] FDA has an enormous budget, an enormous number of personnel and in some ways, they [the FDA and TGA] are functionally doing the same work.
>
> (Interviewee 3:18)

The level of staffing at the TGA was thought not only to be a result of cost recovery requirements but also of difficulties associated with staff recruitment (a historical problem, see Section 2.3). The lack of resourcing was used to rationalise the TGA only using regulatory techniques that are most cost-efficient to administer. Indeed, this economic rationality has been pivotal in hindering the reform of the regime (as discussed in detail in Chapter 6) and is the direct result of the 'commercialisation' of health and medicine regulation in the 1990s (see Section 2.3).

Beyond these resourcing limitations, the TGA is otherwise limited in its capacity to act on non-compliance due to its location within the structure of the Australian Government. The TGA is not an independent statutory authority but a divisional unit within the Department of Health. As such, it is subject to the funding arrangements imposed on it by the government (which are based on the need for cost recovery), as well as to other decision-making priorities (through the Department). Although the TGA carries out pre- and post-market regulation relatively independently of the Department of Health, an interviewee indicated that the Minister for Health can intervene in its decisions and advisory committees. In this regard, the example below concerns the registration of a medicine on the ARTG:

> just in the last meeting, we were asked to comment on it [the drug] again and I thought why are we commenting on this again? Because . . . there wasn't much more to comment, but there were slight[ly] differently worded questions. . . . [It] actually originated in the Health Minister's office. She actually specifically contacted the TGA and said, 'What's this? What's the deal with this?' And so that came up for discussion.
>
> (Interviewee 7:13)

To understand the differences in power between the apparatuses of the state, the work of Poulantzas is particularly helpful—indeed, it was foundational to Jessop's strategic-relational approach to the state. According to Poulantzas (1973:48), state power is assured through its ideological apparatuses (including politicians, political parties, and so on) and the exercise of this power over other apparatuses within the state. In this way, ideological apparatuses elaborate and inculcate the dominant ideas within the state. As a state apparatus, the TGA and its power are shaped by the ideas of the state project because of its location in the state structure, and therefore its relation to the state ideological apparatuses and ideology. Although its lack of autonomy may limit the TGA's susceptibility to direct influence from the industry, this does not necessarily limit its indirect influence (exerted through the government—see more discussion on this point in Section 5.5). It is the power relations across the state apparatuses that ensure the realisation of neoliberal ideas (e.g. expediting the TGA's approval of a medicine).

## 4.7 Disempowering the TGA and regulatory regime

Risk has been integral to rationalising limited intervention by the TGA in Australia's medicine regulatory regime. Product risk has been used to rationalise the deprioritisation of risks that do not directly pertain to the medicine. In so doing, it prioritises techniques that target products (rather than sponsors), high (rather than low) risk products, techniques specific to regulating product (over compliance) risks (in particular, laboratory testing compared to compliance reviews) and pre-market (over post-market) techniques. The prioritisation of product risk rationalised limiting regulatory techniques to those that were commensurate in severity with this type of risk classification. Techniques that did not align with this classification on product risk (e.g. those that might address the high compliance risk of the sponsors of listed medicines) were (re)aligned to the classification assigned. As a result of product risk rationality, the regime lacked centralisation or hierarchy in relation to regulatory techniques for low product risks and non-product risks, which in turn reduced the applicability and deterrent effect of these techniques for sponsors. This decentralisation and lack of hierarchy also diffused responsibility for regulatory failure (because the number of actors responsibilised for governing was increased). This approach to regulation diminished the overall deterrent capacity of the regime, and therefore its capacity to compel compliance.

The regime was self-reinforcing in that it rationalised sponsors as responsibilised, cooperative and capable of self-regulating. The use of self-regulatory techniques was justified by the lack of TGA post-market regulatory techniques to identify and act on non-compliance. Self-regulatory techniques were in turn justified by sponsors seemingly identifying and acting on their own non-compliance voluntarily. In this way, the responsibilisation–cooperation nexus was discursive in limiting the intervention of the regulator.

Combined, risk-based and responsive governmentalities justified limiting the regulator's intervention in ways that were both compatible and incompatible with one another. Both rationalised limiting the use of punitive techniques and in this way were compatible. However, they were incompatible—and therefore further limited intervention—because the associated techniques were required to be both risk-based (i.e. proportionate in their severity to the risk) and cooperative (i.e. provide sponsors with the opportunity to cooperate first before escalating to more severe techniques). This had the potential to trap the regulator—where the regulator refrains from using higher-level punitive techniques because they might increase non-cooperation and non-compliance, but the lack of such techniques might also encourage non-cooperation and non-compliance. Together, the use of these techniques effectively rationalised limiting intervention by the regulator, aligning the regime closely with a neoliberal governmentality.

This neoliberal governmentality forms part of a larger hegemonic project. Because of the TGA's position within the overall structure of the state, neoliberal ideas have come to be exercised through the organisation via the ideological apparatuses of the state. This macro-level neoliberal hegemonic project was maintained at a micro level through governmentality which essentially functioned as a 'regime of truth' (Foucault 1977). By creating a reality that it says already exists, neoliberal governmentality is discursive and rationalises the exercise of particular techniques. It therefore creates and shapes the regime and its subjects in ways that effectively align with the hegemony of industry and the state. In turn, this reinforces the unequal power relations within the regime, not only maintaining the power of industry and the state, but also empowering them.

This failure of regulation in Australia's medicine regulatory regime in fact further rationalises neoliberal governmentality. In Chapter 6, this (re)turn to neoliberal governmentality is explored in the form of 'more effective and transparent' regulation, or more specifically the idea of 'better' and 'bettering' (rather than alternatives to) existing regulation; while in Chapter 5, it is argued that public empowerment facilitates a similar (re)turn. For Joseph (2018:154), 'empowering' and the shifting of responsibility for regulation onto the public, 'where . . . [they] are encouraged to behave in such a way as to better cope with this uncertainty', only increases the emphasis on micro-level techniques of governance.

## Notes

1 For example, each new ingredient proposed for use in listed medicines (i.e. not on the pre-approved list of ingredients) must first undergo pre-approval, which requires the submission of quality, safety and efficacy data (see TGA 2016a:54).
2 In its more recent guidance to sponsors of clinical trials, the TGA stipulates that it can 'request' (in writing) that certain information or documents be provided; the failure to comply with such a request attracts penalties (TGA 2021b:30).
3 For example, in the US, fewer than 34% (926 out of 2,701) of post-market studies were honoured by sponsors (Garattini and Bertele' 2007:804). In Europe, between 2004 and 2014, only 60% of post-market studies for cancer drugs were

completed within five years. These studies were less likely to have randomised designs, have an active (non-placebo) comparator or measure survival as an end point (Cherla et al. 2022).

4 This study also found that the more severe an ADR, the less likely it was to be reported to authorities (Ma et al. 2015:1566).

5 According to the Institute for Safe Medication Practices (2015:2), less than 50% of the ADR reports submitted by companies to the FDA in the US between 2013 and 2014 contained complete information. In contrast, the proportion of complete reports made by the public and health professionals was 85% (Institute for Safe Medication Practices 2015:2). While these data are in no way indicative of the level of compliance by sponsors with ADR reporting requirements in Australia, the lack of compliance monitoring and data collection impacts the TGA's ability to prioritise its resource allocation towards high risks (e.g. to determine the frequency with which it should audit manufacturing sites to identify non-compliance with quality and safety requirements).

6 Non-placebo (or active-controlled) trials are usually mandated in those circumstances where an existing treatment is available and has been shown to improve survival or reduce morbidity as the failure to provide treatment (by offering a placebo) would be unethical and likely to result in detrimental health outcomes for participants (Davis and Abraham 2013:25). Even then, most treatments need only establish non-inferiority—a level of efficacy equivalent to a pre-specified, statistical fraction of the comparative treatment (Davis and Abraham 2013:28).

7 Vioxx was approved on the basis of mostly non-placebo-controlled clinical trials where the active comparator was ibuprofen, diclofenac or nabumetone (non-selective NSAIDs) (see FDA 1999:6; Krumholz et al. 2007). Although some placebo-controlled clinical trials were conducted by Merck, 'these studies were limited in duration because it was not possible to keep patients with chronic painful arthritis on a placebo for very long' (*Peterson v Merck Sharpe & Dohme (Aust) Pty Ltd* (2010) FCR 180:para. 64). According to Vitry et al. (2007:736), there were a lack of studies comparing Vioxx to other common treatments (for example, paracetamol) or 'with a combination of a less selective NSAID and a cytoprotective agent for patients at high risk of gastrointestinal adverse effects'.

8 Sibutramine (Reductil), a prescription drug for weight loss, was withdrawn voluntarily by Abbott Australasia over concerns of increased cardiovascular risk (TGA 2010b).

9 Sitaxentan (Thelin), a prescription medicine for pulmonary hypertension, was withdrawn voluntarily by Pfizer because of the increased risk of acute liver failure (TGA 2010c).

10 It is usually recommended that patients be placed on an ascending dosing schedule to minimise the risk of ADRs (Professional association 24:3). At the time, the PI and CMI for allopurinol provided information that implied that the dosing schedule was discretionary and should be administered in accordance with the severity of the condition (i.e. 100–200 mg per day for mild conditions, 300–600 mg per day for moderate to severe conditions and 700–900 mg per day for severe conditions). An example was provided by this submission of a patient who had selected their own dose and suffered an ADR (Professional association 24:3).

11 Let alone adhere to an industry code of conduct as a condition of registration or listing on the ARTG (as occurs for registered medicines, see Section 3.3.1).

12 A copy of which is available at Pfizer (2010).

13 Threats of defamation, although rare, can also potentially force a complainant to withdraw their complaint.

14 This is despite the fact that age-related testosterone loss is a consequence of ageing and there is little evidence to support the use of testosterone therapies in reversing age-related effects (Academic 218:3). A copy is available at academic (218:5).
15 Interviewee 8 (6) disagreed with this assertion, claiming to have seen a draft audit report for the February Audit that was produced by one of the inspectors but was never provided to Pan.
16 The Macquarie and Oxford dictionaries were used for reference in the interim judgement.

# 5 Public disempowerment

The literature claims that failures of regulation can be overcome simply through empowering the public. Ayres and Braithwaite (1992:54, 57) argue this on the basis that tripartism or 'empowering public interest groups' provides them with the opportunities and information ('all . . . that is available to the regulator') to participate directly in regulation. This participation is said to increase the capacity of public interest groups to hold the regulated and regulator to account (and decrease the potential for capture) (Ayres and Braithwaite 1992). In Australia's medicine regulatory regime, the public and health professionals and their professional associations can participate in standard-setting and decision-making through their positions on advisory boards or committees, and by making submissions to consultations. They can participate in ADR reporting and reporting complaints. The public can also participate in decisions about their health and health care by becoming informed about the medicines they use (health literacy), as well as the ways in which they are regulated (regulatory literacy). However, as Cruikshank (1999:69) warns, 'the object of empowerment is to act upon another's interests . . . in order to conduct their actions towards an end', and so empowerment itself is a form of power relation, 'one deserving of careful scrutiny'. Indeed, the inherent individualism of public empowerment, which '(re)produces citizens . . . capable of governing themselves' and 'acting in their own interests', aligns with neoliberal governmentality and may impede the possibility for more transformative change.

This chapter explores the second of the two overarching themes developed in the thematic analysis: the limited capacity of the public and those representing the public's interests to participate in regulation (which I refer to as *public disempowerment*). These limits on public participation occur by way of the limited transparency (*limited transparency of information* and *the regulator*) and accountability (*limited accountability*), the limited role of the public in regulation (*limited regulatory role of the public*), and the regime's furthering of state–corporate relations (*enhanced state–corporate relations*). These three sub-themes are explored separately in this chapter. What follows is a demonstration of not only how the public and those representing

DOI: 10.4324/9781003285762-5

their interests are rendered largely uninformed, but also how the public's capacity to participate in the regime through a variety of technologies of (dis)empowerment is severely limited due to asymmetries of knowledge/power. These knowledge/power asymmetries render the regime less representative of the public interest and ultimately restrict the capacity of the public, and its representatives, to act and manoeuvre to change these power relations. A major implication of the public's limited knowledge and power is that it may further rationalise a (re)turn to neoliberal governmentality—that knowledge and power need only rebalancing, and therefore increases in micro-level self-regulatory techniques.

## 5.1 Limited transparency of information

Difficulties were reported in the interviews and submissions in relation to accessing certain types of information from the TGA website. This included access to public summary documents, PI and CMI, AusPARs and information on reporting ADRs and complaints. In one submission, the TGA website was described as:

> not particularly user friendly and intuitive to find your way around [as] there is often a need to 'try and see' before finally, often quite by coincidence, finding what you are looking for. This is frustrating as a Health Professional who might actually understand and recognise what I am looking for but would be more so for the general public who are less likely to understand the information that comes up.
>
> (Governmental organisation 79:3)

The search function of the ARTG database was criticised by some for its limited functionality:

> Searching for either an Approved Product Information or Consumer Medicine Information is challenging. For example, when entering 'Aspirin', all products that contain aspirin in combination with other drugs were presented but nothing that related to plain and simple aspirin.
>
> (Governmental organisation 79:3)

> You need specific names/brands rather than just a type of thing (for example you can't search 'baby pillow', you need the actual brand) which makes searching inefficient.
>
> (Journalist 110:8)

Some of the information searched for was not always provided on the TGA website or was out of date. PI and CMI documents, for instance, were not available for each listed[1] and registered medicine in the ARTG site; and when such documents were available, they were described as out of date because they reflected the safety and efficacy profile of the medicine at the time that it was listed/registered or last updated.[2] Between 1 January 2010 and 31 January 2013, only 28% (3,600 out of 12,654) of the PI documents on the ARTG site were approved or re-approved by the TGA, meaning that 'two-thirds of documents . . . [were] not current within the last three years' (Information provider 391:16). An industry association (392:6) insisted that the low rate of re-/approval 'reflects the fact that no new information has been generated on the medicine which would require the PI to be updated'. However, several submissions cited the lack of post-market monitoring by the TGA (i.e. of sponsors' compliance with the requirement that PI or CMI be correct and up to date) alongside the financial cost to sponsors of updating PI or CMI as the reasons why sponsors are disinclined to maintain their currency. The TGA uses an exclusion of liability disclaimer to shift the responsibility for inaccurate or outdated information in a PI or CMI document obtained through the ARTG; and a person must agree to these terms prior to accessing the PI or CMI. This disclaimer reads:

> You acknowledge and agree that You are responsible for making Your own enquiries to determine whether any PI Document or CMI Document is accurate, up to date and fit for Your purposes. . . . You acknowledge and agree that We do not accept any legal liability or responsibility (including for negligence) for any injury, loss or damage incurred by Your use of, disclosure of, or reliance on, the information contained in any PI Document or CMI Document made available to You via Our website (including for any inaccuracy in, or reliance on, the information in a PI Document or CMI Document or use of a PI Document or CMI Document to achieve a medical outcome or therapeutic good supply arrangement) regardless of any involvement by Us including in the creation or approval of any PI Document or CMI Document.

A disclaimer is also provided for AusPARs supplied through the ARTG, which reads: 'The onus is on the reader to verify the current accuracy of the information on the document subsequent to the date shown'.

The findings also revealed that the TGA's communication of safety warnings, alerts, advisories and other monitoring communications is often delayed or lacking entirely. One interviewee recounted an instance where a medicine was approved by the TGA without an explicit safety warning, despite prior knowledge that it had an irreversible ADR:

> My concern was the reason why the drug was approved for use in Australia without the test . . . being available, and also that the safety issues were not more explicitly stated in the product information . . .

> Because there is no antidote for the drug. So, if you develop a bleeding side-effect from it, . . . [there is] no antidote to correct the drug activity.
>
> (Interviewee 7:4)[3]

> [T]he general public don't know, they don't understand . . . The GP thinks there's no testing required.
>
> (Interviewee 7:6)

The TGA does not publish information regarding whether a medicine is subject to a RMP (Advisory committee 3:3).[4] The TGA also does not publish clinical trial and ADR data, despite this being common practice by regulators overseas (e.g. see the FDA's Adverse Event Reporting System or FAERS and ClinicalTrials.gov).

Submissions referred to instances when safety advisories were not issued by the TGA, despite them being issued (or the medicine even being cancelled) by regulators overseas. One such example is that of dronedarone, a prescription anti-arrhythmic medicine:

> American, United Kingdom and European regulatory authorities have raised concerns about an increase in hepatotoxicity[5] from dronedarone (FDA safety alert, 14/1/2011; MHRA safety warning, 21/1/2011; and EMEA notice of benefit/risk review, 21/1/2011 respectively) but there is no mention of any concern relating to dronedarone on the TGA website to date.
>
> (Advocacy group 112:2)

The PI and CMI for dronedarone were later updated to include a warning, but when they were updated is not possible to determine as PI and CMI are not backdated and previous versions are not made available.[6] Historically, the TGA has issued 'fewer advisories than other regulators, [and] often much later'; between 2010 and 2016, the TGA issued less than a quarter of the number of advisories issued by regulators in the UK, US and Canada and by an average of 10.1 months later (Bhasale 2021:x, 167).

The findings drawn from the submissions and interviews indicate that much of the information provided through the TGA website (including the ARTG) is thought to be too technical and therefore inaccessible to the public, even some health professionals. Some of these concerns are outlined as follows:

> there is already a multiplicity of public information available from the TGA website. However . . . the majority of this information is highly scientific in nature and consequently is not provided in a necessarily consumer friendly or simple to understand manner.
>
> (Industry association 81:1)

> AusPARS are written for a technical audience and are unlikely to be used by most consumers and health professionals.
>
> (Advisory committee 3:3)

> Consumers . . . considered current CMI leaflets to be technical and long. These barriers have been identified on many occasions previously.
>
> (Professional association 406:4)

The operation of the regulatory regime was also thought to be highly technical. Many submission authors and interviewees reported a lack of knowledge of spontaneous reporting mechanisms among the public, a concern that is supported by the literature. Robertson and Newby (2013:685) found that just 10.4% (520 out of 4,981) of the Australian public were aware of ADR reporting mechanisms and only 2.9% (145 out of 4,981) were able to correctly identify the TGA as the agency to which ADR reports had to be lodged. It was also claimed that most health professionals[7] have a low level of knowledge of reporting mechanisms, a finding reflected in the literature (Bensoussan et al. 2004; Kelly et al. 2004; Nita et al. 2005; Parella et al. 2013). One study revealed that when rates of ADR reporting were at their greatest among health professionals in Australia,[8] only 34% of doctors and 37% of nurses claimed to be aware of any form of ADR reporting procedure (Kelly et al. 2004:33). There is a lack of research on the extent of the public's or health professionals' knowledge of complaints reporting mechanisms for DTCA and promotion violations, but the submissions and interview transcripts in this study indicated that complaints are rarely lodged. For example, Interviewee 6 (1), who worked for an industry association, claimed that their association had only received one non-industry complaint in the ten years prior to the interview. The technicality of the regulatory regime was thought to prohibit members of the public from participating in consultations or on TGA committees. One submission raised this concern in relation to a consultation for which no submissions were received from the public:

> the audience for the guidance document is medicines manufacturers . . . While the technical aspects of the manufacturing process may not be of significant interest to consumers, the overarching framework should, at a minimum, be easily understandable. The information available on the TGA's website and the guidance and policy documents in this area are not written in a way that facilitates consumer understanding.
>
> (Consumer association 434:5)

> [Our organisation] sees this process as an important, but ill-defined area of Australia's medicines regulatory regime and an area that consumers, traditionally, have had limited scope to provide input to.
>
> (Consumer association 434:2)

> As the end users, and those who will directly experience any adverse effects from poor manufacturing practices, consumers should have access to easy to understand information as well as to be able to comment on how policies affect them.
>
> (Consumer association 434:8)

Regarding representatives of the public on TGA committees, Interviewee 9 (10) stated:

> it's difficult I think for a non-expert consumer . . . unless you know the literature and unless you can counter the bullshit, it can be hard to make an impact . . . [My colleague] she's good but she'll admit that . . . I've got technical knowledge and knowledge of the history that she just hasn't got.

Commercial confidentiality has limited the access to certain types of information. The TGA classes all information not in the public domain that has the potential to undermine the economic and competitive interest of the owner as commercial-in-confidence (TGA 2014h:7). This means that certain information concerning the product,[9] manufacturer or supplier and the sponsor's financial and commercial dealings cannot be disclosed publicly unless it is necessary to warn the public about the product's safety, quality or efficacy (permitted under s. 61 and 61A of the Therapeutic Goods Act) or forms part of a freedom of information request (under s. 11 and 11A of the *Freedom of Information Act 1982* (Cth)). Regarding the latter, commercial confidentiality can still take priority under certain circumstances.[10] While the TGA is permitted to disclose these documents if it so choses, the agency cannot do so unless the sponsor (as the owner of this information) agrees to its release, or until the sponsor has the opportunity to appeal the decision (internally with the TGA and/or externally with the Australian Information Commissioner or AAT) to release the documents, and the documents are not found to be exempt or conditionally exempt (TGA 2014h:20). This scenario arose in the case of Strattera, a prescription drug for attention-deficit/hyperactivity disorder (ADHD), as reported in a submission by an academic (116:6–7). The sponsor, Eli Lilly, was successfully able to argue against the release of documentation it originally supplied to the Pharmaceutical Benefits Advisory Committee on the grounds that the documents were exempt under s. 38(b)(i) of the Freedom of Information Act. A Minister of the Western Australian Parliament was seeking these documents to investigate allegations that Strattera was being over-prescribed and that its side effects were not being appropriately disclosed (Academic 116:6–7).

Ultimately, the information made available to the public about medicines is largely produced by industry. PI and CMI documents, for instance, which are written by the sponsor, are at times accused of containing non-clinical, promotional information. One submission cited two examples in the PI for arthritis medications (Remicade and Prolia) to demonstrate this point:

> The Remicade PI promotes its use 'for the *improvement in* physical function in patients with active disease'—this is not an indication, it is an outcome. The Prolia PI proclaims 'Prolia *significantly reduces the risk* of vertebral, nonvertebral and hip fractures' [but] this is flagrantly promotional language.
>
> (Information provider 391:15, emphasis added)

Public summary documents are also rarely reviewed by the TGA (despite them being written and updated by the sponsor). As a result, it is claimed that they contain information that lacks an evidence base.

Labelling, packaging and DTCA and promotional materials were widely regarded as inappropriate sources for evidence-based information (despite industry and professional associations describing them as a necessary source of information, indeed educational, for both the public and health professionals—see Chapter 6). A listed medicine, for instance, can possess a name that implies that it has a specific effect (such as weight loss accelerate). Listed medicines can employ vague terms on labels and packaging and in DTCA and promotional materials to imply that they have an effect (such as may relieve a certain symptom) or are superior to other medicines (e.g. that they are only available through a practitioner or 'practitioner only' medicines). Listed medicines can also make claims of efficacy based on a medicine's traditional use even if such claims are unsupported by evidence (from the literature or otherwise).

Although listed medicines contain an AUST L label, this label was widely considered in the submissions and by the interviewees as insufficient for communicating the extent to which they are regulated by the TGA. The following communication illustrates this point:

> One of our members brought along to the meeting with the Review Panel a therapeutic goods product that he had recently purchased from his local pharmacy. The packaging of this product looked indistinguishable in appearance from a prescription medicine, which was obviously a marketing ploy. None of us could find any information on the packet as to whether it was a TGA registered or listed product. Even one of the panel members couldn't find this information either, until she took it to another panel member or TGA officer who found the code for a listed product on one side of the packet in small print. The orientation was such as to require the box to be turned sideways to read the 'AUST L' marking.
>
> (Sceptic organisation 86:3)

Indeed, a study of complementary medicine use in Australia between 2008 and 2009 found that 88% (986 out of 1,121) of people who reported having taken these medicines in the previous 12 months did not notice whether the product contained an AUST L label (Braun et al. 2010:243). Of these people, 33% (325 out of 986) thought that the AUST L label indicated that the product was tested by a government agency for safety, 26% that it was tested for quality, and 24% that it was Australian made (Braun et al. 2010:243). Approximately 15% of people thought that the label indicated that the product was tested for effectiveness, while 13% did not know what the label represented (Braun et al. 2010:243).

Because the DTCA of registered medicines is prohibited in the Therapeutic Goods Act, the public depend to a large extent on the information provided by and decision-making of health professionals. However, the range of sources on which health professionals depend for information about medicines includes the pharmaceutical industry. The pharmaceutical industry produces a large amount of medical research and literature, and historically this has tended to portray the products the industry produces more positively than do independent research and literature—an issue that is well documented (Davis and Abraham 2013; Dukes et al. 2014; Faunce et al. 2010; Loder et al. 2013; Lundh et al. 2017; Matheson 2016; Ross et al. 2012). Industry also delivers continuing medical education to health professionals (Adair and Holmgren 2005; Katz et al. 2010; Morgan et al. 2006; Lieb and Scheurich 2014; Rutledge et al. 2003; Sah and Fugh-Berman 2013; Wazana 2000). Drug familiarisation programmes and clinical trials or audits conducted by the industry can be a form of marketing to health professionals, albeit less overt than other forms. Although health professionals receive training in evidence-based medicine and complete a minimum number of hours of professional development (as per their registration requirements), marketing still affects the prescribing practices of general physicians and practitioners. Industry has been found to exert an indirect influence over these practices by offering health practitioners financial or material incentives, such as gifts, free samples, payments for services and profits from sales (Alowi and Kani 2018; Fickweiler et al. 2017; Lieb and Scheurich 2014; Sah and Fugh-Berman 2013). Health professionals are also prone to cognitive biases and filters (see Lewandowsky et al. 2012).

Medicine information, including PI and CMI documents, is freely provided by third-party information providers, including websites such as Health Direct, the NPS's MedicineWise and MIMS, as well as trade medical press like *Australian Doctor* and *Medical Observer*. However, many of these providers rely on the information published on the TGA's website (and thus are limited by those issues previously mentioned). The submission authors and interviewees commonly believed that there is '[p]oor direct availability of information' from the TGA to third-party information providers; for example, there is 'no direct communication' by the TGA when a safety alert is issued and the safety alert is likely to result in more requests from the public for information from third-party information providers about the medicine and its safety (Information provider 87:3–4).

These limitations in information provision exacerbate the knowledge/power asymmetries between those who know 'the objects to be known' (Foucault 1977:27–28) (the regulator and industry) and those who do not (the public, and to an extent, health professionals). These asymmetries are due in part to technical knowledge/power—by which I mean both the technicalities of knowledge and the power that comes with knowing these technicalities. Insofar as these technicalities are intrinsic to medicine itself, so too are these asymmetries, although the latter are also determined by the fact that information is not accessible (or transparent). These asymmetries of knowledge/power produce what Rose and Miller (1992:188) refer to as enclosures, or 'bounded locales or types of judgement', whereby knowledge is not just created, but concentrated.

Far from being a technology to empower, health literacy is a technology to disempower, to limit the participation of the public in the regime and to shape this participation in line with neoliberal governmentality. The deprioritisation of certain types of risk, and reducing the responsibility of the state for regulating them, requires risks to be individualised and persons to be responsibilised (or 'empowered'). Through rationalising them not as social risks that are a result of the regime itself (regulatory failure) but as individual risks to health that the person ought to know (and which result from their decision not to know and act on them), the state is able to rationalise the reallocation of some of its responsibilities for regulating these risks. People come to be responsibilised for (and therefore, participate in) the self-regulation of risks posed to them through health literacy; through becoming aware of and knowing their health risks and the extent to which the state is responsible for them, and indeed by not taking on more responsibility, their health may be at risk. In this way, health literacy internalises risks and compels people to act on them. Because a person is responsible for their own literacy, illiteracy, or not knowing the risks to their health, becomes a failure on their part. However, there are limits to their knowledge/power. Their knowledge is bounded and they depend on those with knowledge/power—the regulator, industry and to an extent health professionals (although their knowledge is also bounded)—to provide them with information necessary to their literacy, or being informed. Yet this information, and its transparency, is neither neutral nor value free. The imbalance of and dependency on those with knowledge/power is thus a means to control, to disempower, 'to mete out unwanted behaviour', and thus produce 'a homogeneity whose behaviour and even affectations can be anticipated, controlled and capitalised [on]' (Adams 2020:3). In this way, health literacy only permits a particular type of participation by the public within and not counter to neoliberal governmentality. It controls how people are informed and compels them to act on the information they are provided with. A similar argument can also be applied to regulatory literacy—for both the public and health professionals.

## 5.2 Limited transparency of the regulator

In this research, the TGA was described variously as 'closed', 'secretive' and 'unwilling to engage' publicly (Journalist 110). These sentiments were captured best in submissions by journalists and media organisations with prior experience engaging with the TGA:

> All questions we want to put to the TGA have to be put in writing. Sometimes those responses can be very detailed. Yet at other times we can end up asking ourselves whether it was worthwhile even writing out the questions in the first place either because the answers come too late for deadlines or the answers don't fully address the questions asked.
>
> (Media organisation 17:1)

> Answers do not often address questions asked. We have to address all questions to the media unit at the DOH [Department of Health], rarely [do we] get to actually talk to the people involved, and instead get short, written responses that sometimes do not address all the questions asked.
>
> (Journalist 110:8)

> Many [of our] journalists complain that they do not have access to TGA officials with the relevant expertise for stories they are researching. All requests must be put in email to a PR consultant, who typically then provides a response in writing.
>
> (Journalist 110:4)

These accounts reflect my own experiences with the TGA. When I first approached individuals and organisations for the purposes of conducting interviews, I contacted the TGA's principal medical advisor and the head of each office within the TGA's monitoring and compliance group by email with information regarding my research project and a request for the TGA's assistance (by having either themselves or a member of staff within the office consent to participate in an interview). Within two hours of having sent the emails, I was contacted by phone by the TGA's Chief Operating Officer, who stated that I had to go through the 'appropriate channels' of obtaining consent—via the TGA's external relations team for the purposes of 'centralising' this process. I was prohibited from contacting TGA staff members directly and was assigned an escort, the Chief Operating Officer's Assistant, for this purpose (personal communication, 13 February 2013). My communication with the TGA, including the distribution of information regarding the project and consent forms to TGA staff, occurred first through this Assistant. I was permitted to conduct an interview with a group of TGA staff, but not individual interviews, which required me to submit an ethics modification request to the university's research ethics committee (the first of three such requests). All but one person who consented to participate held a managerial position in their respective office or unit. These participants were from offices or units within the TGA that were not part of my original target sample, and they were therefore what I considered to be 'safe' participants to which the information and consent forms could be distributed and who could provide me with 'safe' data. I was prohibited from making a recording despite initial assurances (from the Assistant in personal communication, 22 February 2013) that this was possible and had been done previously.[11] I negotiated to bring a scribe to the interviews to take notes, which meant that I had to submit a second ethics modification request. A third modification request was submitted because participants were then prohibited from giving written consent (and so verbal consent was obtained from each participant on the day of and prior to commencing the interview).

During the interview, participants answered questions before I had finished asking them, were selective in their answers (i.e. did not address questions in full) and asked to have several questions put on notice (which were answered in writing by the Assistant at a later date).[12] Many of the answers provided portrayed the TGA and its actions positively. One participant, a non-manager, who interjected in ways that brought into question what other participants had said, was frequently 'corrected'. Two days after the interview, this participant contacted me directly by phone requesting to have a particular statement removed from the transcript because they had been 'a bit grumpy' on the day of the interview (implying that their answers had not been objective). I was not in a position to determine whether there were external factors that may have influenced this call—a known problem in research involving a group of participants—but I agreed to remove the statement as a precaution, nonetheless.

The TGA's position within the structure of the Australian Government contributed to perceptions among my interviewees that the Department of Health exercises control through the TGA via its media and public communication:

> all media and public affairs inquiries go to the Department of Health spokesperson, they then get filtered to the TGA who may respond. It goes then back to the Department of Health media person who then determines whether the response will be made public or not . . . the TGA doesn't have control over its own messaging.
>
> (Interviewee 11:12)

> they sit under DoHA [Department of Health and Ageing]. They may give the appearances of being independent, but they are actually sitting under DoHA . . . the way they communicate with the world and how the TGA presents itself is filtered through DoHA.
>
> (Interviewee 3:17)

> they can't talk to anyone by themselves . . . they can't put out a press release without it going through [the Department].
>
> (Interviewee 3:18)

There was also a perceived lack of disclosure by the TGA with regard to its decision-making and activities, including the results of its post-market enforcement activities and its issue of warning letters, suspensions, cancellations[13] and civil and criminal penalties. Criticism was targeted particularly at the TGA's reporting of complaint outcomes. In addition to those issues identified in Chapter 4, several submissions noted that little to no information was provided by the TGA on the outcomes of complaints referred to it by the CRP and industry associations. In particular, the organisation fails to report the receipt, progress and outcome of complaints to complainants. A sceptic organisation (127) and Interviewee 9 made explicit reference to occasions when the contents and outcome of a complaint were withheld from the complainant on the basis that it was commercial-in-confidence.

The TGA's committees were likewise criticised because they are not compelled to publish their meeting minutes. When meeting minutes are published, it is usually in the form of public summaries, which one submission described as 'totally useless' for information purposes (Academic 417:2). Interviewee 7 (11), a member of one of the TGA's committees, indicated that these summaries are 'carefully worded' to remove details, such as the name of a medicine:

> they couldn't really say that we spoke about [this drug] and we said this, but . . . say that the committee considered an application on [this class of drug].
>
> (Interviewee 7:11)[14]

Here, the asymmetries of knowledge/power reduce participation by the public to the point where the potential for questioning TGA decisions or actions is diminished. Because certain types of information are not made available—such as whether the TGA made a decision, sponsors are complying with the TGA's decision, or the TGA is heeding or acting contrarily to the advice of its committees—the public are less able to hold either the regulator or industry to account. Ayres and Braithwaite (1992:146) argue that making information accessible is essential to tripartite accountability and to the 'explicit involvement' of the public (e.g. through public interest groups) in regulation. They acknowledge that while it is not possible for every person to participate actively in regulation, 'all that is . . . required is for *enough* people to absorb the information made available and take up the opportunities for participation to supply countervailing regulatory power' (Ayres and Braithwaite 1992:83, emphasis in original). Information on regulatory decision-making must be accessible; otherwise 'tripartism will not work' (Ayres and Braithwaite 1992:59).

However, transparency, which is the mentality that by making information more accessible the regulator and regulated will be more accountable, is discursive; while transparency implies that there is a capacity to see/know the regulator and regulated, this seeing/knowing is mediated by them (Adams

2020:24). Transparency is asymmetrical in that it requires the regulator to be transparent 'to those which it holds power over' (Adams 2018:16). Not only does the regulator have the power to control what is disclosed but also how it is disclosed—that is, the very processes by which certain types of information come to be made transparent, which are obscured by the rationality of transparency (that frames such processes as objective and without bias). Therefore, as Adams (2020) argues, transparency is a fallacy and not truly achievable in reality. Both transparency and the lack thereof thus maintain asymmetries of knowledge/power between the state, industry, and the public.

## 5.3 Limited accountability

The legislation provides no capacity for civil action against the TGA for harmful acts or omissions. S. 61A of the Therapeutic Goods Act provides the Commonwealth and protected persons with immunity from civil action for acts and omissions, unless such acts or omissions are committed in bad faith (i.e. with the *intent* to cause harm). For sponsors, 61A reduces the perceived fairness of the regime and therefore has the potential to impact upon regulator–regulatee cooperation. Interviewee 8 (10–11) cited an example of such impact:

> [the manufacturer] had to make the transition from [the old] PIC/S code . . . And that was very difficult for it [the manufacturer] to do and it was slowly making that transition. Anyway, cut a long story short, there was a series of audits . . . which finally led to the TGA imposing a licence condition on this manufacturer that they weren't allowed to sell product, release product for sale, unless certain criteria had been met . . . [The manufacturer had] worked with a well-known external GMP consultant who was helping them become GMP compliant to [the new] PIC/S, and they wrote to the TGA three times giving them an update on where their state of compliance was. . . . [A]fter a personal meeting with Skerritt [head of the TGA], tended by a regulatory consultant . . . they suddenly accepted, with no explanation, that the most recent explanation of GMP compliance by [the manufacturer] was acceptable. And therefore, the licence condition could go away. . . . [F]or about five or six weeks, [the manufacturer] couldn't release any product . . . I can take them to the AAT . . . I can get an order that they made the wrong decision, but if that wrong decision cost [the manufacturer] 10 million . . ., bad luck.

However, s. 61A reflects a risk-averse approach that also has implications for the public. S. 61A has been construed by the (TGA 2014h:14) as being in the 'public interest' by allowing the TGA to 'carry out their statutory functions . . . without fear of being subject to civil action in the courts', for example, in response to a 'breach of confidence' arising 'from the release of information alleged to have resulted in commercial damage'. However, because the legislation limits civil liability to acts and omissions committed by the TGA in bad faith, unless bad faith is proven, responsibility for the risk (and therefore the harm) of acts and omissions committed by the TGA is displaced onto the public (as well as sponsors), away from the state.

There are other ways in which the regulatory regime is structured to reduce the risk of opposition and critique. In some areas of the regime, there is a lack of complaint and appeal mechanisms to enable the public to challenge the decisions of the TGA or its associated bodies. For instance, in the listed medicines space, there is no mechanism that allows members of the public to lodge complaints about medicines approved and listed on the ARTG that have inappropriate indications, only the capacity to lodge a complaint about the subsequent advertisement of such medicines. Complainants dissatisfied with a CRP determination also have no recourse to appeal a determination; sponsors, on the other hand, can 'in effect' appeal the CRP's determination with the TGA delegate and then 'further appeal a delegate's decision at the AAT or in court' (Complaints body 341:3). As such, 'there is arguably some bias inherent in the regulatory [regime]' (Complaints body 341:3) that prohibits certain types of opposition (those enabling the public to hold the regulator, and by extension industry, to account).

The submissions and interview transcripts also revealed a widespread belief that TGA committees are gradually being delegated advisory, rather than decision-making, responsibilities:

> when ADRAC was the committee, ADRAC made decisions. . . . They actually made decisions. Now ACSOM in this new iteration does not make decisions; they give advice.
>
> (Interviewee 3:15)

> We don't have any sort of statutory or executive powers. It's more the TGA's reviewed some applications, they've got some questions and asked us for advice.
>
> (Interviewee 7:2)

> the ACPM resolution no longer carries the same weight or signal of a pending decision as it previously did.
>
> (Industry association 81:3)

Interviewee 3 suggested that this is likely a risk-averse approach introduced in response to the Pan settlement (see Section 2.3.1) to limit the TGA's liability when it chooses to act contrary to committee advice. Interviewee 7 stated that the TGA is not always transparent on the types of action it takes following committee advice:

> the TGA will ask us for some advice and we'll provide it, but it may not follow this through or [we don't] hear about . . . the outcome or how the information is used.
>
> (Interviewee 7:5)

> the comments made by the committee . . . it's hard to know whether any of those recommendations were implemented.
>
> (Interviewee 7:5)

The lack of public accountability is in part due to knowledge/power asymmetries and also the fact that such accountability is mediated by the state. Through law, the state determines not only the extent of its transparency but also its accountability to the public. In this way, and as an exercise of power, the state acts upon the actions of others, permitting a particular type of participation that is prescribed by and does not challenge neoliberal governmentality.

## 5.4 Limited regulatory role of the public and public interest representatives

A range of factors have limited the participation of the public and health professionals in the reporting of ADRs and complaints. As mentioned at the outset of this chapter, few members of the public and health professionals are aware of ADR and complaint reporting mechanisms or know how to report an ADR or make a complaint. A lack of regulatory literacy, or knowledge or understanding of regulatory requirements (around registration, listing, DTCA, promotion and so on), can also make it difficult for the public and health professionals to differentiate between what is appropriate and inappropriate for the purposes of reporting.

Other factors include the decentralisation of reporting. Decentralisation has increased the complexity of making a report because '[t]here are too many avenues for lodgement of complaints . . . [so that] identifying where to complain in the first place appears too difficult' (Complaints body 299:7). Similarly, decentralisation has diffused the responsibility for reporting. When it comes to ADRs, sponsors are legally required to report serious ADRs to the TGA and non-serious ADRs as part of a periodic safety update report (in a table as required or requested by the TGA, see Section 3.4.1). Therefore, reporting by industry could (in part) make up for the lack of reporting by the public and health professionals. However, industry reporting is driven by self-interest, which does not always align with the greater public interest. As Interviewee 4 (5) argued:

> the highest number of reports come from industry because most people report back to the company who they assume report back. Now that's

> fine if you trust that process, but how do they know [that the company reports back]?

In terms of DTCA and promotion complaints, which are also largely made by industry, Interviewee 9 (4) argued that '[i]t's industry concerned about, someone's got a competitive advantage, so they'll put in a complaint. . . . if everyone's doing it [not complying] then no one's going to complain'.

A factor that has discouraged reporting by the public and health professionals is the perception that the TGA is disinterested in collecting such reports. According to Interviewee 3 (8), historically, the TGA was:

> all in favour of clerks taking consumer medicine complaints over the phone and just cataloguing them . . . . So they are not actually interested in saying, 'well that sounds a bit scary' or you know, actually giving support or [obtaining] the important detail of the story since there can be a good deal of information gleaned from hearing the story.

Even if this perception is incorrect and the TGA is interested in collecting such reports, Interviewee 3 (3) was of the opinion that there is a widespread perception, especially among health professionals, that 'they're [the TGA] not particularly interested'.

The outcomes of reporting are also perceived to be poor, as these interviewees explained (in relation to DTCA and promotion complaints):

> I lodged a complaint and it took about six months for it to wind its way through the process and they came back and said, 'Well we don't have any evidence to say that any of these things were committed. So we are unable to uphold your complaint or sanction this person in any way' . . . So I mean really it got me nowhere, the fact that I took the trouble to do it even was probably more than many other people would do.
>
> (Interviewee 1:7)

> [S]he put in a complaint and it didn't get up . . . I had to fly to Sydney at my own expense to go to the appeal. . . . it got up and eventually a $40,000 fine was put against the company . . . so I mean, it's not surprising that very few medics or consumer people complain.
>
> (Interviewee 9:4)

Although a fear of reprisal was not explicitly referred to in the submissions or by interviewees, a case such as that of SensaSlim (see Section 4.4) could have had the effect of discouraging complaints by the public and health professionals. With the exception of sponsors, complainants can submit complaints anonymously to the CRP and industry associations. However, the SensaSlim case set 'dangerous precedents' for those complainants who choose to identify themselves (Dowden 2012:39). Although the cases brought against the complainant of SensaSlim by the company and its director were eventually dismissed, and damages were awarded, the complainant was left to pay the legal costs when the company went into liquidation (Dowden 2012:39). Furthermore, as this complainant had lodged complaints previously, they were dubbed a 'serial complainant' by the TGA, CRP and MA (Creswell 2010:20). According to an industry consultant (98:7), the CRP refused to hear further complaints from this person because they were thought to be motivated by a 'personal political agenda'.

Participation in public consultations by the public and those claiming to represent their interests, including consumer associations and advocacy groups, was also perceived to be limited, a perception supported by the descriptive data for the 12 consultations analysed in this book. Most submissions were made by sponsors and industry associations. While professional associations represent the third largest category of submissions, health professionals and professional associations have interests that are separate to (and do not always align with) the greater public interest (see Sections 2.2 and 6.1.2). A lack of participation by the public and those claiming to represent their interests can result from the information barriers mentioned earlier in this chapter. In addition, 'limited resources and the high costs of developing submissions' (Professional associations 76:4), as well as the time required to develop submissions—'who's got the time?' was a question asked repeatedly by Interviewee 9 (20)—can act as further disincentives to participation.

Representation by and of the public and their interests on committees that either include industry representatives or are industry led was also perceived to be limited. Interviewee 9 (5), for instance, who identified as a consumer advocate, indicated that some of the committees formed previously by the Department of Health and TGA had up to nine representatives from industry, one per industry association. Based on their experience, they only ever recalled there being one or two consumer representatives on committees that also had representation from industry, and industry representation was greater than consumer representation (Interviewee 9:10).

These technologies designed to (dis)empower have had both an enabling and constraining effect on participation in regulation. As Cruikshank (1999:20) affirms, the exercise of these technologies occurs within 'a tangled field of power and knowledge'. Indeed, the 'inequality' of power such technologies create is a key feature of the neoliberal rationality of 'equal inequality for all', which seeks to 'multiply and expand entrepreneurial forms within the body social' (Lemke 2001:195). The effects of these technologies include the unequal representation of the public and their interests in reporting and consultative and committee processes and the regime becoming increasingly organised 'around the core interests of the hegemonic fraction' (Mahon 1979:192).

## 5.5 Enhanced state–corporate relations

Several submissions expressed the view that the TGA and industry are in a 'client' relationship, such that industry is *the* client of the TGA. This perception arose in part because the regime is structured to be fully cost recovered by industry. These claims were refuted by several of the submissions made by industry and by interviewees who were from industry. Interviewee 6 (3–4), for example, argued that the TGA's reliance on cost recovery could not result in a benefit to industry because cost recovery does not allow the TGA to make a profit from the services it provides to industry. However, in a small number of the submissions, industry explicitly framed themselves as the clientele of the TGA:

> It may be fair to say that the consumer is the TGA's principal stakeholder. It may also be fair to say that industry in general is a client rather than a stakeholder, and we believe that the service levels provided to a client in a cost for service situation should be constantly monitored to ensure that the services are delivered in the most efficient, timely and cost-effective manner.
>
> (Industry association 50:3)

> Given the entire Biologicals Sector will become paying customers of the TGA . . ., the provision of timely services, appropriate information and clear communication will be expected and needs to be provided.
>
> (Industry association 11:2)

Historically, industry was framed as among the clients of the Department of Health (see Section 2.3).

Another aspect of state–corporate relations evident in this sector is that industry associations and sponsors are known to make regular donations to the two major political parties. In the 2015–2016 financial year, Roche (AU\$70,600), MSD (AU\$68,130), Boehringer Ingelheim (AU\$66,455), Novartis Pharmaceuticals Australia (AU\$62,781), Pfizer Australia (AU\$45,600) and Medtronic Australasia (AU\$24,720) made donations to political parties (Hanrahan et al. 2017). Marcus Blackmore, Chairman of Blackmores Limited, made an individual donation of AU\$113,900 (Hanrahan et al. 2017).

Two interviewees (10 and 11) mentioned a 'revolving door' between industry and the TGA (i.e. the movement of TGA staff to jobs in the pharmaceutical industry, and vice versa); however, this was not believed to be the norm because of the historically low levels of staff turnover at the TGA (see Section 2.3). Yet a revolving door was said to be more evident between Australia's state and federal governments and industry, from which therefore arises a conflict of interest insofar as the TGA falls under the Australian Government's Department of Health, and 'industry influences the politicians' (Interviewee 10:16). State and federal ministers and their employees have transitioned from jobs in government to the pharmaceutical industry (Ferguson and Johnston 2010; Pash 2014). Historically, many of the largest pharmaceutical companies in Australia were based in John Howard's electorate of Bennelong (dubbed the 'Bennelong Group'—see Jackson 2001 and Moynihan 2001), a seat that Howard held from 1974 to 2007 and while he served as treasurer (1977–1983), leader of the Liberal Party (1985–1989 and 1995–2007) and prime minister (1996–2007). Furthermore, relationships between politicians and industry are not uncommon. For example, Interviewee 11 (11) stated that their industry association would 'fully fund' an Annual Parliamentary Dinner:

> where we invite a number of key decision-makers and bureaucrats and politicians from both parties, or all parties rather, and provide opportunities for people to, you know, discuss their issues and, and talk about their policy concerns.

Interviewee 11 (11) also stated that their association would attend events hosted by politicians and their political parties in full knowledge that it would mean 'pay[ing] for that privilege and that constitutes a donation'. According to Interviewee 11 (11):

> we have attended a number of fundraising events or, or business forums which we have had to pay to attend knowing that that money does go into that . . . political party.

Interviewee 11 (11) believed that such opportunities are 'provided fairly evenly', and that these types of interactions are exclusive to neither the pharmaceutical industry nor certain industry sectors:

> it's part of our democratic political process to allow those opportunities to occur . . . people will go to fundraising events . . . [our] political process allows people to meet with them for free at Parliament House or at their electoral offices. So I don't think that our democratic process denies anyone the opportunity to have some exclusive time with the people they think will influence the decision-making in their sector.
>
> (Interviewee 11:11)

> [our] industry doesn't deny other parts of the sector opportunities to interact with influencers and decision-makers in the political and bureaucratic sphere.
>
> (Interviewee 11:11)

With respect to the Annual Parliamentary Dinner, Interviewee 11 (11) claimed that they would invite people from other sectors of the medicine industry, as well as from 'public health, nursing, medicine, [and] patient support groups'. However, not all industry associations and sponsors take up such opportunities; this was emphasised by Interviewee 6 (5), who stated that their association does not make political donations or fund events attended by politicians.

There was also potential for conflicts of interest arising from industry representatives sitting on TGA committees and industry-led committees, irrespective of whether these conflicts were necessarily acted upon. The submissions and interviewees made no reference to any formal complaints disputing the quality of a given decision made by a committee on the basis of its industry membership or the committee being industry led. However, clearly, conflicts of interest could arise from having industry associations participate in decisions concerning their members. For example, in terms of advertising pre-approval, 'for advertisers that may be members of their organisation . . . [a] decision to approve an advertisement may have implications for not just that particular advertiser, but for others seeking approval who may be members' (Consumer association 344:6). The extent of the representation of industry and its interests on such committees could, depending on the proportion of committee members, result in a 'majority decision' (Academic 246:2).

Interactions between politicians and industry, and the fact that members of the public cannot generally have such interactions with politicians, have given rise to unequal relations of power in the regime, which has rendered the regime more amenable to the interests of industry. Industry representation and industry-led committees are problematic when industry is placed in a position where it is expected to act in ways consistent with the public interest. When public interests happen to conflict with private interests, industry may be more inclined to act in its own interests in the first instance. Even if these conflicts are not necessarily acted upon by industry representatives, the degree of representation industry receives over other interest groups can lead to an over-representation of private interests in these decision-making processes. This over-representation generates unequal relations of power, which provides industry with more opportunities to assert its interests.

## 5.6 Technologies of (dis)empowerment: disempowering the public and representatives of public interests

Technologies of (dis)empowerment, or the means through which to (dis)empower the public and its representatives, are shaped by asymmetries of knowledge/power. The limited transparency in the regulatory regime is exacerbated by the knowledge/power asymmetries between the state, industry, and the public. The public, which have the least knowledge/power, are limited in their capacity to responsibilise (despite being obligated to take on more responsibility) because their subjectivity (health and regulatory literacy) is tied to their subjection (the control of their knowledge/power). As such, the capacity of members of the public to rationalise the costs and benefits regarding their health, vital to their literacy and to being informed, is bounded by and contingent on those with the most knowledge/power. Asymmetrical knowledge/power also limits the public's capacity to act as a regulator or 'third player' to the TGA and industry, and thus to hold them publicly accountable. Although health professionals have technical knowledge/power, the asymmetries created by the lack of transparency in the regime likewise limit their capacity to rationalise the costs and benefits of particular medicines, and therefore to fully inform their patients. They also limit their capacity to act as a regulator and 'third player' on the public's behalf when representing the public interest. In this respect, these sets of actors have been disempowered, rather than empowered, through the very technologies that seek to utilise their agency. The knowledge/power said to be indispensable to such technologies, and therefore participation in the regulatory regime, both individually and collectively, has contributed to the unequal relations of power that have rendered the regime less representative of the public's interest.

Conversely, these technologies and the asymmetrical knowledge/power relations they produce empower the TGA and industry. This has enabled the TGA and industry to shape the content, form and timing of information in ways that align with their interests, in particular, to limit the potential for opposition and therefore to maintain existing relations of power. The lack of equal representation within the regime has furthered the opportunities for the exercise of this power by these actors because it effectively restricts the ability of the public and their representatives 'to maneuver and to act to change' these relations of power (Hayward 1998:21). Indeed, knowledge/power in this context has increasingly become enclosed and concentrated.

The findings presented in this and the previous chapter indicate an apparent lack of power and knowledge. Chapter 4 revealed how regulation has failed because the TGA is disempowered by its limited capacity to regulate and respond to non-compliance by sponsors. This chapter has demonstrated the variety of ways in which the public and those representing their interests have been disempowered through their limited knowledge/power relative to that of the TGA and industry. This lack of power and knowledge implies that the solution is quite simply the redistribution of both, and that what is really needed is 'better' regulation and provision of information that empowers the public. Of course, this conclusion also rationalises the (re)turn to (and continuing to work within) existing neoliberal techniques of governing—the ultimate aim of neoliberal hegemony.

Since the period of data collection for this research, the TGA has attempted to reform the regime to address its failures in securing compliance, as well as to increase its transparency to the public. Chapter 6 critically examines the TGA's attempts at reforming the regime in the more than ten-year period following data collection. This chapter is informed by an additional four themes identified in the thematic analysis, which submitters to the public consultations and interviewees believed would 'better' the medicine regulatory regime. At the time of writing, however, many facets of the regime remain unchanged, and in some cases, neoliberal governmentality has only intensified.

## Notes

1 The provision of PI or CMI is not a legal requirement for listed medicines.
2 PI documents are updated when a variation is made to a medicine or its ARTG entry by the sponsor, when a variation to the PI is requested by the sponsor (e.g. to extend product indications, register a new generic medicine or add a new trade name to a medicine), or based on a safety-related change mandated by the TGA (TGA 2013b, 2013f). Whether a variation is self-assessed or approved by the TGA is dependent on the type of change requested. Self-assessable changes are generally permitted when variations are not safety related; do not reduce the quality, safety or efficacy of the product; and do not require the submission and evaluation of data by the TGA (TGA 2013g:46). These changes include corrections to ARTG entries, minor editorial changes, and some safety-related requests (TGA 2013g:18). Anything that generally requires the submission and evaluation of data is not self-assessable (TGA 2013b:18). Outside these updates, the onus generally falls on sponsors to ensure that PI documents contain correct and updated information. No independent mechanisms are in place to ensure the currency of CMI documents either; the TGA simply mandates that sponsors ensure that CMI documents are consistent with the approved PI (TGA 2013f:9).
3 The brand name of this medicine was removed from the extract to protect the anonymity of the interviewee.
4 The TGA website provides some information on the types of evidence supplied by sponsors at the time of registration, but 'these are not referenced as specific citations' to enable their location (Advocacy group 112:1).
5 Chemical or drug-induced liver damage or injury (Martin 2007:349).
6 Dronedarone was cancelled from the ARTG in 2017. In the year after its cancellation, the PI and CMI were accessible from the ARTG, and current as of January 2015. The ARTG entry has since been removed.
7 Excluding pharmacists, who demonstrated significantly higher levels of awareness of ADR reporting mechanisms than any other practitioner group in Australia (Kelly et al. 2004; Nita et al. 2005).
8 Which was between 1998 and 2003, when reporting was as high as 26% (Department of Health and Aged Care 1999a; Department of Health and Ageing 2003, 2005; Department of Health 2016b).
9 For example, information or data about its formulation or active ingredient, manufacture, testing or investigations into its performance, provided as part of a recall, certain information about clinical trials or ADR reports, or 'post-market studies/performance/safety information about the product' (TGA 2014h:8).
10 See s. 31B, 45(1), 47(1) and 47G(1)(a) and (b) of the Freedom of Information Act.
11 The justification for this change given to me was that the Chief Operating Officer had 'left' the TGA and my interview request was (re)scrutinised by members of the TGA Executive (personal communication, 11 and 18 April 2013).
12 The answers provided did not address the questions and mostly restated information provided on the TGA website.
13 Details of those goods and manufacturing licences that are cancelled by the TGA are published in the Australian Government Gazettes; however, the availability of the Gazettes is not widely publicised, and few authors of submissions believed that the public are aware of their availability or would intuitively turn to Gazettes to locate this information (Submissions 33, 72, 127 and 240).
14 The brand name and class of this medicine were removed from the extract to protect the anonymity of the interviewee.

# 6 The regime 'reformed'

In identifying the perceived failures of the regime in regulating medicines, the thematic analysis also identified recommendations in the submissions and transcripts to 'improve', 'enhance', 'strengthen' and 'better' the regime (TGA 2011c). Broadly, these recommendations can be grouped into four main proposals for reform: *increasing regulation* (by government, and through centralisation and co-regulation), *penalties* (in severity and range), *resourcing* of the TGA, and *transparency* of the TGA and medicine regulatory regime. Each of these proposals requires relatively small, modest reforms to (and therefore, working within) the existing regime, rather than larger structural reforms. This chapter examines the government and TGA reforms to the regime to 'better' regulation that were implemented following the period of data collection and up until mid-2024. The analysis demonstrates how these reforms were shaped by (and subordinated to) neoliberal rationalities, such as product risk and economic rationality, and responsibilisation, and how neoliberal governmentality also increased (and, indeed, became more hegemonic). The chapter argues against the notion that the regime (and even neoliberalism itself) can merely be 'better regulated'; instead, it asserts that overcoming the failures and harms of medicine regulation will only be possible through much wider social transformation.

## 6.1 Increasing government regulation, co-regulation and centralisation

There was a consensus that the regulation of listed and registered medicines, and of their DTCA and promotion, needed to be increased, and that the TGA needed to play a larger role, particularly where its role has been limited or non-existent. Due to space limitations, this section cannot examine all the increases to regulation recommended in the submissions and by the interviewees. Instead, it focuses on three of the areas where increased regulation was frequently recommended: the pre- and post-market regulation of listed medicine efficacy, the regulation of the promotion of medicines to health professionals and the regulation of DTCA (the pre-approval of advertisements and complaints).

DOI: 10.4324/9781003285762-6

### *6.1.1 Pre- and post-market listed medicine efficacy*

Most of the submissions and interviewees recommended that the TGA evaluate the efficacy of listed medicines prior to their approval by requiring sponsors to submit evidence of efficacy at the point of application for listing. These submissions and interviewees also recommended an increase in the rate of post-market compliance reviews. Evaluating efficacy prior to approval and increasing the rate of review were justified for several reasons. By obtaining the evidence used by sponsors to substantiate their efficacy claims (and which they are otherwise required to hold) at the point of application, the TGA could initiate a review at any time and without first having to approach the sponsor to supply this evidence voluntarily. Having this evidence available upfront could facilitate the TGA's risk-based approach to compliance review, particularly the determination of a sponsor's compliance risk (e.g. by prioritising for review those applications that provide fewer sources of evidence, supply outdated evidence or forms of evidence superseded by newer sources of evidence, or are not reputable). The capacity of the TGA to initiate a review immediately and the increased likelihood of an application being subject to a review could increase the regime's deterrent effect. Most importantly, these reforms would decrease the likelihood that the public will be exposed to inefficacious listed medicines.

The TGA responded to the findings of the consultations instead by attempting to clarify the type of evidence that sponsors are required to hold at the point of approval. In the first part of a two-part consultation on *Evidence Required to Support Indications for Listed Medicines*, the TGA introduced a proposal requiring sponsors to produce, but not submit, an expert report summarising the evidence of the medicine's efficacy. This report would have to be prepared by an expert independent of the sponsor and take the form of either 'a literature review of the existing body of evidence backing an indication for a particular ingredient' or an 'analysis of new, unpublished clinical trials' (TGA 2012b:10). However, industry stakeholders criticised this proposal on numerous grounds. The majority of sponsors and industry associations argued that this increase in the evidence requirements was not commensurate with the level of product risk. Examples of these sentiments are provided as follows:

> government action should be proportional to the issue being addressed. The requirements . . . appear to be equivalent to or higher than those for registered over-the-counter medicine, yet are applied to listed medicines which may only carry listable indications/claims. [Our organisation] considers this to be inappropriate for listed medicines which are low risk by definition.
>
> (Industry association 162:7)

> [L]istable complementary medicines are at the lower end of the risk continuum and any regulatory intervention should be consistent with that level of risk.
>
> (Industry association 160:2)

> any indication previously considered to be general, such as a health maintenance claim, will now require the same rigour of evidence to be presented as a claim to cure or treat, which was previously considered a high level claim. By this reasoning a claim that Vitamin C may assist with the maintenance of immune function will require a full literature review . . . to validate this claim. In this way the level of evidence and analysis required is beyond the scope of the types of indications allowed to be made, or that are intended to be made on listed products.
>
> (Sponsor 178:5)

As the listed medicines contain a combination of active ingredients, each of which varies in strength (and therefore size of effect from batch to batch), it was argued (e.g. by Sponsor 178:3) that their complexity makes it difficult for sponsors to conduct clinical trials for, and apply conventional clinical indicators to, listed medicines in the same way that a sponsor would for registered medicines. These difficulties, in turn, were said to limit the amount of literature available to sponsors to support indications for listed medicines, as well as the pool of suitably qualified experts independent of sponsors who could produce reports on their behalf (according to Industry consultant 165:4). Industry stakeholders often argued that this increase in the evidence requirements would 'drive up the cost to sponsors' (Sponsor 191:5)—in terms of the cost of compiling a report for each ingredient and/or indication, hiring an expert to compile the report and carry out clinical trial(s), and complying with the requirements unique to Australia (which are greater than those overseas). Some argued that such evidence requirements could prompt regulatory evasion and avoidance through sponsors cancelling the listing and 'presenting products as foods' (Sponsor 170:4).[1]

In the second part of the consultation, the TGA removed several of the requirements initially proposed for the expert report, including that reports be based on the outcomes of new or unpublished clinical trials (reviews of existing literature would suffice) and written by an expert independent of the sponsor (TGA 2012c:14–15). Sponsors were also offered the option of using established sources of evidence already recognised by the TGA (rather than produce an expert report) to support an indication (TGA 2012c:12–13). Yet industry maintained that these requirements remained disproportional to the level of product risk. They also argued that the report would still be too costly to produce, for many of the same reasons provided by industry in the first part of the consultation. One submission made anonymously (195:2) described what the production of a report would entail for a sponsor of a multi-ingredient homoeopathic product: in addition to being 'costly', the report was said to be 'very time-consuming to complete, taking up to 20 hours for each ingredient where it was necessary to search for primary sources'. This submission also claimed that '[t]he tracing of primary sources in homeopathy is difficult, requires enormous research and may sometimes not be possible at all' (Anonymous 195:2).

The idea of an expert report was abandoned, and instead, a list of established sources of evidence and permissible or coded indications was created by the TGA to restrict industry to using TGA-approved evidence sources and indications. Under the Liberal government, the Therapeutic Goods Act was amended in 2018 to provide the Minister for Health with the power to create legislative instruments on permissible indications (via the *Therapeutic Goods Amendment (2017 Measures No. 1) Act 2018* (Cth) and s. 26BF). Not long after, a legislative instrument for permissible indications was created (Therapeutic Goods (Permissible Indications) Determination (No. 1) 2021). The significance of this reform was that it effectively abolished the use and exploitation of the free text fields in the ELF, which was a major limitation of the previous application process for listing medicines. But according to Haggan (2018:para. 13), only 14% (153 out of 1,091) of the indications developed by the TGA require substantiation by scientific evidence; traditional evidence suffices for the vast majority of indications approved by the TGA.

In 2018, the Therapeutic Goods Act was also amended to create a second 'TGA-assessed' approval process for listed medicines (through the Therapeutic Goods Amendment (2017 Measures No. 1) Act (Cth) and introduction of s. 26AB). These applications are directly assessed by the TGA, including assessment of the evidence supporting the medicine's indications (efficacy) that is supplied as part of the application process. Following confirmation by the TGA of the medicine's efficacy, these medicines are designated with an 'AUST L(A)' number and 'TGA assessed' symbol on their packaging. This TGA-assessed approval process is only available to new listings and is more expensive compared to the existing listed medicine approval process (which results in the designation of an 'AUST L' number). In 2024, listing an assessed listed medicine on the ARTG requires sponsors to pay a minimum of AU$2,498[2] in application and evaluation fees, as well as AU$1,429 in annual fees. This compares to AU$983 in application fees and AU$1,429 in annual fees for listed medicines using the existing approval process (TGA 2024d:13–15). At the time of writing, few sponsors have opted for this higher level of approval. Up to 30 June 2024, just three applications for listed medicines were TGA assessed: Care Pharmaceuticals' Hydralyte Effervescent Electrolyte tablets, Caruso's Prostate Eze Max and Swisse's Ultiboost High Strength Krill Oil. This is in stark contrast to the 6,175 applications for listed medicines[3] approved through the existing process between 1 January 2020 and 30 June 2024 (the period in which all three assessed listed medicines were approved) (ARTG 2024).

There is also a reason to be sceptical about the level of assessment that TGA-assessed listed medicines receive. According to Harvey and Dwyer

(2021), there is only one published article assessing the effectiveness of Caruso's Prostate Eze Max for which it is indicated—which is '[f]or the relief of nocturia (night-time urinary frequency) associated with medically diagnosed benign prostatic hypertrophy or [enlarged prostate]'. This study was funded by Caruso's Natural Health Pty Ltd and has limitations in relation to its design and the reporting of statistical tests, including its small sample size and lack of inclusion of 95% confidence intervals and zeros in the *y*-axis (the latter exaggerating small trends and differences in the graphs published in the article) (Harvey and Dwyer 2021). Although a statistically significant result was reported for night-time urinary frequency, and a *P*-value was provided, no raw data was provided (meaning the significance of the result is not verifiable). Harvey and Dwyer (2021) argue that insofar as the TGA does not publish or summarise the studies used to substantiate indications in listed medicine applications, it prohibits health professionals and the public from making informed comparisons between Prostate Eze Max and other prescription (registered) medicines (which remain the primary treatment option).

In its response to the *Review of Medicines and Medical Devices Regulation*, the Department of Health (2016a:34–35) indicated its intent to increase the rate of random and targeted compliance reviews, as part of an overall increase in the TGA's post-market regulation of medicines. The number of compliance reviews completed by the TGA more than doubled between 2014 and 2017 (from 212 to 551 reviews, per year—see *Table 6.1*). However, by the second half of 2017, the TGA (2017a:6) conceded that the increase in the number of reviews alone had 'not driven an improvement in compliance rates'. The TGA has since doubled down on the number of reviews it completed. A slight decrease in the rate of non-compliance is observable from the 2017–2018 financial year, although it is not clear from the data what caused this decrease. Non-compliance rates, nevertheless, continue to average above 70% (and therefore at rates similar to those seen prior to and during the 2010–2014 reform period).

*Table 6.1* Number of compliance reviews conducted by the TGA and % of compliance breaches, per year, between the 2014–2015 and 2022–2023 financial years

| | *2014–2015* | *2015–2016* | *2016–2017* | *2017–2018* | *2018–2019* | *2019–2020* | *2020–2021* | *2021–2022* | *2022–2023* |
|---|---|---|---|---|---|---|---|---|---|
| No. completed | 212 | 473 | 551 | 243 | 181 | 195 | 76 | 78 | 203 |
| No. where compliance status was determined | 161 | 408 | 417 | 171 | 140 | 160 | 45 | 71 | 185 |
| No. of compliance breach(es) | 118 | 327 | 330 | 129 | 102 | 118 | 39 | 50 | 128 |
| % compliance breach(es) | 73% | 80% | 79% | 75% | 73% | 74% | 87% | 70% | 69% |

*Source*: Adapted from TGA (2015b, 2016e, 2017a, 2018a, 2019a, 2020a, 2021c, 2022d, 2023b)

### *6.1.2 Promotion of medicines to health professionals*

A prevalent view in the submissions and interview transcripts was that the self-regulation of promotion to health professionals by industry associations was ineffective or of limited effectiveness and it was recommended that there be greater regulation of such activities by the TGA. From the outset, the Labor government stated that it 'supports self-regulation of industry conduct' when it comes to regulating promotion to health professionals (Department of Health 2011:1–2). In the *Position Paper on the Promotion of Therapeutic Goods*, the government proposed:

> in the first instance, that industry strengthen and standardise self-regulation through developing an industry framework for universal adherence to consistent industry-wide codes based on a common set of high level principles. . . . [I]f consistent arrangements are not realised, then legislative options consistent with the Government's policy objectives, including universal coverage and consistency across the sector, could be put in place in 2012. This could include enforcement arrangements to ensure compliance with these objectives.
>
> (Department of Health 2011:1–2)

The Labor government first established a Working Group on Promotion of Therapeutic Goods in late 2010 to respond to the Position Paper and submissions it received, and to develop 'a high level statement of principles to be incorporated into each industry code' (Australia, Senate Finance and Public Administration Legislation Committee 2013:6). The Codes of Conduct Advisory Group was then established in January 2013 to oversee the incorporation of these principles into industry association codes. It was allocated AU$1.4 million over a four-year period to support this work (Australia, Senate Finance and Public Administration Legislation Committee 2013:8). The Labor government went so far as to appoint the members of the Codes of Conduct Advisory Group (comprising representatives from industry associations, and health professional and consumer associations—see Parliament of Australia 2013), but no further information has been published on the Advisory Group and its meetings or other activities since these appointments were made (the Liberal Party assumed government in late 2013).

In February 2013, the Therapeutic Goods Amendment (Pharmaceutical Transparency) Bill 2013 was introduced in the Senate by Senator and former general practitioner Richard Di Natale (Australian Greens) proposing a number of amendments to the Therapeutic Goods Act. The Bill introduced civil penalties for sponsors that arranged or sponsored conferences, conventions or educational or other similar events held overseas at which the majority of attendees were registered medical practitioners and that paid for medical practitioners to attend such events (including covering their travel and/or accommodation fees), unless the practitioner was representing the sponsor at the event, or otherwise paid for the hospitality of medical practitioners at such events (including the payment of meals or entertainment valued at more than AU$100 per head) (Australia, Senate Finance and Public Administration Legislation Committee 2013:2–4). The Bill also required sponsors to publicly report each payment made to a medical practitioner and publish these on their websites, including payments for attending conferences, conventions and educational or other events; the provision of a service, travel or accommodation; medical research; charitable donations on behalf of or in relation to a medical practitioner; and gifts valued at more than AU$25 (Australia, Senate Finance and Public Administration Legislation Committee 2013:2–4). The Bill was referred by the Senate to the Senate Finance and Public Administration Legislation Committee in March for public inquiry and report. Of the 25 submissions received to the public consultation, 14 were made by sponsors and four by industry associations (representing 72% of the total number of submissions received). In these submissions, it was generally argued that the Bill would undermine industry self-regulation and industry efforts to strengthen self-regulation; was less comprehensive than what industry associations were considering (e.g. MA was considering establishing a single repository for these reports) or existing industry codes (e.g. it would only apply to medical practitioners and not health professionals broadly); and framed industry–health professional relationships, said to be essential to health professionals' continuing professional development and education, as unlawful. Regarding the last point, the only submission by a professional association (254:1–2) agreed, arguing that:

> interactions between medical practitioners and pharmaceutical and medical companies are a necessary and legitimate part of ensuring that patients have access to new and improved medicines, treatments and medical devices . . . Australian medical practitioners' engagement with international colleagues and experiences improve patient outcomes in Australia. Industry sponsorship is an important element in assisting these activities to take place. By its very nature, the Bill provides the perception that the interactions between medical practitioners and pharmaceutical companies are not legitimate. If passed the Bill will make particular interactions illegal.

But the lone submission from a consumer association (257:2) countered this argument by stating that the Bill simply prohibited industry's arrangement and sponsorship of such events and sponsorship of doctors' attendance or hospitality at them:

> [t]he Bill does not prohibit Australian doctors from attending events outside Australia, nor would it prevent companies from hosting events within Australia or overseas (provided the latter are not aimed exclusively at Australian prescribers).

Some of the submissions also argued that the proposals of the Bill were cost ineffective and disproportionate, especially for lower-risk, non-prescription medicines. For example, an Industry association (255:4) representing the non-prescription medicines industry claimed that:

> any change in regulation should be risk-based and that the tendency to prescribe a 'one-size-fits-all' solution must be resisted. . . . [I]t is . . . essential that any compliance measures are proportionate to the risks and that they do not introduce unnecessary complexity. So for example, a complex and expensive compliance system set up to monitor something which rarely occurs in a particular industry sector would place an unnecessary burden on that sector and would result in increased costs to consumers, without any corresponding increase in their protection.

In its own submission to the consultation, and in challenging the assumption that the TGA would adopt a 'supervisory role' if the Bill were to pass, the Department of Health argued that:

> [t]he TGA's current enforcement powers are not designed or adapted to detect, enforce and prosecute contraventions of the type proposed. As well as requiring additional amendments to the [Therapeutic Goods] Act, development and implementation of such a monitoring and enforcement role would require significant resources and would result in additional costs to industry through TGA's cost recovery arrangements.
>
> (Government department 258:8)

The final report of the Senate Finance and Public Administration Legislation Committee in June 2013 recommended that the Bill not be passed.

MA has required that its members report certain types of payments to health professionals since 2007. Initially, these reports were provided to MA and published on its website as separate PDF files (e.g. see MA 2024a, 2024b), which made it difficult to compare the spending of different sponsors. Health professionals were also de-identified, so the public was not able to determine which health professionals were in receipt of payments. However, this practice changed with the release of the 18th edition of the MA Code, which came into effect in March 2015, after which MA members were required to publish the details of those health professionals in receipt of payments (with the agreement of the health professionals to publish their information). It was not until late 2019 that all of this information was consolidated into a single database. As per the 19th edition of the MA Code, the latest in effect, members are required to report payments and transfers of value paid to health professionals—in the form of speaker or consultancy fees; airfare, accommodation or registration fees; or fees to participate in market research—as well as their sponsorship of educational events (MA 2019:19–20). Although it is the most detailed reporting of such relationships to date in Australia, this reporting regime has a couple of limitations. Most notably, it is only mandatory for members of MA, even though some sponsors of prescription medicines in Australia, albeit a minority, are not members of MA. At the time of writing this book, the database contains the reports of just 39 pharmaceutical companies.[4] Another limitation is that payments for food and beverages are excluded from the reporting requirements. Prior to the 18th edition of the Code, MA had required that food and beverage payments be reported by its members. Historically, these types of costs have made up to 34% of the total expenditure reported to MA[5] (Parker et al. 2019). Food and beverages were also paid for at over 90% of the industry-sponsored events reported to MA (Fabbri et al. 2017). Research from the US (where such payments are reported) has shown that physicians' receipt of food and beverages paid for by industry at events was associated with an increase in the prescribing of the medicine promoted at these events (DeJong et al. 2016). For these reasons, the number of payments reported in the MA database is likely to underestimate the amount of spending that actually occurs. Although the Consumer Healthcare Products Australia (CHP Australia, formerly ASMI) and CMA Codes contain provisions on payments to health professionals, they do not contain provisions on reporting these payments (unlike the MA Code); and these payments do not appear to be reported publicly by either association.

In the consultation *Regulation Impact Statement: Regulating the Advertising of Therapeutic Goods to the Public* in 2013, the TGA proposed to limit the promotion of listed and registered non-prescription medicines to health professionals by replacing the term 'health professional' in the Therapeutic Goods Act with 'healthcare practitioner', thereby narrowing its application to those practitioners who are registered under the National Registration and Accreditation Scheme (NRAS).[6] The NRAS, administered by the Australian Health Practitioner Regulation Agency (APHRA), not only maintains a national (and searchable) register of health practitioners but also generally requires those who register with the NRAS to have a minimum level of training and qualifications, complete a minimum level of continuing professional development each year and be insured (against professional indemnity) (Chinese Medicine Board, APHRA 2024). NRAS practitioners were therefore thought to be 'appropriately qualified' and 'able to exercise specialist judgement when either treating consumers with advertised therapeutic goods, or advising consumers about the use of advertised therapeutic goods' (TGA 2013a:28). Their NRAS registration also restricts them to using and administering only those therapeutic goods that they are qualified to use. While a large number of submissions saw merit in this proposal, industry and health professionals whose professions were not included on the scheme (such as naturopaths, Western herbalists and homeopaths) condemned the move, mainly because these promotional activities and materials were thought to contribute to health professionals' knowledge and understanding of these medicines. In one submission, it was argued that:

> [t]he proposed changes . . . mean that complementary medicine practitioners will *no longer* have access to appropriate advertising or educational material from Complementary Medicine sponsors. Complementary medicine Health Professionals must be able to access technical and scientific information, including contraindications, around the medicines they prescribe . . . if health professionals were not able to access this information, . . . this would increase the potential for harm to consumers.
>
> (Industry association 342:13 [emphasis in original])

The TGA has since backed down on this proposal. Other than in a limited number of circumstances, promotion otherwise remains self-regulated through industry association codes (TGA 2013a, 2021a).

### *6.1.3 DTCA pre-approval and complaints*

The majority of submissions and interviewees agreed that the management of advertising pre-approval and complaints should be centralised so that there is a single body responsible for pre-approving and handling complaints for advertisements. Such reforms would reduce the complexity of the current regime and remove the perceived inconsistencies between the approaches of those bodies charged with pre-approval and complaints handling. However, there was little consensus among the submissions and interviewees as to who should be charged with this responsibility.

Many preferred that the TGA or a new statutory officer or agency be made responsible for both advertising pre-approval and complaints handling. In the case that the TGA did assume such responsibility:

> TGA staff assessing pre-approvals would provide the expertise currently lacking in industry delegates to assess claims of efficacy, would eliminate inconsistency between the two industry delegates currently employed and ensure that advertisement approval, sponsor submitted ARTG indications and post-marketing product reviews were all assessed under a common framework. . . . [A]ll complaints [need] to be handled by the TGA. This eliminates concerns expressed about the CRP, removes duplication in the current system and would allow earlier identification of repeat and major offenders and advertisements posing a high risk to public health and safety.
>
> (Consumer association 340:5–6)

Industry, however, preferred to maintain some responsibility for advertising pre-approval and complaints, partly because it was more 'cost-effective'

(Industry association 126:1). For example, one sponsor (359:2) argued for the 'maintenance of the current system for regulation of advertising . . . with amendments' because:

> [w]e are satisfied that the industry bodies provide timely and efficient service to the industry (regardless of membership) and consider the pre-approvals process an exemplar of co-regulation. We do not consider that there is a need for closer TGA oversight and quality control and are concerned that such involvement could slow the advertising approval process, increase cost to industry and lengthen pre-approval timelines.

To eliminate the inconsistencies between industry associations in connection to pre-approving and handling complaints for advertisements, these submissions generally called for greater alignment of industry association codes (e.g. through the incorporation of high-level principles) and making adherence to these codes mandatory (e.g. as a condition of listing on the ARTG). For instance, an industry association (229:1) argued that in general 'industry should strengthen and standardise self-regulation through developing an industry framework for universal adherence to consistent industry-wide codes based on a common set of high level principles'. Non-industry submissions and interviewees agreed that incorporating the same high-level principles into all of the codes and making the codes mandatory were necessary to increase their consistency, even if advertising pre-approval and complaints were not self-regulated. While such a proposal, if it were implemented, would have the benefit of standardising industry codes and enable industry associations to act on non-members who fail to comply, advertising pre-approval and complaint handling processes would continue to be decentralised under this model, and thus open to inconsistency by virtue of having multiple bodies adjudicating them. However, little progress has been made around increasing code consistency since the establishment of the Codes of Conduct Advisory Groups in 2013. The Australian Government has also opposed mandatory adherence to industry codes of conduct for non-prescription medicine sponsors. In response to these recommendations in the Transparency Review, the Labor government reinforced its support for industry self-regulation and initiatives to harmonise all industry codes, stating that:

> [f]urther changes will [only] be considered if it is found that there is a need to provide greater encouragement to non-members of industry associations to nominate and sign up to an appropriate industry code, including . . . notification of a sponsor's nominated code of conduct at the point of including a product on the ARTG.
>
> (TGA 2011c:12)

In response to the *Position Paper on the Promotion of Therapeutic Goods*, the Labor government further stated that companies should 'not be obliged to become members to elect to be covered by a code of conduct' and that all code breaches, irrespective of whether they are committed by members or non-members, can simply be referred to the relevant code of conduct committee (Department of Health 2011:2). At the time of writing, adherence to industry codes for non-prescription medicine sponsors remains voluntary.

There were a large number of submissions and interviewees that also called for expanding the pre-approval process to all advertising mediums. These submissions and interviewees believed the demarcation between the forms of advertising that require and those that do not require pre-approval to be 'arbitrary' and reflective of 'a practical decision regarding resources rather than a decision based on protecting consumers' (Industry association 126:4). Expanding the pre-approval of advertising to all mediums would increase consistency in the standard of advertisements; decrease the burden of responsibility on the public and health professionals (to identify non-compliant advertisements) and in turn on complaints processes (because advertisements would be vetted prior to their publication); decrease the likelihood of the public being exposed to inappropriate advertising; and provide sponsors with increased regulatory certainty (that a complaint about an advertisement will be less likely). However, opponents of this proposal argued that expanding advertising pre-approval had cost implications (for sponsors, as well as for the body that would be charged with pre-approving advertisements):

> [we] would not support arrangements that required pre-approval for all advertising material as this is practically not possible with the range of advertising and marketing communications within a campaign or new forms of advertising e.g. social media. It would also be an unacceptable cost and imposition to commercial operations.
>
> (Industry association 121:4)

> To subject all advertisement[s] to pre-approval would greatly increase the cost of advertising. . . . Removing the restriction on pre-approval would mean that advertisers of non-prescription medicines would be able to get to market much quicker and with less cost.
>
> (Industry association 141:6)

Several submissions also argued that if advertising pre-approval were to be expanded, it 'must be commensurate with the risk profile of the products' (Industry association 347:1).

In October 2014, the then Minister for Health Peter Dutton and Assistant Minister for Health Fiona Nash (Liberal Party) jointly announced an Expert Review of Medicines and Medical Devices Regulation 'to remove ineffective regulation and encourage greater competition and innovation in the medicines and medical devices sectors' (Department of Health and Ageing 2014:1). The committee appointed by Dutton and Nash to preside over the Review (herein, referred to as the Expert Panel) was led by Emeritus Professor

Lloyd Sansom AO[7] and comprised Mr Will Delaat AM[8] and Professor John Horvath AO.[9] At the Expert Panel's recommendation, the Liberal government agreed to abolish the requirement that advertisements be pre-approved (TGA 2016b).[10] Instead, the government 'left it open for industry associations . . . to implement a self-regulatory regime for providing pre-approvals' (TGA 2016b:9). The decision to abolish advertising pre-approval was rationalised on the basis of the need 'to ease [the] regulatory imposts on sponsors' and the conditions that post-market monitoring and complaints processing be increased, penalties be increased, permissible or coded indications be introduced and advertising claims be consistent with the coded indications (Sansom et al. 2015:60). The changes came into effect on 30 June 2020. The CMA declined to accept further applications for advertising pre-approval. However, CHP Australia introduced a (voluntary) advertising advisory service called AdCheck whereby sponsors, irrespective of their industry association membership, could get compliance-related advice on all forms of advertising. AdCheck fees for new advertisements vary between AU$100 and AU$1,705, depending on the medium (CHP Australia 2024a). According to the 2020–2021 Annual Report of CHP Australia (2021:7), the latest available through its website, more than 110 sponsors used AdCheck in the first year of its operation. Data on the proportion of 'AdChecked' advertisements subject to advertising complaints is not published by either CHP Australia or the TGA; and therefore, it is not possible to evaluate the impact of this voluntary service on compliance rates.

The abolishment of mandatory pre-approval has had several implications, nonetheless. First, because industry associations no longer have the official capacity to pre-approve advertisements under law (because pre-approval is no longer mandatory), CMA was not inclined to introduce pre-approval processes of its own. Second, the voluntary advisory service provided by CHP Australia could appear to have less merit from the perspective of some sponsors, and therefore discourage its use, because of the time and cost of obtaining this advice relative to the level of assurance provided (i.e. that an advertisement will not be subject to a successful complaint). This is particularly so given that the Terms of Agreement for AdCheck include indemnity to CHP Australia, requiring the user to agree to not bring a claim in respect to the services provided (CHP Australia 2022:s. 4.2, 7). This is not to suggest that such advice would not be beneficial, but that it could be perceived by some sponsors as having less weight compared to an advertisement that is pre-approved under the former system.[11] Finally, the abolishment of mandatory pre-approval and its replacement with a voluntary advisory service increases the public's exposure to inappropriate advertisements and claims (through an increased reliance on post-market regulatory techniques to identify non-compliance). Ultimately, it has only shifted responsibility further away from the state and onto the public.

To compensate for the lack of pre-approval, and at the recommendation of the Expert Panel, the Liberal government abolished the co-regulatory approach to handling advertising complaints (Sansom et al. 2015:64). In doing so, the CRP was disbanded and the TGA took on the responsibility for managing advertising complaints (through the Advertising Management System, or AMS) on 1 July 2018 (Department of Health 2016a:17). The government introduced penalties for advertising non-compliance through multiple amendments to the Therapeutic Goods Act (explained in detail in Section 6.2.). The minimum requirements for non-prescription medicine advertisements were formally established through the introduction of the Therapeutic Goods (Therapeutic Goods Advertising Code) Instrument 2021.

Removing the requirement that advertisements be pre-approved, and thereby increasing the reliance on post-market regulation to identify non-compliance, has likely contributed to the increase in the number of complaints received by the TGA. Prior to its cessation, the CRP received 261 and 190 complaints[12] in the 2016–2017 and 2017–2018 financial years, respectively (CRP 2016–2017, 2017–2018). This compares to the 1,468 complaint reports received by the TGA through the AMS in the 2018–2019 financial year (TGA 2019d:12), which doubled to 3,064 reports in the 2022–2023 financial year (TGA 2023c:10). It is important to note that this increase may be the result of multiple causes. Previously, the CRP had received complaints for advertisements of therapeutic goods in *specified media* only. The centralisation of complaints reporting and its publicising by the TGA (see Section 6.4) have likely increased knowledge and understanding of the processes for reporting complaints among the public. Indeed, consumers make up more than 60% of the complainants for the reports received by the TGA (TGA 2023c:10). This increase could also be due in part to the number of advertising complaints in relation to COVID-19.[13] Nevertheless, the lack of pre-approval and reliance on complaints reporting has likely contributed to this increase.

## 6.2 Increasing (the strength and range of) penalties

Due to the lack of penalties available to the TGA, the majority of the submissions and interviewees, including TGA staff members, called for stronger and a more extensive range of penalties. Broadly, these calls ranged from the introduction of on-the-spot fines to civil and criminal penalties (including jail terms) where these did not exist previously under the Therapeutic Goods Act, and the publication of these enforcement actions on the TGA's website. There were calls to require corrective statements to be published in the same medium as the original advertisement. There were also calls for additional enforcement actions, such as the power to issue substantiation notices (e.g. to require sponsors to provide the information or documentation used to support a claim) and prevent the re-listing and re-registration of medicines previously cancelled from the ARTG for non-compliance.

Since 2014, there have been multiple amendments to the Therapeutic Goods Act to include criminal and civil penalties, and other forms of enforcement action. The *Therapeutic Goods Amendment (2016 Measures No. 1) Act 2017* (Cth) introduced a criminal penalty for failing to comply with a request by the Secretary of the Department of Health for information regarding a therapeutic good and its manufacture,[14] as well as an offence and a civil penalty for providing false or misleading information or documentation in response to such a request.[15] The *Therapeutic Goods Amendment (2017 Measures No. 1) Act 2018* (Cth) increased the range of enforcement actions available in responding to advertising (and other forms of information disseminated to the public) by introducing written (substantiation) notices[16] and directions.[17] Criminal and civil penalties and other general offences were introduced for advertising a medicine for an unapproved indication;[18] advertisements containing a prohibited or restricted representation, a representation implying that the medicine is government recommended or approved or a representation that otherwise includes an unauthorised reference to substances;[19] advertisements that do not comply with the Therapeutic Goods Advertising Code;[20] and a sponsor's failure to comply with a notice requesting information or documentation[21] or with a direction.[22] Civil penalties were introduced where previously criminal penalties only applied for advertising offences.[23] There was also an increase in the penalty for the ongoing offences under the Therapeutic Goods Act.[24] In addition, injunctions[25] were introduced, complementing the existing range of enforcement actions (including infringement notices and enforceable undertakings, which were first added to the Act in 2006 but historically were rarely used). In the *Therapeutic Goods and Other Legislation Amendment (Vaping Reforms) Act 2024* (Cth), introduced under the Labor government, enforceable directions[26] were also added to this existing range of enforcement actions. An updated version of the TGA's enforcement pyramid was published to reflect the increase in the range of penalties (see *Figure 6.1*). Although the overall number of levels has increased, the TGA pyramid in 2022 is rather similar in height to the pyramid in 2012 (see *Figure 3.1*). It also appears to integrate risk rationality more so into its design (potentially furthering the incompatibility issues with risk-based techniques, see Section 3.2.3).

While the expansion of the number and range of penalties and enforcement actions goes some way towards increasing punishment severity, they have little deterrent effect if the likelihood of punishment (i.e. punishment certainty) is low. Further, as one sponsor (7044:3) pointed out, 'it is not enough to have the powers available; the TGA must have the appetite to enforce those powers'. Data indicates that the lack of enforcement remains an ongoing problem. A study examining the TGA's response to advertising complaints between July 2018 and September 2019 (the period immediately after it took over from the CRP) found that 91.6% of the complaints were classified by the TGA as low priority and 'closed by merely sending an obligations letter with no follow-up', meaning that 'the TGA's new powers were rarely applied' (Harvey et al. 2021:87). This was despite the complaints and annual reports of the TGA detailing specific breaches of the Therapeutic

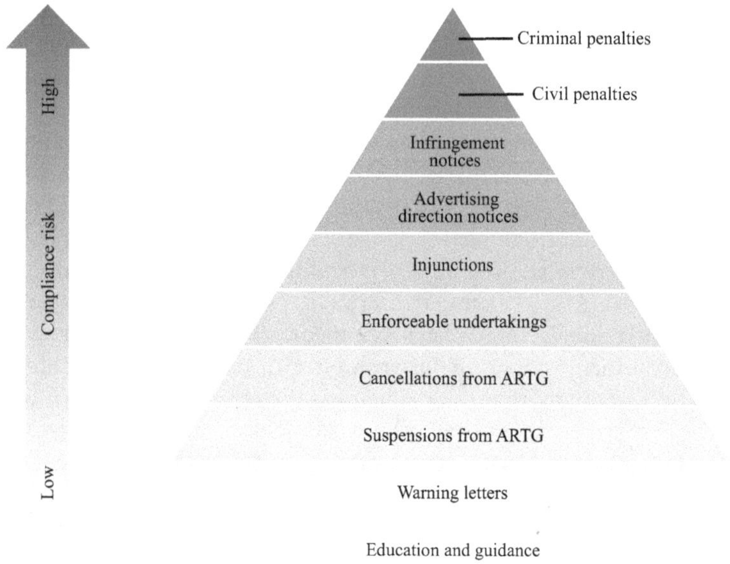


Adapted from TGA (2022c [shading direction in original]).

*Figure 6.1* The TGA's enforcement pyramid in 2022

Goods Act and Regulations and Therapeutic Goods Advertising Code (irrespective of their priority level assigned by the TGA). The authors identified several other issues. First, the priority level of complaints was determined on the basis of the product risk or direct physical harm to the public, not other forms of harm (such as financial harm or indirect physical harm caused by forgoing evidence-based treatment options). Also, the determination of these priority levels did not appear to take into account compliance risk, such as that indicated by previous CRP determinations or repeated non-compliance. Second, the TGA's publication of its actions on complaints was believed to be less transparent than the CRP's. Often the TGA only published the reference number and a statement of the action taken; rarely was information published about the complaint lodged or the product or advertiser subject to the complaint (Harvey et al. 2021:87). Finally, staffing and resourcing were identified as a concern.

Data from the TGA's annual reports indicates that the number of reports alleging advertising non-compliance has doubled since the TGA assumed responsibility for managing complaints in July of 2018. *Table 6.2* shows that between 2020–2021 and 2022–2023, the majority of complaints resulted in a request that the advertisement be removed or a warning letter. Of note is the higher proportion of infringement notices used by the TGA, typically 'as an alternative to undertaking formal court action' (TGA 2024e:para. 1). In 2022–2023, the total value of the infringement notices issued was AU$2,152,512 (an average of AU$9,440 per notice).

*Table 6.2* Number of enforcement actions by the TGA following advertising complaints between 2020–2021 and 2022–2023 financial years, by action type

| | *2020–2021* | *2021–2022* | *2022–2023* |
|---|---|---|---|
| No further action taken (e.g. no breach identified) | 328 | 334 | 1,589 |
| Number of advertisements requested for removal | 569 | 1,174 | 16,328 |
| Warning letter issued | 421 | 343 | 256 |
| Infringement notice issued | 127 | 110 | 228 |
| Civil cases commenced/in progress | 4 | 2 | 1 |
| Civil cases finalised | 0 | 2 | 0 |
| Criminal cases commenced/in progress | 0 | 0 | 1 |
| Criminal cases finalised | 0 | 2 | 1 |
| Referred to another internal or external party for action | 68 | 6 | 78 |
| Direction notice issued | 0 | 0 | 4 |
| Enforceable undertaking negotiated and/or entered | 2 | 0 | 1 |
| **Total** | **1,519** | **1,973**[a] | **18,487** |

*Source*: Adapted from TGA (2021d, 2022e, 2023c).

*Note.*

[a] In the annual report, the TGA (2022e:18) lists this total as 1,976. It has been adjusted in this table to reflect the total cumulative number of compliance actions recorded, as reported in the annual report.

Data on the outcomes of the TGA's compliance reviews indicates that notices (proposing to cancel a listing) or warning letters remain the primary action carried out (see *Table 6.3*). In 2022–2023, a small number of civil (two) and criminal (one) actions were commenced for non-compliant imported, exported, manufactured and supplied therapeutic goods; however, in the overwhelming majority of cases, warning letters were issued by the TGA (94%) and the goods were either not registered or listed on the ARTG (i.e. 98% were unauthorised therapeutic goods) (TGA 2023b:109–110).

In sum, despite the introduction of further penalties, these penalties are rarely used. The TGA (2022b:para. 2) has made it clear that '[i]n the first instance, the TGA will . . . work with the responsible entity to provide education and advice in order for that entity to achieve compliance' and that 'escalation' will only be considered if the sponsor 'has repeat breaches and is not willing to comply, and/or the alleged breach is such that there is a likely impact on the consumers' ability to use [the] therapeutic goods safely or appropriately'.

## 6.3 Increasing resourcing

While most of the submissions and interviewees agreed that further resourcing of the TGA was necessary to enhance its capacity to regulate, suggestions

*Table 6.3* Number of compliance actions recorded by the TGA following compliance reviews between the 2015–2016 and 2020–2021 financial years, by action type

| *Action(s) following a request for information* | *2015–2016* | *2016–2017* | *2017–2018* | *2018–2019* | *2019–2020* | *2020–2021* |
|---|---|---|---|---|---|---|
| Medicines found to be compliant and review concluded | 81 | 87 | 42 | 38 | 41 | 6 |
| Medicines cancelled by the TGA without a proposal to cancel notice | 0 | 0 | 0 | 0 | 0 | 0 |
| Proposal to cancel notice or warning sent by the TGA | 327 | 330 | 129 | 102 | 119 | 39 |
| **Total** | **408** | **417** | **171** | **140** | **160** | **45** |
| **Actions following the proposal to cancel notice** | | | | | | |
| Medicines cancelled by the TGA | 44 | 17 | 10 | 3 | 7 | 6 |
| Medicines cancelled by sponsors after being notified of compliance breaches | 76 | 84 | 45 | 29 | 38 | 18 |
| Reviews concluded after compliance breaches assessed | 207 | 229 | 74 | 70 | 59 | 15 |
| **Total** | **327** | **330** | **129** | **102** | **104** | **39** |
| *Medicines no longer on the ARTG* | *0* | *0* | *55* | *32* | *45* | *24* |

*Source*: Adapted from TGA (2016e, 2017a, 2018a, 2019a, 2020a, 2021c).

on how best to source the required funding were contentious and varied. Industry has consistently opposed an increase in fees and charges to cover the cost of any reform proposal from which they will not derive benefit. For example, sponsors stated that:

> access to TGA information will largely be for public benefit rather than the benefit of industry who are reasonably familiar with the details. . . . These costs, which could be quite substantial, should not be from industry.
>
> (Sponsor 4:1)

> These activities should . . . be subject to government funding as general public health initiatives are not as [sic] part of TGA fees for evaluations.
>
> (Sponsor 105:6)

Although the Australian Government has stated that it prefers to maintain the current cost recovery arrangement, funding was allocated to the TGA in recent federal budgets to meet the costs of specific government initiatives. In the 2016–2017 Budget, the Liberal government allocated a total of AU$20.4 million to fund the implementation of the recommendations of the *Review of Medicines and Medical Devices Regulation* over the following four years; the ongoing costs of implementation, however, were to be met by the existing cost recovery arrangements (Australian Government 2016:106). In the 2019–2020 Budget, AU$33 million was allocated for a four-year period and an additional AU$15 million per year from 2022 to 2023 to fund the Orphan Drugs, Special Access Scheme and Authorised Prescribers programmes, all of which are aimed at increasing access to prescription medicines. It was not until the 2023–2024 Budget of the incumbent Labor government that funding was allocated to those 'public good activities' that cannot be cost recovered (TGA 2023a:5). Over the next four years, AU$61 million in funding is being allocated to meet the costs of 'compliance and enforcement for products and companies *outside* the regulatory system', meaning, unauthorised therapeutic goods and sponsors, and 'providing information to consumers and healthcare professionals', as well as other aspects of therapeutic goods regulation (TGA 2023a:5 [emphasis added]). How much funding is being allocated to each area is not clear. However, the TGA's Cost Recovery Implementation Statement indicates that 'freed up cost recovered funds' will be used by the TGA 'to increase its service delivery to industry' (TGA 2023a:5).

## 6.4 Increasing transparency

The submissions and interviewees overwhelmingly agreed that there must be increased transparency of both the TGA and the regulatory regime. They highlighted the need for greater communication by the TGA about the extent to which it regulates prescription and non-prescription medicines; the information that is available through its website (e.g. on PI, CMI and AusPARs); and ADR and complaints reporting. There was also agreement that the information provided by the TGA had to be more accessible to the public and independent (i.e. not industry produced), and that the TGA's website had to be redeveloped to increase its accessibility. Moreover, the submissions and interviewees called for the transparency of medicine information and data to be increased, including greater access to and disclosure of the information provided to and evaluated by the TGA during applications for listing and registration, and in relation to evaluations, ADR data and TGA committee meeting minutes, as well as information otherwise relating to the medicine's safety and efficacy. This included calls to review current commercial confidentiality policies to reduce the barriers to accessing information and expand PI, CMI and AusPARs to a wider range of therapeutic goods. In addition, the submissions and interviewees referred to the need for greater transparency of the TGA's enforcement, including increased access to and disclosure of information relating to its enforcement actions and their results and the basis (or decision-making) for such actions.

### *6.4.1 TGA website and ADR reporting*

Over the past decade, the TGA website has been updated to include 'education resources' using 'plain English' and 'infographics and videos'; but as the Labor government conceded, the 'TGA's industry cost recovery model . . . limits a very significant extension of [these] consumer outreach activities' (Australian Government 2023:19). The TGA website is undergoing a complete redevelopment. As part of its Digital Transformation Strategy, first announced in late 2019, the TGA indicated that it will carry out an audit and rewrite of the content on its website, redevelop the website's architecture (to improve access to information), and develop 'digital self-service options' (Australian Government 2023:19). The TGA has also indicated that it will implement a Consumer Engagement Strategy to 'positively influence consumer health' by 'providing quality and tailored information' and 'designing solutions that meet consumers' needs and empowers [*sic*] them to have informed decisions with health professionals', among other stated aims (Australian Government 2023:18–19). The implementation of these strategies will likely be funded using part of the AU$61 million the TGA received in the 2023–2024 Budget.[27] Since they remain ongoing, it is not possible to evaluate their implications for the public or for regulatory and health literacy (except, perhaps, in terms of the length of time it has taken to enact such changes). However, it is possible to evaluate the impacts of these strategies in relation to ADRs and their reporting, given that ADRs have been under-reported historically and there have been attempts by the TGA to improve reporting during the past decade.

In 2013, the TGA established the Database of Adverse Event Notifications (DAEN), which contains information on the ADR reported to the TGA. As of 30 June 2024, DAEN contains just under 630,000 ADR reports (accessible as far back as 1971—see TGA 2024c). The homepage of the TGA website was updated to include direct links to DAEN and the online Adverse Event Management System to report ADRs. This system is accompanied by information tailored to the public on how to report an ADR and what to include in the report (separate information is also provided for health professionals and sponsors). In 2018, the TGA also introduced the Black Triangle Scheme. This scheme, which is similar to those used in the UK and EU, requires sponsors to display a black triangle on the PI, CMI or similar materials (including AusPARs) to communicate to health professionals and the public that a medicine is newly registered or registered for a new use and to report ADR associated with it (TGA 2022a, 2024b). Sponsors must use a black triangle on these materials for up to five years (TGA 2022a).

Since the introduction of the Black Triangle Scheme, there has been a 'marginal' increase in adverse event reporting (Li et al. 2020). The TGA's annual reports indicate that adverse event reporting by health professionals has remained relatively consistent over the past decade—between 10% and 20% of the overall number of reports submitted (TGA 2014c and 2014d to 2023b). Reporting by the public, however, increased from as low as 3% in 2018–2019 to as high as 23% in 2021–2022 (TGA 2019a:38, 2022d:70). There was also an increase in the number of reports made by state and territory health departments during this period (from 15% to 55%—see TGA 2019a:38, 2022d:70). But most of the adverse events reported in 2021–2022 were for vaccines (86%), COVID-19 vaccines in particular (more than 79% of the total number of adverse events reports) (TGA 2022d:9, 70). Therefore, the recent increases in adverse event reporting are likely due to the increased and active monitoring of COVID-19 vaccines and their adverse events by the TGA and state and territory health departments, and the communication and ready availability of information to the public on the adverse events associated with COVID-19 vaccines and the reporting of them (i.e. in the materials provided to members of the public at the point of vaccination). In the latest TGA annual report, adverse event reporting appears to be on the decline, with less than 10% of all adverse events reports made by the public in 2022–2023 (TGA 2023b:84).

### *6.4.2 Medicine information*

Most of the submissions by industry demonstrated a reluctance to publish information about medicines beyond the level that is already provided. Some of these submissions argued that such disclosure will increase the cost to sponsors and may in fact hinder health literacy because of the misconceptions the public and health professionals could draw from its release. For example, with regard to updating and maintaining a record of updates for PI documents, a sponsor (402:3–4) commented that:

> [t]he cost of an application [to vary a PI and/or ARTG entry], the lack of company-sponsored trials, the resource intensive process of conducting a systematic literature review to support a literature-based submission and the lack of patent protection are barriers to updating PI documents for older ingredients to better reflect new indications and current practice. . . . The suggestion of maintaining a file of superseded PI documents is not supported as it may lead prescribers to outdated information about a medicine and/or cause unnecessary confusion.[28]

Some industry submissions classed the information that is typically sought by the public as commercial-in-confidence, even if this information is not necessarily defined as such in law. For example, the following statements were provided in the submissions:

> [Our organisation] does not support disclosure of product information in relation to ingredients/formulas as this encroaches on commercial-in-confidence details. The complementary medicine industry already struggles with the lack of exclusivity/data protection available impacting on competitiveness and innovation in the market. . . . [P]ublicly disclosing additional product information would not benefit consumers but lessen the forces of competition.
>
> (Industry association 41:1)

> [T]he process for supporting indications should be carefully explained to the public, [as] a sponsor's information on evidence for specific products is commercially sensitive, and should not be made public. Considerable time, expertise and expense can be involved in obtaining suitable evidence of efficacy, therefore, details should remain confidential.
>
> (Sponsor 4:1)

> Most product registration information is a trade secret, except for the limited information published by TGA after registration. To the extent to which any of the information in a product dossier is not a 'trade secret', that information is nevertheless of significant commercial value (for example, but without limitation, the filing date, shelf life, bioequivalence justifications, indications claimed, formulation and manufacturing process information).
>
> (Industry association 418:8–9)

> [T]he CCI [commercially confidential information] property interests at stake represent fundamental rights accorded the owners of the information. Setting these rights aside by disclosing CCI, even in cases of

> an overriding public interest, results in total destruction of the property right, and consequently real injury. This means that an abstract 'public interest in transparency' cannot justify release of CCI in any specific case.
>
> (Sponsor 412:2)

Some submissions by industry also argued that the type of information commonly sought by the public is already made available and that the issue was simply that there is a need to communicate the availability of this information and/or increase its accessibility. In this regard, the industry submissions included the following observations:

> the focus of the transparency initiatives should be on providing existing information in a more consumer friendly format rather than disclosing ever more details where there is already broad disclosure . . . The TGA should approach extended information disclosure with caution, to ensure that unintended consequences of unnecessary and inappropriate disclosure does [sic] not unduly damage the innovative capability of the pharmaceutical industry and act as a disincentive to bring medicines to Australia. . . . AusPARs appropriately provides detailed disclosure on a product including the objective assessment of benefit and risk.
>
> (Industry association 81:2)

> We strongly believe that if the TGA would clearly and effectively communicate to the consumer the way it assesses and regulates CM [complementary/complementary medicines] listed medicines compared to registered medicine—including why different considerations apply and highlighting the strong safety record of CM, [and] the different nature and purpose of these types of medicines—the consumer could make a better informed choice.
>
> (Sponsor 92:4)

The TGA, nonetheless, has proceeded with making a number of changes to the way in which prescription medicine information is communicated to the public and health professionals. In 2017, it made multiple changes to the format of the PI, which came into effect in 2018. Among these changes were a reordering of the content, with key information moved to the front of the document, and the inclusion of a date of revision section (including a table summarising the changes made) located at the end of the document (TGA 2024h). But Yuan (2020) believes that this change to the format of the PI (which closely resembles that within the documentation used in the EU) was made with minimal consultation within or 'user testing' among health professionals and was based on the TGA's own reviews and assessments. Interviews conducted by Yuan (2020:134–135) with health professionals found that the new PI format did not overcome the existing issues associated with

PI regarding length, technicality, amount of text and difficulty in locating information. Moreover, these health professionals expressed a preference for using CMI (updates to which are not evaluated by the TGA) and the Australian Medicines Handbook, because these were simpler, only using PI when they required more detailed information (Yuan 2020:139).

In addition, the TGA developed a database that lists those applications for prescription medicines under evaluation by the TGA (see TGA 2024g). A separate database containing the decision summaries following the TGA's evaluation of these applications was also developed, and the summaries are available for evaluations made as far back as late 2019 (TGA 2024f). The summaries provide a general or broad statement of the TGA's evaluations. For example, they usually state that a decision was 'based on quality (chemistry and manufacturing), nonclinical (pharmacology and toxicology), clinical (pharmacology, safety and efficacy) [data] and [the] risk management plan . . . submitted by the sponsor', but they do not provide further detail. The summaries also state the type of clinical trials submitted by the sponsor as part of their application, including their design (e.g. as being blinded/not blinded, randomised/nonrandomised and/or placebo-controlled/ non-placebo-controlled) and phase (Phase I, II or III), but usually no further detail. PI does provide a detailed summary of the clinical trials supporting a medicine's safety and efficacy but will rarely provide details that enable the reader to locate the clinical trial or publications associated with the data. In the consultation *Mechanisms to maintain the currency of approved Product Information (PI) and Consumer Medicine Information (CMI)*, the TGA (2013f:9, emphasis in original) made clear 'that the PI does *not*, nor is it intended to[,] represent a historical record of all known information or published studies on the particular medicine'.

### *6.4.3 Enforcement*

In 2011, the TGA began publishing on its website information about its enforcement actions and outcomes, including actions taken on advertising complaints (those referred to it by the CRP, from 2011), cancellations (from 2012), court actions (from 2013), enforceable undertakings (also from 2013) and suspensions (from 2015). Initially, these actions were published in a dedicated 'Compliance & other regulatory actions' section on the website (in the 'About the TGA' section), but the types of actions published were primarily those against listed complementary medicines and medical devices[29] and not all of this information appeared to be up to date. As of 1 July 2018, the information on compliance undertakings taken by the TGA available on its website only covered cases up until December 2014 (see TGA 2018c)—either the TGA had not performed any of these types of actions since 2014 or it was not reporting them. Action taken in response to advertising complaints that resulted in the issue of a Regulation 9 Order was likewise only available for cases prior to December 2014 (see TGA 2018d). And as Vickers and Harvey

(2021:80) and Harvey et al. (2021:87) note, there were limitations to the TGA's reporting on advertising complaints, at least up until mid-2018 and September 2019 (the end date for these studies).

At the time of writing (mid-2024), the TGA publishes information on cancellations and suspensions, recalls,[30] advertising directions and notices, infringement notices, undertakings, civil and criminal actions and the general outcomes of compliance reviews and advertising complaints, in a dedicated 'Compliance and enforcement hub'. Many (but not all) of the entries contained in this hub are hyperlinked to a searchable sponsor database (located at TGA 2024i), allowing users to search some of the activities carried out in connection to each sponsor. The TGA's annual 'performance' reports also publish data summarising these enforcement actions.

Some of the information the TGA publishes on these actions still appears to be incomplete. A case in point are infringement notices, which, after warning letters, are one of the most common enforcement actions used by the TGA. Infringement notices are published as an itemised list on a single webpage. This list does not provide a search function or filters (to sort notices by date, sponsor and so on); essentially, you must scroll to the bottom of the webpage or use the control find keyboard shortcut to locate a particular infringement notice (using the correct terms). Each entry on this list states those sections of the Therapeutic Goods Act contravened by the sponsor and the status of the notice (e.g. whether it has been issued, paid, withdrawn or reissued). But the name of the sponsor and the amount of the fine are not always stated. Some (but not all) of the infringement notices listed are hyperlinked to a TGA news item or media release; however, the level of detail provided in each item or release varies. Caruso's Natural Health Pty Ltd, for instance, received five infringement notices in March 2024 for 'an alleged failure to hold information or evidence to support five therapeutic uses in relation to three medicines' (TGA 2024a:para. 1). These notices amounted to a total of AU$82,000. However, the media release does not state the names of the medicines or which indications were found to be unsupported, and these infringement notices do not appear in the sponsor database entry for Caruso's Natural Health Pty Ltd either.

## 6.5 Reinforcing hegemonic neoliberal governmentality

Despite the promise of reform and the consultations that followed, neoliberal governmentality has only increased in the medicine regulatory regime. Risk rationality was used to reject the implementation of techniques that increase the regulation of listed medicines, promotion to health professionals and DTCA on the basis that they were deemed to be incommensurate with product risk. Economic rationality was also routinely used to reject the implementation of techniques on the basis that they were too costly for the government and TGA to implement, and for industry to comply with. In addition, responsibilisation was used to reject forms of government intervention that undermine existing self-regulatory techniques. Because they represent a rationality (and policy) of the government, techniques of regulation need to balance the public's interest with industry's (and therefore, industry viability). As a result, the implementation of techniques is regularly rationalised on the basis of product risk, the cost of the techniques and their capacity to responsibilise. Techniques that are in the public's interest are not often able to withstand such rationalities and are therefore easily rejected. In this way, these rationalities privilege the implementation of techniques that are compatible with neoliberal governmentality (and derogate those techniques that are incompatible with it). The extent to which these rationalities shape the regime to align with the neoliberal rationale of limiting state intervention—except when such intervention happens to be compatible with the neoliberal project—reflects not only the pervasiveness but also the embeddedness of hegemonic neoliberal governmentality and the extent to which the state is conditioned (indeed, neoliberalised) in terms of its facilitation of this project.

Some reforms were made to benefit the public's interests, but in ways that did not undermine the interests of industry (or other groups whose interests also happened to be compatible with the neoliberal project). Established sources of evidence and permissible indications were implemented for listed medicines, rather than requiring sponsors to supply evidence substantiating their efficacy claims. The majority of the indications developed do not require substantiation by the scientific literature. A second, TGA-assessed approval process was implemented for listed medicines instead of having the TGA assess all applications for listing. This approval process has rarely been used by sponsors and the extent to which applications are assessed by the TGA is not clear. The number of random and targeted compliance reviews for listed medicines was only temporarily increased; the lack of punishment certainty (and reliance instead on punishment severity or threat) has led to a negligible change in compliance rates and subsequently a reduction in the number of reviews. Rather than place further restrictions on the payments made by industry to health professionals, a database listing these payments was implemented (at the initiative of an industry association). Reporting is only mandatory for members of that association and excludes certain types of (and therefore, under-reports) payments. TGA intervention in DTCA complaints coincided with the abolishment of advertising pre-approval (in spite of calls to expand it to all advertisements). It also coincided with an increase in the number of complaints. Penalties (punishment severity) were increased, but their use (punishment certainty) was minimal by the TGA; and the focus of the TGA continues to be on getting sponsors to cooperate so that it can avoid the use of penalties. The TGA was provided with further funding, but largely for the purpose of providing the public and health professionals with more information (in terms of the former, to 'positively influence' and 'empower' them). The information provided is often incomplete and lacking detail (and therefore continues to be shaped by asymmetries of knowledge/power).

These reforms only reinforce—even, increase—the shift in regulatory responsibility and the turn to micro-level techniques. In the case of the public, making more information available (transparent) and accessible incentivises increased participation by the public in the regime—to accumulate the information provided (and increase their health and regulatory literacy), to make reports and so on. Information transparency and accessibility are therefore indispensable to neoliberal governmentality; they facilitate the deregulation of the regime and increased responsibilisation and thereby micro-level techniques of governance that only reinforce (and do not work contrary to) neoliberal governmentality (Adams 2018:4). In so doing, neoliberal governmentality shapes (and facilitates an illusion of) agency.

Neoliberal governmentality in the medicine regulatory regime is not just an industry-led project either. When the interests of health professionals and the government and TGA did not align with those of the public, this increased the alignment and incorporation of these interests with those of industry, and the formation of a common interest. Together, these interests further lent support to and facilitated the implementation of neoliberal governmentality.

These findings suggest that not only is medicine regulation not 'better' but also that neoliberalism itself is not regulatable. In fact, it is reinforcing of itself. 'Better' techniques of regulating that are inherently unable to withstand neoliberal rationality, and economic rationality in particular, will continue to be shaped (indeed, rejected) by this project. As such, neoliberal rationality is particularly difficult to disrupt (hence its pervasiveness and hegemonic status). The implication, then, is that harm reduction is likely only achievable through more substantive, social transformation, and not by way of reforming and continuing to work with the existing neoliberal project.

## Notes

1 For example, a sponsor (174:10) argued that if they 'cannot reasonably bring these low risk products to market without great expense . . . [they] may have to opt out of the complementary medicine side of the business and focus on other aspects of the business (e.g., food manufacturing)'.

2 Starting at AU$520 for the application fee and AU$1,978 for the evaluation fee. However, the application fee can be up to AU$2,136 and evaluation fee up to AU$16,387 (TGA 2024d:13–15).

3 A further 1,088 applications were for export-only listed medicines (ARTG 2024).

4 The database contains some of the reports made from 2016 to 2019, but mostly those made from 2020. Listed alphabetically, those companies with reports in this database are as follows: A. Menarini Australia Pty Ltd, AbbVie, Alexion Pharmaceuticals Australasia Pty Ltd, Amgen, Astellas Pharma, AstraZeneca Australia, Bayer Australia, BeiGene, Besins Healthcare, Biogen Australia, BioMarin Pharmaceutical Australia Pty Ltd, Boehringer Ingelheim, Bristol-Myers Squibb, Celgene Pty Ltd, CSL Vifor, Eisai, Eli Lilly Australia, Gilead Sciences, GlaxoSmithKline Australia Pty Ltd, Ipsen Pty Ltd, Janssen-Cilag Pty Ltd, Merck Healthcare Pty Ltd, Merck Sharp & Dohme (Australia) Pty Ltd, Norgine Pty Ltd, Novartis Pharmaceutical Australia Pty Ltd, Novo Nordisk, Organon Australia, Pfizer Ltd, PTC Therapeutics Australia Pty Ltd, Roche, Sanofi, Takeda Pharmaceuticals Australia Pty Ltd, UCB Pharma and Vertex Australia.

5 In the form of payments made to health professionals for hospitality (food and beverages) and small amounts of travel (e.g. taxis) to attend or provide services at an educational event and to administer an industry-run event (which includes hospitality, but also venue hire, event organisation and so on); this also includes payments made to health professionals for hospitality at third-party (non-industry) run events (Parker et al. 2019:5).

6 This includes Aboriginal and Torres Strait Islander health practitioners, Chinese medicine practitioners, chiropractors, dental practitioners, medical radiation practitioners, medical practitioners, nurses, midwives, occupational therapists, osteopaths, paramedics, physiotherapists, podiatrists and psychologists (Department of Health and Aged Care 2023).

7 Formerly the Chair of the Australian Pharmaceutical Advisory Council (1991 to 2000) and Pharmaceutical Benefits Committee (2001–2012), during which time he was involved in the development and review of the NMP (University of Sydney 2014).

8 Formerly held executive positions at MSD and AstraZeneca in Australia and Europe, a board member and the chairman of MA, and a director at Pharmaxis (MA 2020).

9 Formerly the Australian Government's Chief Medical Officer (2003–2009).

10 The exception being advertisements containing restricted representations.

11 It is worth noting that the lack of officiality provided to industry associations to pre-approve advertisements and the potential risk of liability in the event that incorrect or adverse advice is provided may have contributed to the production of these terms (and indemnity provisions) by CHP Australia.

12 For advertisements in specified media, see Section 3.4.5.2.

13 The way in which the data is reported in the TGA's annual reports—that is, as the total number of *reports* received versus the total number of *allegations* received relating to COVID-19—does not facilitate an accurate comparison of this data to determine the proportion of complaints that were COVID-19 related.

14 Amounts to 400 penalty units (s. 41AC of the Therapeutic Goods Act).

15 This includes up to 12 months' imprisonment or 1,000 penalty units or both for an offence (s. 41AD, 41AE) and up to 5,000 penalty units for an individual and 50,000 penalty units for a body corporate for a civil penalty (s. 41AF).

16 That is, to request that the sponsor provide information or documentation regarding an advertisement (see s. 42DR of the Therapeutic Goods Act).

17 For advertisements, such direction can include ceasing the advertisement, making a retraction or correction, recovering an advertisement in circulation, destroying an advertisement or ceasing a claim or representation made in the advertisement. Directions for other forms of information disseminated to the public can include its withdrawal, making a retraction or correction, recovering information in circulation, destroying the information or ceasing a claim or representation made in the information disseminated (see s. 42DV of the Therapeutic Goods Act).

18 That is, up to 5,000 penalty units for individuals and 50,000 penalty units for body corporates for a civil penalty (s. 21B(4) of the Therapeutic Goods Act) or five years' imprisonment or 4,000 penalty units or both for an offence (s. 22(2), (3)).

19 Up to 5,000 penalty units for an individual and 50,000 penalty units for a body corporate for a civil penalty (s. 42DLB of the Therapeutic Goods Act, complementing the existing criminal penalties in s. 42DL).

20 For advertising, 5,000 penalty units for individuals and 50,000 penalty units for body corporates for a civil penalty (s. 42DMA of the Therapeutic Goods Act, complementing the existing criminal penalties in s. 42DM). The penalties for offences are less for generic information disseminated in non-compliance with the Therapeutic Goods Advertising Code—up to 12 months' imprisonment or 1,000

penalty units or both for offences (s. 42DP). Civil penalties for disseminating such information are otherwise the same as those for advertisements (s. 42DQ).

21 Up to 500 penalty units for offences (s. 42DS(1) to (3) of the Therapeutic Goods Act), except where the information provided to the Secretary is false or misleading—this offence can include up to 12 months' imprisonment or 1,000 penalty units (s. 42DS(4) to (6)). Civil penalties for providing false or misleading information are up to 5,000 penalty units for an individual and 50,000 penalty units for a body corporate (s. 42DT).

22 Up to five years' imprisonment or 4,000 penalty units or both for an offence (s. 42DW of the Therapeutic Goods Act) or up to 5,000 penalty units for an individual and 50,000 penalty units for a body corporate for a civil penalty (s. 42DX).

23 For example, s. 22(5) of the Therapeutic Goods Act.

24 These revisions are specific to s. 22, 42DL, 42DM and 42DP. In all of these provisions except the last one, the penalties were increased to up to five years' imprisonment or 4,000 penalty units or both.

25 To restrict a sponsor from engaging in non-compliance (restricting injunction), for continuing not to comply (performance injunction), or on an interim basis (interim injunction) (s. 42YN and 42YO of the Therapeutic Goods Act).

26 If the Secretary believes that a sponsor is not complying with the Act, they can give enforceable directions to the sponsor (by written notice) to take steps to rectify the compliance issue within a specified time period. Such directions can include (re)labelling or repackaging the good so that it complies, destroying or disposing of the good, or other directions as specified elsewhere in the Act (s. 42YT of the Therapeutic Goods Act).

27 The Australian Government referred to the Strategy alongside this funding in its response to the *Inquiry into Approval Processes for New Drugs and Novel Medical Device Technologies in Australia* (see Australian Government 2023:19).

28 This sponsor (402:3) suggested an alternative approach whereby the findings of recent peer review journal articles be added 'via an abridged evaluation process with associated reduced fees'.

29 For example, the cancellations page in the 'Compliance actions' section listed the cancellations of complementary medicines and medical devices only (TGA 2017b). The TGA did have a separate page containing a list of cancellations that were conducted at the request of sponsors, which included cancellations requested by sponsors of registered medicines (see TGA 2018b); but these cancellations did not necessarily occur on compliance grounds.

30 In 2012, the TGA established a database for recalls called the System for Australian Recall Actions (SARA).

# 7 Conclusion

Weeks before the first recorded cases of COVID-19, Mundipharma Pty Ltd (Mundipharma) was issued 24 infringement notices by the TGA for the 'misleading, imbalanced and otherwise inaccurate' advertising of Targin to health professionals, totalling AU$302,400 (TGA 2019b:para. 2). Targin, a prescription pain reliever containing both oxycodone (an opioid) and naloxone (used to treat opioid-induced constipation), was first registered in Australia in May 2010 (TGA 2024j). In a media release published on 20 December 2019, the TGA (2019b:paras. 3–4) stated that the promotional materials 'appeared to positively encourage' health professionals to prescribe Targin, representing it 'as a core component' of a pain management strategy using multiple medications for chronic (long-term) pain. It is recommended that opioids only be used to treat acute pain or chronic pain caused by cancer because the evidence of their effectiveness in treating non-chronic, non-cancer pain is lacking and they are addictive and can cause opioid dependence, overdose, hospitalisation or death (Australian Institute of Health and Welfare (AIHW) 2018:viii, 3). The TGA noted that the advertising breached the MA Code and emphasised that sponsors agree to comply with the Code as a condition of registration, irrespective of their membership of MA.

However, there is more to this case than the media release. Mundipharma is a subsidiary of Mundipharma International, which is based in the UK and owned by the Sackler family. The Sacklers also own Purdue Pharma based in the US. In the US, Purdue Pharma and the Sacklers face ongoing civil litigation for 'injuries allegedly caused by their deceptive marketing' of OxyContin, a prescription pain reliever and opioid found in 2007 to be misbranded as 'less addictive' and 'less subject to abuse . . . than other pain medications' (Harrington, United States Trustee, Region 2 v. Purdue Pharma L. P. et al. 2023:3).

Mundipharma had been a member of MA up until the 2015–2016 financial year (see MA 2016:9), after which it withdrew its membership. In the 2017–2018 financial year, MA received three complaints about a 'non-member', which it later told *Pharma in Focus*[1] had been made against Mundipharma (Ma 2019). According to MA (2018:3), it invited the non-member to participate in the adjudication of the complaint at its Code

DOI: 10.4324/9781003285762-7

of Conduct Committee but the non-member declined, and so MA referred the complaint to the TGA. Dr Simon Holliday, a NSW-based general practitioner, confirmed to the *ABC* and *Pharma in Focus* that he had submitted one of the three complaints to MA in 2017–2018 and that the complaint had concerned a brochure for Targin (Branley 2019a; Ma 2019). He alleged that the brochure had claimed that weaker opioids (such as codeine) were less effective than stronger ones (like oxycodone) for the fictitious patient depicted in the brochure, described as suffering from moderate to severe chronic osteoarthritis (Branley 2019a). The Faculty of Pain and Royal Australian College of General Practitioners also alleged that the brochure to have made inaccurate claims about their recommendations regarding the appropriate use of opioids (Branley 2019a; Dow 2018). When the complaint did not proceed to the MA Code of Conduct Committee, Dr Holliday claimed that he took the complaint to the TGA but did not receive a response; he had been waiting for a response for more than a year at the time the *ABC* published the article on 9 July 2019 (Branley 2019a). According to the *ABC* article, a spokesperson from the TGA stated that the agency had written to Mundipharma but implied that the TGA could do little more because therapeutic goods advertising laws explicitly exclude advertising to health professionals. The TGA spokesperson argued that practitioners have the 'critical analytical skills' to 'question claims in promotional materials that may be perceived to mislead a consumer' (Branley 2019a). The spokesperson also said that '[t]he TGA expects prescription medicine sponsors to engage constructively with the self-regulatory system, irrespective of whether they are members of the industry body concerned' (Branley 2019a). A spokesperson from Mundipharma rejected the article's claim that the brochure was misleading.

The *ABC* was not the first media outlet to publish on this potentially misleading brochure. Dow (2018) published an article on the same brochure for *The Sydney Morning Herald* more than a year earlier, on 3 April 2018. It was not the first time that Mundipharma had been subject to this type of complaint at the MA Code of Conduct Committee either. In 2002–2003, the Committee found that a visual used in promotional material for OxyContin 'had the potential to mislead prescribers and encourage broader use of this product than was appropriate', and it requested that Mundipharma withdraw and no longer use this material (MA 2003:11). Two other complaints for Norspan (an opioid patch) in 2007–2008 and Targin in 2013–2014 were not upheld by the Committee (MA 2008:55–56; 2014:35–37). The former concerned a presentation at a continuing medical education event hosted by Mundipharma and alleged the non-disclosure of side effects by the company. In the latter case, which went to appeal, the health professional who made the complaint contended that the claim in the promotional material 'was misleading by omission because it was not qualified by a statement that the product [Targin] gives short-term relief from pain . . . [and did not provide] any statement that there was no long term quality of life improvement or improvement in function' (MA 2014:37). Members of the Appeals

Committee were unanimous in their agreement that Mundipharma's advertising material did not breach the Code; however, the Committee:

> suggested that Mundipharma consider whether any qualification of the term 'chronic' [used in the promotional material] would assist other healthcare professionals to correctly interpret that the advertisements do not encourage the long term use of opioid analgesics and do not imply that these products are effective for the long term.
>
> (MA 2014:37)

Mundipharma maintained that it was not in breach of the MA Code in this and the two other complaints heard by the Code of Conduct Committee. All three complaints were determined against sections 1.1 (responsibility) and 1.3 (false or misleading claims) of the Code.

On 1 August 2019 in the Senate, Senator Stirling Griff (Centre Alliance) questioned Senator Michaelia Cash (Liberal Party), who was representing the Minister for Health, on the TGA's response to Mundipharma following the publication of the *ABC* article. Senator Griff asked Senator Cash why the Therapeutic Goods Advertising Code did not also apply to advertising directed at health professionals. In her reply, Senator Cash stated that it is the expectation of the government that sponsors 'engage constructively' with self-regulation (Australian Senate 2019:1471). Senator Cash also confirmed that the TGA was 'currently seeking further information from Mundipharma' to determine whether the advertising of Targin had violated a condition of Targin's registration (Australian Senate 2019:1471), which, as discussed previously in this book (e.g. see Sections 3.4.1 and 3.4.5.3), can result in a medicine's cancellation from the ARTG, as well as civil or criminal penalties. In a follow-up question, Senator Griff asked whether the Liberal government would 'actually commit' to redrafting the Therapeutic Goods Advertising Code to address this 'loophole', to which Senator Cash responded by saying that 'in the event that there was a loophole or there was something that was discovered, the minister obviously would take the appropriate action' (Australian Senate 2019:1472).

Following the receipt of the infringement notices, a spokesperson from Mundipharma stated publicly that although the sponsor 'respectfully disagrees' with the determination made by the TGA, it otherwise 'respects' the importance of the TGA and MA in regulating sponsors of registered medicines and 'will continue to strengthen' its practices to ensure its compliance (Branley 2019b). Over the decade to 2016, opioid-induced deaths 'increased substantially' in Australia, accounting for 62% (1,119) of drug-induced deaths in 2016, with '[l]egal or pharmaceutical opioids (including codeine and oxycodone) . . . responsible for far more deaths and poisoning hospitalisations than illegal opioids (such as heroin)' (AIHW 2018:viii, 46). In 2018, opioid-induced deaths further increased, accounting for 64.5% (1,123) of drug-induced deaths, with pharmaceutical opioids accounting for 70%

of these deaths (ABS 2019). This compares to the 'peak' total number of opioid-induced deaths in 1999 of 1,245 (AIHW 2018:46). Before the end of the 2018–2019 financial year, Mundipharma earned AU$461 million pre-rebate for medicines it supplied on the Repatriation PBS, with 'its biggest earner' being Targin, at over AU$70 million per year (Brodie 2019:para. 10).

The harms resulting from the regulatory failure in the Mundipharma case are far from exceptional; indeed, they have a long-standing and well-established cause.

## 7.1 Why regulation regularly fails

Neoliberal governmentality has been a state-led and state-facilitated hegemonic project in Australia, including in the context of Australia's medicine regulatory regime. It is a product of the Australian settler colonialism/capitalism that emerged in the late 18th and early 19th centuries and the pursuit for a 'new' liberal capitalism in the mid- to late 20th century, as detailed in Chapter 2. Perceived racial differences in health (and immunity) and the development of techniques of governing quarantine (and incidentally, race) through the Quarantine Act enabled the objectification of people, medicines and health. Ultimately, this objectification led to the commodification of health and subjectification of individuals. The creation of these colonial differences represents the underlying historical cause of the 'modern' harms of hegemonic neoliberal governmentality. Health and medicines became increasingly defined by economic rationality. Since the mid-20th century, the costs of medicines have been negotiated directly with prescription medicine sponsors to obtain a reduction in prices and savings, and general patients have been required to cover some of these costs through the PBS co-payment. This is because hegemonic governmentality is and always has been inherently capitalist in the Australian context and has an emphasis on individualism (hence, why it is best described as social liberal capitalism). Towards the end of the 20th century, these costs were passed increasingly onto the public, rationalised on the basis of further individualising responsibility (or indeed, 'helping yourself'). Not only did this make technologies of health, such as the PBS, more economical, but participation in health by the public also became more individualised and active (and therefore less socialised and passive). Health promotion became a technique to increase the participation of (or more accurately, subject) the public, specifically, by supplying and requiring the public to accumulate the information necessary for their health literacy.

Economic rationality was pivotal to hegemonic governmentality becoming neoliberal in the later 20th century. The Department of Health became 'leaner' and 'more economical', rationalising the decentralisation of the medicine regulatory regime and increasing the use of self-regulatory techniques in the late 1980s and throughout the 1990s. Responsibility was delegated to MA (formerly the APMA) and CHP Australia (formerly PMAA and ASMI) for promotion to health professionals and pre-approving DTCA in *specified media*, respectively. Although a legal requirement was introduced obligating sponsors to register or list medicines prior to sale, listed medicines could be self-assessed by sponsors (through the ELF). The Department of Health was effectively 'commercialised' through the creation of the TGA and it becoming 100% cost recovered (by way of charging approval and annual fees to sponsors for registering and listing medicines).

Rights discourse, including the increasing preoccupation of the Australian Government with the rights of the population as the object of its intervention, further supported the development of neoliberal governmentality. The compatibility of (neo)liberal rationality (i.e. the real respect of freedom, including private freedoms) with human rights (the 'legitimate' rights of the individual to freedom from and through the state) increasingly facilitated the development of techniques designed to limit intervention by the state, indeed to responsibilise regulatory (and health) governance. Techniques that entailed intervention by the state on the basis of the right to health were rationalised not only as rights violating (i.e. violating private rights and the rights of the economy), therefore justifying the imposition of limits on them, but also as a form of unfreedom (by relieving the individual of their responsibility for governing their own health, and instead increasing their dependence on the state). When these assorted 'rights' happened to align—such as the alignment of the right to access medicines (preconditional to the right to health) with timelier and reduced barriers to medicines approval—these 'common interests' further supported the implementation of techniques to limit state intervention, thereby advancing hegemonic neoliberal governmentality.

Relations between the state and the medicines industry based on a cooperative rationality of governance were established long before neoliberal governmentality became hegemonic in the late 1980s and 1990s but were formalised following the regulatory failures in the Travacalm and Vioxx cases through the adoption of a 'tiered offence regime' (and therefore less-punitive techniques) and 'responsive regulation'. Chapter 3 considered how adopting such techniques could result in failure simply because the TGA may be unwilling or unable to escalate its enforcement as this would affect the extent to which sponsors cooperate with it. However, the increasing decentralisation of the regulatory regime may also affect cooperation insofar as it results in the interactions between the TGA and sponsors becoming too infrequent and less intense and direct. Regulation may also fail because the techniques used are disproportional to the harm caused (meaning that non-cooperation comes to be treated more punitively than non-compliance itself). In addition, tripartite techniques used by the public and public interest groups to regulate the TGA and industry (and therefore to overcome the biases of cooperation) may fail because of knowledge/power asymmetries (between the public and its representatives, on the one hand, and the Australian Government and industry, on the other).

Risk rationality, in contrast, became central to hegemonic neoliberal governmentality through rationalising the reallocation of some of the responsibilities for governing, thereby reducing the costs. This reallocation occurred through the two-tiered risk classification scheme, which included the classification of some risks as 'low', and the rationalising of micro-level techniques, such as decentred and deregulated (self-regulated) forms of governing. In Chapter 3, the reduction in the resources directed at lower risks was identified as having the potential to cause regulatory failure. However, this risk prioritisation may also result in failure simply because there is less interaction between the TGA and sponsors and less information obtained by the TGA from sponsors for the purposes of (re)classifying risks. A preoccupation with risk can trump and render meaningless all other criteria used to determine the TGA's response. But the main implication of using risk-based techniques is that it increases the individualisation of responsibility and risk (of the potential harms).

Both risk-based and responsive regulation are congruent with the neoliberal rationale of limited state intervention. The focus on risk provides a means of rationalising the non-intervention of the TGA in the regime and the use of micro-level self-regulatory techniques. The emphasis on cooperativeness rationalises limiting intervention in a similar, but self-reinforcing way—through the TGA's apparent failure and incapacity to identify and act on non-compliance and sponsors' supposed capacity to identify and act on these 'voluntarily'. The TGA's enforcement pyramid is an adaption of the original enforcement pyramid and is therefore less complete (and more limited in terms of the extent to which the TGA can deter and intervene on non-compliance). The incompatibility of risk-based regulation with responsive regulation, and their use as part of a hybrid strategy of governing, has the potential to further limit intervention in the regime. Because risk-based techniques are rationalised on the basis of product (and not compliance) risk, risk-based governance is typically commensurate with the severity of product risk. Responsive regulation, which escalates to punitive techniques when cooperative techniques fail, is incompatible with governing medicines that are deemed low risk. This can lead the TGA to be reluctant to escalate or refrain from escalation altogether.

These possibilities for failure were mostly evidenced by the findings of the thematic analysis, discussed in Chapters 4 and 5. Regulation failed because intervention by the TGA in the regime and the regime's capacity to limit non-compliance were both reduced (reflecting a form of *regulatory disempowerment*). Product risk became a means by which to limit regulatory techniques to those commensurate with the risk classification—for example, through prioritising techniques targeting the medicine itself (rather than the sponsors), targeting high risk (rather than low risk) medicines, specific to regulating product (over compliance) risks (in particular, laboratory testing rather than compliance reviews) and pre-market (over post-market) risks. Consequently, the findings revealed that there was limited evaluation by the TGA of medicines quality, safety and efficacy, and DTCA and promotion, both pre- and post-market, particularly for low-risk listed medicines, and also where risk did not directly pertain to the medicine itself (e.g. in relation to DTCA and promotion to health professionals). In these areas of the regime, the TGA's risk-based and cooperative techniques were mostly reactive, disproportionate to the severity of the non-compliance and incapable of escalation when non-compliance persisted. The lack of centralisation in these areas of the regime increased the disproportionality of and lack of hierarchy in the techniques used because responsibility for regulation was distributed across multiple bodies. This led to regulatory gaps (e.g. a lack of application to non-members, mechanisms for referral and so on) and an overall diffusion of responsibility when regulation failed. (Indeed, this appeared to be the case with Mundipharma insofar as the TGA intervened and escalated its response after the details of the complaint were publicised in the Australian media and increasing public and political pressure was applied). Decentralisation also contributed to perceptions among sponsors of their unequal treatment by the TGA, which had the potential to affect their cooperation. The TGA is also limited as a result of constraints on its resourcing arising from the prioritisation of 'risk management' and economic rationality. The TGA was otherwise constrained due to its relative positioning within the overall structure of the Australian Government (and thus its ideological apparatuses), which can shape its decision-making. For these reasons, non-compliance persists in these largely self-regulated areas of the regime.

The capacity of the public, and of those representing their interests, to participate in the regime is limited (representing a form of *public disempowerment*). This, in turn, limits their capacity to make up for the failures of regulation. Chapter 5 discussed how knowledge/power asymmetries limit the public's access to the information needed to develop health and regulatory literacy, and in the case of the latter, the possibility of holding either the TGA or industry to account. Much of the information on medicines is produced by industry (which in itself represents an asymmetry of knowledge/power). The complexity of such information often requires a level of technical knowledge (and power), making it less accessible. Furthermore, this information is not always available on the TGA website; and when it is, it may be outdated or its communication delayed. Sometimes, this information is considered commercial in confidence. The same types of limitations apply to information on the outcomes of the TGA's regulatory and enforcement actions. The harms resulting from this failure to disclose information are nevertheless shifted onto the public as a result of a responsibilisation rationality and through technologies limiting the TGA's liability, such as s. 61A of the Therapeutic Goods Act and the use of exclusion of liability disclaimers.

The regime is structured to reduce the potential for opposition and critique, but not just in terms of its limited transparency and accountability. Public interest groups and individuals who do participate in the regime are typically under-represented compared to industry, as demonstrated by the proportion of ADR reports, complaints and submissions provided to consultations, as well as their limited representation on some TGA committees and industry-led. This contributes to the unequal power relations that render the regime less representative of the public's interests. Therefore, although the regime allows for some participation by the public and the representatives of their interests, this participation has limits and occurs in ways that align with (and do not pose a serious challenge to) neoliberal governmentality. The forms of participation, such as health and regulatory literacy and ADR reports, complaints, consultation submissions and committee representation, instead of empowering the public, therefore function as technologies that contribute to their continued disempowerment.

The medicine regulatory regime is the culmination of reforms by successive Liberal and Labor governments. It is therefore not aligned with any particular Australian political party or its policies. The regime is also partly the culmination of the alignment of various sets of interests over time—those of sponsors, industry associations, health professionals, professional associations and patients and patient interest groups. However, the regime prioritises the interests of capital and its accumulation above all others. In these respects, it can be considered the product of a mostly consensual hegemonic project.

## 7.2 The limits of regulating neoliberal capitalism

The Australian Government and TGA responded to these regulatory failures by attempting to reform the existing regime, purportedly making it 'more effective and transparent'. Yet these reforms have ultimately reinforced and further embedded hegemonic neoliberal governmentality. Despite more than a decade having passed since the public acknowledgement of regulatory failure in certain aspects of the regime, and the initiation of public consultations intended to reform it, Chapter 6 demonstrated that little has changed, and the same types of non-compliance persist. Listed medicines remain almost entirely self-regulated; and the level of non-compliance remains at around 70% for these medicines following a compliance review. The review rate has also remained relatively unchanged compared to the pre-consultation and reform period. The TGA still relies on warning letters despite an increase in the number and severity of penalties available. Requests to remove advertisements and warning letters are still the primary responses to DTCA, despite an increase in complaints. Promotion to health professionals remains self-regulated, with limited intervention by the TGA and limited application to non-members.

Neoliberal rationalities remain influential in limiting further intervention by the TGA in these areas of the regime. Product risk rationality is employed to reject proposals that would require a higher level of evidence demonstrating the efficacy of listed medicines, including the submission of this evidence at the time of application to allow for the TGA's assessment prior to approval. Proposals to expand DTCA pre-approval and promotion to health professionals for listed and registered non-prescription medicines have also been rejected on the basis of product risk rationality, which emphasises that the requirements be 'commensurate' with the product risk. Economic rationality is at the same time employed to reject proposals for reporting the evidence supporting listed medicines' efficacy claims. Instead, a second voluntary approval process was established to evaluate such evidence, although it is rarely used by sponsors. Economic rationality has also rationalised the non-expansion of DTCA pre-approval to cover all forms of advertising and to limit promotion to medical practitioners. In the case of DTCA, the requirement for approval was abolished altogether. Responsibilisation in DTCA and promotion has further rationalised limiting the TGA's intervention by having industry associations implement their own solutions. However, self-regulation by industry associations continues to have limited application, operating on a voluntary basis for DTCA and being mandatory only for MA members in relation to promotion. The implication, then, is that proposals to reform the regime to align more with the public's interest will continue to be shaped by and subordinated to neoliberal rationalities, such as product risk, cost effectiveness and responsibilisation. These rationalities align with and privilege techniques that are congruent with hegemonic neoliberal governmentality.

While certain types of information have been made more available and accessible to the public to encourage their participation in the regime (and their own health governance), the public cannot be omnicompetent and know all. The availability of information is limited by what is disclosed (and thus mediated) by the TGA and industry. Having to accumulate information is 'time consuming' and, at times, not possible for sponsors (e.g. see Section 6.1.1), or even the TGA. Yet, paradoxically, this is expected of the public, who possess less technical knowledge/power and whose knowledge/power is contingent on that of others. Having to accumulate and process the large amounts of information available, regardless of whether it is complete or not, limits their participation. In these ways, transparency both enables and constrains participation to align with and reinforce neoliberal governmentality. Indeed, transparency itself is a form of liberalisation (i.e. the liberalising of information—see Adams 2018). Transparency facilitates the shifting and individualising of responsibility through technologies like health and regulatory literacy, thereby reducing the state's responsibility for the risks and harms resulting from the failures of regulation. Product labels, such as the 'AUST L' label, along with other published materials supplied with the medicine, therefore become a means of *informing*; to inform the public of the extent to which the medicine has been assessed by the TGA, without changing the assessment process and therefore the harms that this process causes. The idea that the public can access information about medicines and their regulation encourages them to seek out such information. At the same time, the trust in the information discloser that this process fosters can lead to public 'complacency' and 'indifference', and thereby to decreased levels of public participation (Adams 2018:17).

Although the TGA and regulatory regime have relatively limited power when it comes to compelling compliance from sponsors, this power is nonetheless a form of 'governing through failure' (Joseph 2018) because it reinforces the use of micro-level self-regulatory techniques. In other words, governing at the macro level, in line with hegemonic neoliberal governmentality, is reinforced through the failure of governing at the micro level. In this way, both the government and industry are empowered by failure as it further embeds hegemonic neoliberal governmentality. Micro-level techniques, such as responsibilisation, also shift and diffuse responsibility for the risks and harms resulting from state-corporate regulatory failure. In a similar way, the public, with its limited knowledge/power relative to others within the regime, become subject to micro-level self-empowerment techniques. Both government and industry are empowered by these asymmetries of knowledge/power, not just because they possess more of it but also because it is something they mediate. Thus, the failure of regulation, including its transparency failures, is a tool for reinforcing neoliberal governmentality and maintaining its hegemony. Hegemonic neoliberal governmentality is thus a self-reinforcing and unregulatable project.

## 7.3 Do we need a more transformative solution?

Historically, the literature has proposed solutions to the harms of regulatory failure that require working within existing (neoliberal) capitalism. For example, Braithwaite—one of the most published and widely cited criminologists in the fields of regulation and pharma-crime—is a proponent of 'new capitalism' (see Dukes et al. 2014:363). He is also a proponent of regulatory capitalism, asserting that '[t]hose who believe we are in an era of neoliberalism . . . are mistaken' (Braithwaite 2008:26). According to Braithwaite (2008:27):

> markets in fits and starts have tended to become progressively more vigorous, as has investment in the regulation of market externalities. Not only have markets, states, and state regulation become more formidable, so has non-state regulation by civil society, business, business associations, professions and international organizations. . . . Both markets and the state [have] become stronger, enlarged in scope and transaction density, at every stage. . . . [N]on-state forms of governance by firms . . . [have] expand[ed] alongside growth in state governance capability.

Braithwaite and his colleagues propose regulatory capitalism as a form of 'new' capitalism, arguing that medicine regulation should become more 'responsive and networked' so that the strengths and limitations of the approaches adopted by different actors compensate for each other (Dukes et al. 2014:382). Moreover, they claim that the key to making capitalism 'more ethical' lies 'within the very corporations responsible for the most criminal conduct' (Dukes et al. 2014:379).

The findings of this book suggest otherwise. The areas of the regulatory regime that are the focus of this book, including listed medicines, DTCA and promotion to health professionals, have historically been subject to lesser amounts of government regulation, with self-regulation almost always prioritised. Although criminal and civil penalties for non-compliance do exist, they are rarely used, as the TGA generally opts for more cooperative rather than punitive techniques. Yet this strategy has not led to high rates of compliance, particularly for listed medicines. In the decentralised areas of the regime where both the TGA and industry associations share responsibility for regulating, there has been little interdependence and complementarity between them. In fact, inconsistencies in decision-making and the application of penalties, particularly in relation to DTCA, are often reported. In the area of promotion to health professionals, there is little intervention by the TGA. This is in stark contrast to the compliance rates in those areas of the regime where the TGA has historically retained most (if not all) of the responsibility for regulating and intervenes more often, such as in registered medicines approval. Therefore, there is little evidence, at least in the context of this study, to suggest that medicine regulation is responsive or networked (let alone formidable enough to actually deter non-compliance). And this is despite the regulator in this study, the TGA, claiming that 'responsive regulation' underpins its rationale for governing (TGA 2020c).

In the research on pharma-crime, the solutions proposed to counter the 'profit motivations' of the pharmaceutical industry have included establishing non-profit and/or publicly owned corporations (Lexchin 1984); enhancing the independence of regulators from industry (Davis and Abraham 2013; Lexchin 1984); publicly funding regulators (Angell 2004; Gøtzsche 2013); increasing the transparency of regulators and medicine information (Abraham 1995; Gøtzsche 2013); imposing stricter limits on the relationships between industry and health professionals, including around the disclosure of payments (Goldacre 2012; Gøtzsche 2013; Lexchin 1984); imposing stricter limits on DTCA and advertising to health professionals (Gøtzsche 2013; Law 2006; Lexchin 1984); and increasing penalties (such as cancelling medicines) (Lexchin 1984). This is not an exhaustive list; however, it illustrates that although many authors identify the 'profit motives' of pharmaceutical companies as the underlying cause of medicine-related harms, their proposed solutions do not necessarily address the underlying historical and structural causes of these harms. Indeed, it further illustrates that the same types of solutions have long been suggested but without resulting in any meaningful change over time.

Many scholars within the field of regulation have also advocated for greater citizen co-regulation and empowerment (Ayres and Braithwaite 1991, 1992; Dukes et al. 2014; Grabosky 2017; Hutter 2006; Scott 2017). However, this literature, as Gray and van Rooij (2021) point out, often overlooks the power asymmetries between the public and the regulator and industry, which, as Rawlinson (2017a) notes, tend to be more pronounced when it comes to the state-pharma nexus. This is because the capacity to understand medicine information requires a level of technical knowledge/power that in many ways is bounded by and contingent on those who possess this knowledge/power. Medicine information is essentially produced by the creator of the medicine itself—the sponsor. The TGA relies in part on the sponsor to disclose this information, and so there exists a level of knowledge/power asymmetry between the sponsor and TGA. However, the TGA also creates information on medicines when regulating them (for example, through laboratory testing, assessing the merit of complaints or ADRs, and so on). Although medical practitioners have training in medicines and therefore have some technical knowledge/power, this knowledge/power is also bounded by and contingent on the extent to which the sponsor and TGA disclose medicine information. Further, this is similar for other types of health professionals, irrespective of their level of medical training. The knowledge/power of the public is contingent on all of these relations of power. Ultimately, this knowledge/power rests upon the full disclosure of this information as is and without alteration, which Adams (2018, 2020) argues is not truly achievable because this disclosure is mediated by its creator. This means that industry and the TGA would provide the required information to those they exercise power over so that those in receipt can then critique them and hold them to account.

Garside (2013:253) is critical of solutions that seek to 'better' regulate capitalism as they still work within the existing capitalist project, rather than offering an alternative. He argues that expecting states to simply choose to pursue laws and policies that are different from and go against the interests of capital is 'unrealistic' since 'capitalist states are not neutral' (Garside 2013:253). As this study has shown, neoliberal—and particularly, economic—rationality shapes state work, indeed the reason of state (*raison d'état*). It is for this reason that 'abolishing corporations' (through abolishing corporate personhood or more simply legal recognition of corporate 'persons' in law, see Tombs and Whyte 2015) alone will not be enough. The pervasiveness of neoliberal rationality and its capacity to shape every aspect of the social domain and *raison d'état* suggests, as Garside (2013) implies, the need for more substantive social transformation. Hegemonic neoliberal governmentality cannot simply be rendered 'more ethical', as regulatory reforms that run counter to neoliberal rationality are continuously shaped by and subordinated to it. Given that neoliberal (and economic) rationality is foundational to the adoption and coalescence of neoliberal governmentality at a macro level—and therefore to it becoming hegemonic—arguably, it is only by instigating a much larger transformational agenda, whereby the historical and structural causes underlying such rationality are dissolved, that an alternative regime rationalised on the basis of health (and not capital) can be achieved.

The solution, then, to neoliberal capitalism may therefore lie in its notional opposite. For Adler-Bolton and Vierkant, this is health communism.

Adler-Bolton and Vierkant (2022:xv) argue that health has become increasingly defined 'under' and 'by' capital (what they call health capitalism) and so it must be separated from capital. Drawing on mostly Marxist (but also Foucauldian) concepts, they argue that health must be (re)defined around the 'surplus population'—essentially, those who typically are or come to be excluded from (and thus surplus to) the health policies of states—in order to achieve 'all care for all people', or indeed, 'a radical abundance of care' (Adler-Bolton and Vierkant 2022:xiii–xiv). They deliberately define the surplus population broadly and not on the basis of a particular illness, disability or other debility because of the tendency historically to pathologise, categorise, certify and therefore include or exclude certain people on the basis of their health. Instead, this 'surplus' status should be defined relative to the health policies of states, and therefore to the people these policies typically exclude and from which health capitalism profits the most (what the authors call 'extractive abandonment'). Adler-Bolton and Vierkant also emphasise the importance of defining care beyond a needs basis which, like health, has also come to be defined by capital. This of course has appeal for scholars of social harm, particularly in light of the criticisms directed at needs-based definitions of harm, often seen as potentially subjective and overly individualistic (see Lasslett 2010a; Raymen 2022). However, their definition of care could still include a degree of subjectivity because it is partly defined by the 'social determinants of health', which are again defined broadly (as non-medical factors affecting health, such as air, water, food and sanitation). In addition, care has historically been defined by the state—that is, in relation to the health policies of states and those they exclude.

Although Adler-Bolton and Vierkant discuss racism and colonialism and their relation to health capitalism and the production of the surplus population, these are not the primary focus of their discussions on health communism. Because Adler-Bolton and Vierkant's definition of care is partly state-defined, this is potentially problematic in the context of colonial/Western states. For example, historically, Aboriginal and Torres Strait Islander people have had limited self-determination, as the extent of its exercise is determined by the colonial/Australian state (see Watson 2017, 2018). Aboriginal and Torres Strait Islander people have also been subject to the white/colonial health law and policies of the Australian Government, variously described as 'civilising' and 'humanitarian' interventions (Watson 2017). Therefore, health law and policies that historically excluded certain populations could unintentionally lead to newer law and policies for their inclusion, which in turn could be harmful. Although there is overlap between communism and decolonisation, particularly in that the former is generally anti-imperialist, communism is nevertheless Euro- and Western-centric in origin. This is not to deny the radical potential of health communism, only that it may be susceptible to reinforcing existing colonialisms.

While not the primary focus of this book, the solution to the harms of neoliberal capitalism may well lie in decolonising medicine—and by extension, health. As this is an emerging field, there is still considerable debate about the best way to define health decolonisation and what decolonising entails (for a good overview of these debates, see Hales 2024). A thorough account of these debates and their implications for understanding the harms caused by the failures of medicine regulation is beyond the scope of this book and really merits its own study. However, for the purposes of proposing this as a concept to guide future research, decolonising health (and medicine) can generally be understood as the reversal and dismantling of the systems (or regimes) of health colonialism/capitalism. It involves not only decolonial thinking and being but also the repatriation of previously marginalised knowledges and practices. Given that the 'modern' harms of hegemonic neoliberal governmentality in the medicine regulatory regime stem from colonialism and the creation of racial differences in health (which led people to be objectified, commodified and subjected), decolonisation is central to the dismantling of neoliberal rationality and re-rationalising hegemonic governmentality on the basis of health (and medicine).

There is a lack of research into the harms of medicines and their regulation experienced by Aboriginal and Torres Strait Islander people, as well as other peoples of colour (Thomas 2004; Thynne and Gabb 2016). Watego and Whop (2022) argue that there is also a lack of research on the racism within public health research itself; for example, there is a tendency within this literature to focus on excess death and less so on other racialised health disparities. In terms of medicine regulation in Australia, there are known racial differences that cause disproportionate harm among Aboriginal and Torres Strait Islander people. For example, the TGA did not include an option to select Aboriginal and Torres Strait Islander (written as 'ATSI') in its online ADR forms until 2008; and regardless, this section of the form is not always completed (Thynne and Gabb 2016). Thynne and Gabb (2016:16) point out that research and development and clinical trials rarely include Aboriginal and Torres Strait Islander participants. Furthermore, sponsors are not required to report post-market ADRs among Aboriginal and Torres Strait Islander people, or any other person from communities of colour, to the TGA, even though such reporting is required for older people, pregnant and breastfeeding women, infants, children and young people (Thynne and Gabb 2016). This is despite known racial differences in drug response and disease burden that disproportionately affect Aboriginal and Torres Strait Islander people (Thynne and Gabb 2016; Watego et al. 2021).

Decolonising health by dismantling colonial differences, starting with (but by no means limited to) racial difference, is necessary to re-rationalise and therefore transform the medicine regulatory regime so that capital and its accumulation is no longer the basis for regulation.

## 7.4 Contributions, limitations and future directions

The aim of this book was to provide a deeper and more complex understanding of neoliberalism and its effects on prescription and non-prescription medicine regulation, state–corporate power relations and the commission of harm (through the failure of regulation). It also attempted to disrupt the thinking that the solution to such failures is simply to reform (and therefore continue to work within) existing neoliberal capitalism. The book makes several important contributions to the literature in this regard. It adds to criminological inquiry on the state–corporate crimes and harms of the pharmaceutical industry, an area that, many note, has largely been neglected within the criminological literature (Braithwaite 1984; Dukes et al 2014; Friedrichs and Vegh Weis 2021; Rawlinson 2017a, 2017b). It expands on this literature by incorporating a focus on all medicines (not just prescription medicines). The findings lend support to the state–corporate crime/harm literature and the concept of state–corporate symbiosis and regimes of permission which detail the symbiotic relationship between the state and corporations in the commission of crime/harm (Bernat and Whyte 2017; Kramer et al. 2002; Tombs and Whyte 2015; Tombs 2016). The findings also add to critical debates on compliance-based approaches to regulation, which first emerged in the scholarship of Pearce and Tombs (1990, 1997) and were developed further in works such as Mascini (2013), Tombs and Whyte (2015) and Tombs (2016), reinforcing the critique of the compatibility of such approaches with neoliberalism. Since the TGA is not the only industry regulator to employ a hybrid risk-based and responsive framework in Australia or overseas (see Gunningham 2011), the findings have broad applications.

The book builds upon the existing literature on neoliberalism, state–corporate crime/harm, and medicine regulation in multiple ways. First, the analysis employed a unique conceptual framework comprising Foucauldian governmentality, Gramscian–Jessopian hegemony and critical realist ontology to understand hegemonic neoliberal governmentality. This conceptual framework has primarily only been employed in the political science and international relations literature by scholars such as Joseph (2004, 2010, 2017). Given that scholars of regulatory and state-corporate crime/harm have previously used Foucauldian (Davies 2011; Scott 2004) and Marxist (Pearce and Tombs 1990, 1997; Tombs and Whyte 2015; Tombs 2016) concepts, this conceptual framework offers a potentially useful lens for approaching future scholarship. Second, this book draws on this conceptual framework to examine the historical basis and development of the regulatory regime, and therefore its harms, starting in Australian settler colonialism/capitalism. The analysis is thus not limited to examining neoliberalism at a particular point in time and space, but rather across time and space and in the various iterations of this project (albeit under different names). This approach is different from that used in previous scholarship, which, Garside (2013:253) notes, has had a tendency to fixate on neoliberal forms of regulation (and not capitalism in all of its forms), closing it off to the possibility of more transformative solutions to the harms of regulation. Third, the book develops its critique from the abductive starting point of regulatory failure. This abductive line of reasoning allows the book to search for premises for the high rates of non-compliance long seen in Australia's medicine regulatory regime, instead of engaging in the usual debates of whether or not particular regulatory strategies, like risk-based or responsive regulation, generate actual compliance. Finally, this analysis broadens the scope of inquiry by examining medicine regulation beyond the regulator–regulatee binary. In particular, it incorporates an analysis of the participation of the public and representatives of the public's interest in medicine regulation, as well as that of other groups, like health professionals. The book therefore builds on the literature that critiques public empowerment in regulation, particularly Gray and van Rooij (2021) and Albert and Gray (2023), by examining public disempowerment through the conceptual lenses of hegemonic neoliberal governmentality and knowledge/power.

The limited transparency and the knowledge/power asymmetries within this regime mean that this book will no doubt contain some mistakes and misinterpretations, although I have done my best to minimise these. Even so, the potential mistakes and misinterpretations on my part speak to some of this book's underlying themes: that transparency and knowledge/power are key to the maintenance of hegemonic neoliberal governmentality by reducing the potential for literacy and dispelling critique.

Other similar limitations include the lack of quantitative data and the reliance instead on qualitative data from secondary sources (submissions to public consultations published on the TGA's and other Australian Government websites) and interviews. The book is therefore restricted in its ability to evaluate the effectiveness of risk-based and responsive regulatory techniques in reducing actual rates of non-compliance. This includes the inability to evaluate such effectiveness where documented evidence of non-compliance has been unavailable. This book has focused only on those aspects of the Australian medicine regulatory regime where non-compliance was high and documented evidence of these non-compliance rates was available. The findings presented herein should not be treated as evidence that risk-based and responsive regulatory techniques are unable to compel compliance at all. The intent of this book is to demonstrate that, in the particular context of medicine regulation in Australia, risk-based and responsive regulatory techniques are susceptible to being weakened by hegemonic neoliberal governmentality, in much the same way as deterrence-based techniques, so that they limit intervention by the state and therefore conform with the neoliberal project. Future research should focus on exploring the use of risk-based and responsive regulatory techniques and their hybridity by drawing on quantitative data to determine whether they are feasible in practice. Such a depth of analysis would provide greater support to the arguments that risk-based and responsive regulatory techniques are vulnerable to degradation by hegemonic neoliberal governmentality and that a much larger program of social transformation is necessary to overcome these interests.

It is due to the previously mentioned data limitations that this book has not been able to focus more on colonialism and its links to neoliberal capitalism, or on decolonising health, which is something I would have preferred to do. The contradiction of using a conceptual framework comprising concepts drawn from Foucault, Gramsci and Jessop, and based on the work of Joseph—scholars who are all located in Europe/the West—while ultimately advocating for the decolonisation of health and medicine is also not lost on me. As I alluded to at the outset of this book, this conceptual framework of hegemonic neoliberal governmentality will not be without its critics. Hegemonic neoliberal governmentality therefore suffers similar limitations to those I raise in my critique of Adler-Bolton and Vierkant's concept of health communism. Again, my intent here has been to spark a re-thinking of this book's themes of neoliberalism, (medicines) regulation, state–corporate power and the harms resulting from regulatory failure.

The book also reaches its conclusions with a number of questions remaining unanswered. How exactly do we decolonise health? What does a decolonised medicine regulatory regime look like? Is decolonisation possible within the existing neoliberal capitalist project and given the pervasiveness of its rationality? Finding the answers to these difficult questions is not a simple task and only achievable when scholars engage with it. Critics may well say that this is too idealistic and difficult to implement in practice. However, such criticisms only limit the possibility of and potential for transformative change, which Garside (2013) first argued many years ago now. Having studied this regime in some shape or form for more than a decade and witnessed the same types of failure and reform repeated over time, resulting in little change and ongoing harm, I am of the opinion that continuing to work within the existing neoliberal capitalist project is no longer the solution. We need to find alternatives to it.

## Note

1 A news service for the pharmaceuticals industry.

# Appendix 1

## Proportion of submissions published in public consultations sampled

| *Consultation Name* | *Total* | *Published* |
|---|---|---|
| Transparency review of the TGA | Unknown | 118 |
| Improving advertising arrangements for therapeutic goods | 38 | 35 |
| Consultation: Evidence required to support indications for listed medicines (excluding sunscreens and disinfectants) (Part 1) | 50 | 40 |
| Consultation: Evidence required to support indications for listed medicines (excluding sunscreens and disinfectants) (Part 2) | 26 | 24 |
| Position paper on promotion of therapeutic goods | 39 | 32 |
| Therapeutic Goods Amendment (Pharmaceutical Transparency) Bill 2013 | 26 | 26 |
| Consultation: Evaluating the feasibility of a new-to-market risk communication scheme for therapeutic goods | Unknown | 20 |
| Consultation: Regulation Impact Statement: Regulating the advertising of therapeutic goods to the general public | 1,276 | 93 |
| Consultation: Mechanisms to maintain the currency of approved Product Information (PI) and Consumer Medicine Information (CMI) | 25 | 23 |
| Consultation: Draft TGA approach to disclosure of commercially confidential information (CCI) | 13 | 13 |
| Consultation: TGA guidance on release for supply for medicines manufacturers | 16 | 16 |
| Therapeutic Goods Amendment (2013 Measures No. 1) Bill 201 | 11 | 11 |
| **Total:** | **1,658** | **451** |

# Appendix 2

## List of TGA consultations conducted between 1 January 2010 and 31 December 2014 and grounds for inclusion or exclusion

| No. | *Consultation Name* | *Date of Closure (Publication of Submissions)* | *Submissions Published (Y/N)* | *Inclusion/Exclusion from Sample, Grounds for* |
|---|---|---|---|---|
| 1 | Proposed standards and Code of GMP for human blood and blood components, human tissues and human cellular therapies | 12 February 2010 (25–26 July 2011) | Y | Excluded, blood, tissues and biologicals |
| 2 | Regulation impact statement on TGA and NICNAS (National Industrial Chemicals Notification and Assessment Scheme) proposed regulation of disinfectants | 12 February 2010 (Unknown) | N | Excluded, unpublished |
| 3 | Child-resistant packaging requirements for medicines | 19 March 2010 (Unknown) | N | Excluded, unpublished |
| 4 | Proposed changes to the sunscreens section of the ARGOM (the Australian Regulatory Guidelines for OTC medicines) | 18 June 2010 (Unknown) | N | Excluded, unpublished |
| 5 | Proposed changes to Product Information (PI) | 26 July 2010 (Unknown) | N | Excluded, unpublished |
| 6 | Consultation: Seeking information from compounding pharmacies | 30 July 2010 (Unknown) | N | Excluded, unpublished |

(*Continued*)

(Continued)

| No. | *Consultation Name* | *Date of Closure (Publication of Submissions)* | *Submissions Published (Y/N)* | *Inclusion/Exclusion from Sample, Grounds for* |
|---|---|---|---|---|
| 7 | Improving advertising arrangements for therapeutic goods | 27 August 2010 (Unknown) | Y | **Included**, advertising |
| 8 | Joint TGA/PBD (Pharmaceutical Benefits Division) discussion paper on Similar Biological Medicinal Products (SBMPs) | 08 September 2010 (Unknown) | N | Excluded, unpublished |
| 9 | Draft Australian regulatory guidelines for GMP clearance for overseas manufacturers | 15 November 2010 (Unknown) | N | Excluded, unpublished |
| 10 | TGA Internet site redevelopment: consultation on content and structure | 01 December 2010 (Unknown) | Y | Excluded, homepage redevelopment, development of an email newsletter and social media |
| 11 | Reforms in the medical devices regulatory framework | 17 December 2010 (Unknown) | Y | Excluded, medical devices |
| 12 | Proposed standards for human blood and blood components, human tissues and human cellular therapy products | 02 February 2011 (25–26 July 2011) | Y | Excluded, blood, tissues and biologicals |
| 13 | Transparency review of the TGA | 11 February 2011 (Unknown) | Y | **Included**, communication of post-market information |
| 14 | Electronic submission dossier requirements | 01 May 2011 (Unknown) | N | Excluded, unpublished |
| 15 | Required Advisory Statements for Medicine Labels (RASML) update 6 | 13 May 2011 (Unknown) | Y | Excluded, revision to guidance document |
| 16 | Consultation: Risk management plan guideline | 06 January 2012 (Unknown) | N | Excluded, unpublished |

(*Continued*)

(Continued)

| No. | *Consultation Name* | *Date of Closure (Publication of Submissions)* | *Submissions Published (Y/N)* | *Inclusion/Exclusion from Sample, Grounds for* |
|---|---|---|---|---|
| 17 | Consultation: Australian regulatory guidelines for over-the-counter medicines (ARGOM)—Stage 1 | 10 February 2012 (12 October 2012) | Y | Excluded, revision to guidance document |
| 18 | Proposed advisory statements for medicines: Cough and cold medicines for use in children | 22 February 2012 (28 September 2012) | Y | Excluded, revision to guidance document |
| 19 | Consultation: Evidence required to support indications for Listed medicines (excluding sunscreens and disinfectants) (Part 1) | 25 May 2012 (13 July 2012) | Y | **Included**, evidence to support product labelling and advertising claims |
| 20 | Consultation: Fexofenadine and loperamide: proposed advisory statements for medicines | 04 June 2012 (27 September 2012) | Y | Excluded, wording of advisory statements (medicine-specific) |
| 21 | TGA medicine labelling and packaging review | 24 August 2012 (09 November 2012) | Y | Excluded, layout of medicine labelling/packaging |
| 22 | Consultation: Evidence required to support indications for listed medicines (excluding sunscreens and disinfectants) (Part 2) | 22 October 2012 (Unknown) | Y | **Included**, evidence to support product labelling and advertising claims |
| 23 | Consultation: ARGCM (the Australian Regulatory Guidelines for Complementary Medicines) Part A: General guidance | 07 November 2012 (Unknown) | Y | Excluded, revision to guidance document |
| 24 | Consultation: Over-the-counter (OTC) medicines business process reform | 07 November 2012 (Unknown) | Y | Excluded, pre-market application |

(*Continued*)

(Continued)

| No. | *Consultation Name* | *Date of Closure (Publication of Submissions)* | *Submissions Published (Y/N)* | *Inclusion/Exclusion from Sample, Grounds for* |
|---|---|---|---|---|
| 25 | Consultation: Loratadine and desloratadine: proposed advisory statements for medicines | 07 December 2012 (25 February 2013) | Y | Excluded, wording of advisory statements (medicine-specific) |
| 26 | Consultation: Azelastine: proposed advisory statements for medicines | 07 December 2012 (25 February 2013) | Y | Excluded, wording of advisory statements (medicine-specific) |
| 27 | Consultation: Famciclovir: proposed advisory statements for medicines | 07 December 2012 (25 February 2013) | Y | Excluded, wording of advisory statements (medicine-specific) |
| 28 | Consultation: Kunzea ambigua: proposed advisory statements for medicines | 18 January 2013 (Unknown) | N | Excluded, unpublished |
| 29 | Consultation: ARGCM (the Australian Regulatory Guidelines for Complementary Medicines) Part B: Listed medicines | 18 February 2013 (Unknown) | Y | Excluded, revision to guidance document |
| 30 | Consultation: Minor variations to prescription medicines: guidance and application forms | 22 February 2013 (22 May 2013) | Y | Excluded, revision to guidance document |
| 31 | Regulation Impact Statement: Changes to premarket assessment requirements for medical devices | 15 March 2013 (Unknown) | Y | Excluded, medical devices |
| 32 | Consultation: Permitted (coded) indications for listed medicines | 15 March 2013 (19 June 2013) | Y | Excluded, pre-market application |
| 33 | Joint TGA and Medsafe project: Trans-Tasman early warning system of safety concerns with medicines and medical devices | 07 April 2013 (Unknown) | N | Excluded, unpublished |

*(Continued)*

(Continued)

| No. | *Consultation Name* | *Date of Closure (Publication of Submissions)* | *Submissions Published (Y/N)* | *Inclusion/Exclusion from Sample, Grounds for* |
|---|---|---|---|---|
| 34 | Review of the arrangements for the scheduling of medicines and poisons | 29 April 2013 (Unknown) | N | Excluded, scheduling |
| 35 | Consultation: Cetirizine: proposed advisory statements for medicines | 03 May 2013 (16 May 2013) | Y | Excluded, wording of advisory statements (medicine-specific) |
| 36 | Consultation: ARGCM (the Australian Regulatory Guidelines for Complementary Medicines) Part C: Evaluation of complementary medicine substances for use in listed medicines | 14 May 2013 (Unknown) | Y | Excluded, revision to guidance document |
| 37 | Consultation: Regulation Impact Statement: Changes to premarket assessment requirements for medical devices | 03 June 2013 (13 August 2013) | Y | Excluded, medical devices |
| 38 | Consultation: Proposed amendments to the new regulatory framework for In Vitro Diagnostic medical devices (IVDs) | 07 June 2013 (12 August 2013) | Y | Excluded, in vitro diagnostic medical devices |
| 39 | Consultation: Mechanisms to maintain the currency of approved Product Information (PI) and Consumer Medicine Information (CMI) | 13 June 2013 (07 August 2013) | Y | **Included**, communication of post-market information |
| 40 | Consultation: Evaluating the feasibility of a new-to-market risk communication scheme for therapeutic goods | 13 June 2013 (01 August 2013) | Y | **Included**, communication of post-market information |

(*Continued*)

(Continued)

| *No.* | *Consultation Name* | *Date of Closure (Publication of Submissions)* | *Submissions Published (Y/N)* | *Inclusion/Exclusion from Sample, Grounds for* |
|---|---|---|---|---|
| 41 | Consultation: International harmonisation of ingredient names | 10 July 2013 (Unknown) | N | Excluded, unpublished |
| 42 | Consultation: OTC N2 application requirements and OTC medicine monographs for aspirin, paracetamol and ibuprofen | 16 July 2013 (Unknown) | Y | Excluded, pre-market application |
| 43 | Consultation: Regulation Impact Statement: Regulating the advertising of therapeutic goods to the general public | 19 July 2013 (12 March 2014) | Y | **Included**, advertising |
| 44 | Consultation: ARGCM (the Australian Regulatory Guidelines for Complementary Medicines) Part D: Registered complementary medicines | 22 July 2013 (Unknown) | Y | Excluded, revision to guidance document |
| 45 | Consultation: Options for reform of the regulatory framework for pharmacy compounding | 26 July 2013 (04 June 2014) | Y | Excluded, pharmacy compounding |
| 46 | Proposal for automatic adoption of new versions of the PIC/S Guide to Good Manufacturing Practice for Medicinal Products | 12 August 2013 (Unknown) | N | Excluded, unpublished |
| 47 | Consultation: Draft TGA approach to disclosure of commercially confidential information (CCI) | 29 August 2013 (07 May 2014) | Y | **Included**, communication of post-market information |

(*Continued*)

(Continued)

| *No.* | *Consultation Name* | *Date of Closure (Publication of Submissions)* | *Submissions Published (Y/N)* | *Inclusion/Exclusion from Sample, Grounds for* |
|---|---|---|---|---|
| 48 | Consultation: TGA guidance on release for supply for medicines manufacturers | 06 September 2013 (02 December 2013) | Y | **Included**, GMP |
| 49 | ANZTPA (the Australia New Zealand Therapeutic Products Agency) implementation—Release of high-level description of a possible joint regulatory scheme | 21 February 2013 (Unknown) | N | Excluded, unpublished |
| 50 | Consultation: Chloramphenicol, propamidine, dibromopropamidine and sulfacetamide for ophthalmic use: proposed advisory statements for medicines | 10 January 2014 (04 March 2014) | Y | Excluded, wording of advisory statements (medicine-specific) |
| 51 | Consultation: Draft OTC medicine monographs for topical imidazole antifungals, topical nasal decongestants and pholcodine | 10 January 2014 (10 June 2014) | Y | Excluded, pre-market application |
| 52 | Consultation: OTC cough medicines for oral use: proposed advisory statements for medicines | 05 May2014 (09 September 2014) | Y | Excluded, outside sampling timeframe |
| 53 | Consultation: OTC nasal decongestant preparations for topical use: proposed advisory statements for medicines | 05 May 2014 (09 September 2014) | Y | Excluded, outside sampling timeframe |

(*Continued*)

(Continued)

| No. | Consultation Name | Date of Closure (Publication of Submissions) | Submissions Published (Y/N) | Inclusion/Exclusion from Sample, Grounds for |
|---|---|---|---|---|
| 54 | Consultation: Supply of in vitro diagnostic devices for self-testing (home testing) for the presence of human immunodeficiency virus in Australia | 06 May 2014 (Unknown) | Y | Excluded, in vitro diagnostic medical devices |
| 55 | Consultation: Review of the low value turnover exemption scheme | 23 May 2014 (Unknown) | N | Excluded, unpublished |
| 56 | Consultation: Software as a medical device (IMDRF [the International Medical Device Regulators Forum] working group) | 31 May 2014 (Unknown) | N | Excluded, unpublished |
| 57 | Consultation: Draft OTC medicine monograph for guaifenesin | 10 October 2014 (16 December 2014) | Y | Excluded, outside sampling timeframe |
| 58 | Consultation: Draft OTC medicine monograph for loperamide hydrochloride | 10 October 2014 (16 December 2014) | Y | Excluded, outside sampling timeframe |
| 59 | Consultation: Draft OTC medicine monograph for mebendazole | 10 October 2014 (16 December 2014) | Y | Excluded, outside sampling timeframe |
| 60 | Consultation: Draft OTC medicine monograph for ranitidine hydrochloride | 10 October 2014 (16 December 2014) | Y | Excluded, outside sampling timeframe |
| 61 | Consultation: Esomeprazole: proposed advisory statements for medicines | 10 October 2014 (02 December 2014) | N | Excluded, outside sampling timeframe |
| 62 | Review: Pilot phase—Australian eCTD (electronic Common Technical Documents) submissions | 03 November 2014 (Unknown) | N | Excluded, outside sampling timeframe |

*(Continued)*

(Continued)

| *No.* | *Consultation Name* | *Date of Closure (Publication of Submissions)* | *Submissions Published (Y/N)* | *Inclusion/Exclusion from Sample, Grounds for* |
|---|---|---|---|---|
| 63 | Consultation: Medicine labelling | 05 November 2014 (Unknown) | N | Excluded, outside sampling timeframe |
| 64 | Consultation: Review of cardiovascular safety of non-steroidal anti-inflammatory drugs and Safety review of diclofenac | 06 November 2014 (Unknown) | N | Excluded, outside sampling timeframe |
| 65 | Consultation: Draft compositional guidelines | Multiple, starting from 08 August 2014 | N | Excluded, outside sampling timeframe |

# Appendix 3

## List of submissions to the public consultations sampled

Note: multiple submissions were made to the same consultation by some individuals and organisations. Each of these have been treated as separate submissions (and therefore assigned separate numbers).

*Transparency review of the TGA* (2011) TGA website, accessed 16 October 2014. https://www.tga.gov.au/consultation/public-submissions-tga-transparency-review

| *No.* | *Citation* |
|---|---|
| 1 | Accord (Advocate for the Consumer, Cosmetic, Hygiene and Specialty Products Industry) |
| 2 | Advisory Committee on Prescription Medicines (ACPM) |
| 3 | Advisory Committee on the Safety of Medicines (ACSOM) |
| 4 | Amway of Australia |
| 5 | Andrewartha, Shane |
| 6 | Archer Emery & Associates |
| 7 | ARCS Australia Ltd |
| 8 | Arola, Travis, RTI Biologicals Inc |
| 9 | Arthritis Australia |
| 10 | Asthma Australia |
| 11 | Australasian Tissue & Biotherapeutics Forum |
| 12 | Australian & New Zealand Association of Physicians in Nuclear Medicine (ANZAPNM) |
| 13 | Australian Commission on Safety & Quality in Healthcare |
| 14 | Australian Customs & Border Protection Services |
| 15 | Australian Dental Industry Association (ADIA) |
| 16 | Australian Dental Industry Association (ADIA) |
| 17 | Australian Doctor |
| 18 | Australian Health Practitioner Regulation Agency |
| 19 | Australian Medicines Handbook |
| 20 | Australian Nursing Federation |
| 21 | Australian Orthopaedic Association |

(*Continued*)

(Continued)

| *No.* | *Citation* |
|---|---|
| 22 | Australian Pesticides and Veterinary Medicines Authority |
| 23 | Australian Red Cross Blood Service |
| 24 | Australian Rheumatology Association |
| 25 | Australian Self Medication Industry (ASMI) |
| 26 | Australian Self Medication Industry (ASMI) |
| 27 | Australian Skeptics (Victorian Branch) |
| 28 | Australian Society of Anaesthetists |
| 29 | Baxter Healthcare |
| 30 | Breast Cancer Network Australia |
| 31 | Brookman, David |
| 32 | Butler, Shane |
| 33 | Cancer Council WA (Western Australia) |
| 34 | Care Pharmaceuticals |
| 35 | Carers Australia WA (Western Australia) |
| 36 | Carroll, Peter |
| 37 | Clark, John |
| 38 | Cohen, Steve |
| 39 | Coleman, Keith |
| 40 | Collins, Michael |
| 41 | Complementary Healthcare Council of Australia (CHC) |
| 42 | Consumers Health Forum of Australia (CHF) |
| 43 | Consumers Health Forum of Australia (CHF) |
| 44 | Council of Australian Therapeutic Advisory Groups |
| 45 | CRANAplus |
| 46 | Cranswick, Dr Noel |
| 47 | Crossing, Sally, Cancer Voices NSW |
| 48 | Department of Health, Government of WA (Western Australia) |
| 49 | Department of Health, Victoria |
| 50 | Direct Selling Association of Australia |
| 51 | Drug Utilisation Sub-Committee of the Pharmaceutical Benefits Advisory Committee |
| 52 | Dunlop, Dr Rachel |
| 53 | Endocrine Society of Australia |
| 54 | Friends of the Earth |
| 55 | Friends of the Earth |
| 56 | Hanigan, Graeme |
| 57 | Heywood, Jennifer |
| 58 | Holley, Associate Professor Loraine |
| 59 | IVD (in vitro diagnostics) Australia |

(*Continued*)

(Continued)

| *No.* | *Citation* |
|---|---|
| 60 | Jansons, Sergei |
| 61 | Jarman, Julie |
| 62 | Johnson & Johnson Family of Companies |
| 63 | Kelly, David |
| 64 | Kertz, John |
| 65 | Love, Professor Bruce |
| 66 | Lucire, Dr Yolande |
| 67 | Lucire, Dr Yolande |
| 68 | Lucire, Dr Yolande |
| 69 | Lugton, Robert |
| 70 | Maiwald, Matthias |
| 71 | Marcus, Alison |
| 72 | Marron, Loretta |
| 73 | McDonald, Professor Peter |
| 74 | McLeod, Mr Ken |
| 75 | McNeil, Helen |
| 76 | Medical Oncology Group of Australia Incorporated |
| 77 | Medical Technology of Australia (MTAA) |
| 78 | Medical Technology of Australia (MTAA) |
| 79 | Medication Services QLD (Queensland) |
| 80 | Medicines Australia |
| 81 | Medicines Australia |
| 82 | Medtronic |
| 83 | Mental Health Council of Australia |
| 84 | Mills, Bayani |
| 85 | MIMS |
| 86 | Mordi Skeptics |
| 87 | National Prescribing Service (NPS) |
| 88 | Newsome, Brad |
| 89 | NSW Therapeutic Advisory Group Inc. |
| 90 | Optometry Board of Australia |
| 91 | Pfizer Australia Pty Ltd |
| 92 | Pharmacare |
| 93 | Pharmaceutical Society of Australia |
| 94 | Public Health Association of Australia |
| 95 | Ratnayeke, Mr Ranil |
| 96 | Real Health Care Reform Pty Ltd |
| 97 | Real Health Care Reform Pty Ltd |
| 98 | Regulatory Solutions |

(*Continued*)

(Continued)

| *No.* | *Citation* |
|---|---|
| 99 | Reilly, Lesley |
| 100 | Robertson, Geraldine |
| 101 | Rook, Dr Chris |
| 102 | Royal Australian and New Zealand College of Psychiatrists (RANZCP) |
| 103 | Royal Australian and New Zealand College of Radiologists |
| 104 | Royal College of Pathologists of Australasia |
| 105 | Sanofi Aventis |
| 106 | Smallwood, Robert |
| 107 | Standards Australia |
| 108 | Stenning, Gordon |
| 109 | Sweet, Graham |
| 110 | Sweet, Melissa |
| 111 | The Pharmacy Guild of Australia |
| 112 | Therapeutic Guidelines Limited |
| 113 | Thornton, Dr Helen |
| 114 | Tivendale, Charles |
| 115 | Verberne, Daniel |
| 116 | Vitry, Dr Agnes |
| 117 | Williams, Mrs M |
| 118 | Commonwealth Ombudsman, NSW |

*Improving advertising arrangements for therapeutic goods* (2010) TGA website, accessed 16 October 2014. http://www.tga.gov.au/consultation/improving-advertising-arrangements-therapeutic-goods

| *No.* | *Author* |
|---|---|
| 119 | Advocate for the Consumer, Cosmetic, Hygiene and Specialty Products Industry (ACCORD) |
| 120 | Arthritis Australia |
| 121 | Australian Association of National Advertisers |
| 122 | Australian Dental Association Inc |
| 123 | Australian Dental Industry Association |
| 124 | Australian Medical Association |
| 125 | Australian Nursing Federation |
| 126 | Australian Self-Medication Industry Inc |
| 127 | Australian Skeptics, Victorian Branch |
| 128 | Bayer HealthCare |
| 129 | Beverley Snell |
| 130 | Buko Pharma-Kampagne |

*(Continued)*

(Continued)

| *No.* | *Author* |
|---|---|
| 131 | Complementary Healthcare Council of Australia |
| 132 | Consumers Health Forum of Australia |
| 133 | Direct Selling Association of Australia |
| 134 | Dr Ken Harvey |
| 135 | Gavin Mutton |
| 136 | Graeme Hanigan |
| 137 | Graham Sweet |
| 138 | Health Action International Asia-Pacific |
| 139 | Health Action International Global |
| 140 | Hunter Skeptics Inc |
| 141 | IVD (in vitro diagnostics) Australia |
| 142 | John Braithwaite |
| 143 | John Hatfield |
| 144 | Johnson & Johnson |
| 145 | Jon Wardle |
| 146 | Medical Technology Association of Australia |
| 147 | Pharmaceutical Society of Australia |
| 148 | Public Interest Advocacy Centre Ltd |
| 149 | Publishers' Advertising Advisory Bureau |
| 150 | The Communications Council |
| 151 | The Pharmacy Guild of Australia |
| 152 | The Royal Australasian College of Physicians |
| 153 | Robyn Clothier, Assoc Prof Jon Jureidini, Prof Joel Lexchin, Dr Agnes Vitry |

*Consultation: Evidence required to support indications for Listed medicines (excluding sunscreens and disinfectants)* (Part 1) (2012) TGA website, accessed 16 October 2014. http://www.tga.gov.au/public-submissions-evidence-required-support-indications-listed-medicines

| *No.* | *Author* |
|---|---|
| 154 | Advantage Medical Products Consulting Pty Ltd |
| 155 | Amway of Australia |
| 156 | Australasian Society of Clinical and Experimental Pharmacologists and Toxicologists |
| 157 | Australian Homeopathic Association |
| 158 | Australian Medical Association |
| 159 | Australian Naturopathic Practitioners Association |
| 160 | Australian Self-Medication Industry |
| 161 | Australian Skeptics Inc. |
| 162 | Complementary Healthcare Council of Australia |
| 163 | Comvita New Zealand Limited |

(*Continued*)

(Continued)

| No. | Author |
|---|---|
| 164 | Consumers Health Forum of Australia |
| 165 | David Tan & Associates |
| 166 | Direct Selling Association of Australia |
| 167 | Dr Ken Harvey |
| 168 | Ego Pharmaceuticals Pty Ltd |
| 169 | Friends of Science in Medicine Incorporated |
| 170 | Go Vita Distributors Limited |
| 171 | Health World limited |
| 172 | John Miller Consulting |
| 173 | Mary Osborn |
| 174 | Melrose Laboratories Pty Ltd |
| 175 | Name withheld [1] |
| 176 | Name withheld [2] |
| 177 | Name withheld [3] |
| 178 | Name withheld [4] |
| 179 | Name withheld [5] |
| 180 | Name withheld [6] |
| 181 | Name withheld [7] |
| 182 | National Prescribing Service Limited |
| 183 | Naturopathx Pty Ltd |
| 184 | PharmaCare Laboratories Pty Ltd |
| 185 | Pharmaceutical Society of Australia |
| 186 | Quality Matters Safety Matters Pty Ltd |
| 187 | Regulatory Solutions Pty Ltd |
| 188 | Sanofi Consumer Healthcare |
| 189 | Sue Akeroyd & Associates |
| 190 | Swisse Vitamins Pty Ltd |
| 191 | The Hydration Pharmaceuticals Trust |
| 192 | The Pharmaceutical Plant Company |
| 193 | Weleda Australia Pty Ltd |

*Consultation: Evidence required to support indications for Listed medicines (excluding sunscreens and disinfectants)* (Part 2) (2012) TGA website, accessed 16 October 2014. http://www.tga.gov.au/consultation/consultation-evidence-required-support-indications-listed-medicines-excluding-sunscreens-and-disinfectants-0

| No. | Author |
|---|---|
| 194 | Amway of Australia |
| 195 | Anonymous 1 |

*(Continued)*

(Continued)

| *No.* | *Author* |
|---|---|
| 196 | Anonymous 2 |
| 197 | Anonymous 3 |
| 198 | Anonymous 4 |
| 199 | Australasian Integrative Medicine Association Inc (AIMA) |
| 200 | Australian Acupuncture and Chinese Medicine Association (ACMA) |
| 201 | Australian Homoeopathic Association Inc |
| 202 | Australian Naturopathic Practitioners Association (ANPA) |
| 203 | Australian Self-Medication Industry Inc (ASMI) |
| 204 | Bayer HealthCare |
| 205 | Chinese Medicine Industry Council of Australia Ltd (CMIC) |
| 206 | Complementary Healthcare Council (CHC) |
| 207 | Comvita New Zealand Limited |
| 208 | Consumer Health Forum of Australia (CHF) |
| 209 | Direct Selling Association of Australia (DSAA) |
| 210 | Health World Ltd |
| 211 | Lipa Pharmaceuticals Ltd |
| 212 | Nestlé Australia Ltd |
| 213 | NPS Medicinewise |
| 214 | Quality Matters Safety Matters Pty Ltd |
| 215 | Royal Australasian College of Physicians |
| 216 | Sanofi Consumer Healthcare |
| 217 | Swisse Vitamins Pty Ltd |

*Position paper on promotion of therapeutic goods* (2010) Department of Health website, accessed 16 October 2014. https://www.health.gov.au/internet/main/publishing.nsf/Content/Consultation%3A+Position+Paper+ on+the+Promotion+of+Therapeutic+Goods

| *No.* | *Author* |
|---|---|
| 218 | Assistant Prof Barbara Mintzes |
| 219 | Assoc Prof Tom Faunce |
| 220 | AusBiotech |
| 221 | Australian Dental Association |
| 222 | Australian Dental Industry Association |
| 223 | Australian Nursing Federation |
| 224 | Australian Orthopaedic Association |
| 225 | Australian Self Medication Industry |
| 226 | Australian Skeptics (Victorian Branch) |

(*Continued*)

(Continued)

| *No.* | *Author* |
|---|---|
| 227 | Beverly Snell |
| 228 | BUKO Pharma-Kampagne |
| 229 | Complementary Healthcare Council |
| 230 | Chronic Illness Alliance |
| 231 | Consumers Health Forum |
| 232 | Dr Ken Harvey |
| 233 | Dr Peter Parry |
| 234 | Generic Medicines Industry Association |
| 235 | Health Action International Global |
| 236 | Healthy Skepticism |
| 237 | IVD (in vitro diagnostics) Australia |
| 238 | John Braithwaite |
| 239 | Johnson & Johnson |
| 240 | Loretta Marron |
| 241 | National Blood Authority |
| 242 | Pharmaceutical Society of Australia |
| 243 | Pharmacy Guild of Australia |
| 244 | Prof Philip Morris |
| 245 | Public Health Association of Australia |
| 246 | Robyn Clothier |
| 247 | Royal Australasian College of Physicians |
| 248 | Royal College of Pathologists of Australia |
| 249 | Sanofi-aventis Australia |

*Therapeutic Goods Amendment (Pharmaceutical Transparency) Bill 2013* (2013) Parliament of Australia website, accessed 16 October 2014. https://www.aph.gov.au/Parliamentary_Business/Committees/Senate/Finance_and_Public_Administration/Completed_inquiries/2010–13/therapgoodsamendbill2013/submissions

| *No.* | *Author* |
|---|---|
| 250 | Abbott Australasia Pty Ltd |
| 251 | Abbvie Pty Ltd |
| 252 | Allergan Australia Pty Ltd |
| 253 | Amgen Australia Pty Ltd |
| 254 | Australian Medical Association |
| 255 | Australian Self-Medication Industry Inc |
| 256 | Bristol-Myers Squibb |
| 257 | Consumers Health Forum of Australia |

(*Continued*)

(Continued)

| *No.* | *Author* |
|---|---|
| 258 | Department of Health and Ageing |
| 259 | Dr Ken Harvey |
| 260 | Dr Mary Osborn |
| 261 | GlaxoSmithKline |
| 262 | Australian Dental Industry Association |
| 263 | GMiA (Generic Medicines Industry Association Pty Ltd) |
| 264 | Assoc Prof Ian Haines |
| 265 | Janssen-Cilag Pty Ltd |
| 266 | Lundbeck Australia Pty Ltd |
| 267 | Medical Technology Association of Australia and IVD (in vitro diagnostics) Australia |
| 268 | Medicines Australia |
| 269 | Merck Serono |
| 270 | MSD |
| 271 | Pfizer Australia |
| 272 | University of Sydney |
| 273 | SANOFI |
| 274 | Vifor Pharma |
| 275 | Department of Health and Ageing (Supplementary Submission) |

Note: The Department of Health and Ageing website lists 25 submissions in total for this consultation. However, two submissions were supplementary submissions made by the Department of Health and Ageing and so it has been treated as two separate submissions (and therefore as 26 submissions in total) for the purposes of this study.

*Consultation: Evaluating the feasibility of a new-to-market risk communication scheme for therapeutic goods* (2013) TGA website, accessed 16 October 2014. https://www.tga.gov.au/submissions-received-evaluating-feasibility-new-market-risk-communication-scheme-therapeutic-goods

| *No.* | *Author* |
|---|---|
| 276 | Accord (Advocate for the Consumer, Cosmetic, Hygiene and Specialty Products Industry) Australasia |
| 277 | Amgen Australia Pty Ltd |
| 278 | Australasian Compliance Institute (ACI) |
| 279 | Australian Self-Medication Industry Inc (ASMI) |
| 280 | Consumers Health Forum of Australia (CHF) |
| 281 | Cook Medical Australia Pty Ltd |
| 282 | CSL Limited |
| 283 | GlaxoSmithKline Pty Ltd |
| 284 | GS1 Australia |
| 285 | Medical Technology Association of Australia (MTAA) |

(*Continued*)

(Continued)

| *No.* | *Author* |
|---|---|
| 286 | Medicines Australia |
| 287 | Medicines New Zealand |
| 288 | Mylan New Zealand |
| 289 | National Electronic Health Transition Authority (NEHTA) |
| 290 | Novartis Pharmaceuticals Australia Pty Ltd |
| 291 | Pfizer Australia Pty Ltd |
| 292 | Pharmaceutical Society of Australia Ltd |
| 293 | Pharmacy Guild of Australia Ltd |
| 294 | ResMed Ltd |
| 295 | Society of Hospital Pharmacists of Australia (SHPA) |

*Consultation regulation impact statement: regulating the advertising of therapeutic goods to the general public* (2014) TGA website, accessed 16 October 2014. https://www.tga.gov.au/submissions-received-consultation-regulation-impact-statement-regulating-advertising-therapeutic-goods-general-public

| *No.* | *Author* |
|---|---|
| 296 | AbbVie Pty Ltd |
| 297 | Accord (Advocate for the Consumer, Cosmetic, Hygiene and Specialty Products Industry) Australasia Limited |
| 298 | Advertising Standards Authority of New Zealand (Inc.) |
| 299 | Advertising Standards Bureau |
| 300 | Aldridge, Rachel |
| 301 | Amway of Australia |
| 302 | Anonymous 1 |
| 303 | Anonymous 2 |
| 304 | Anonymous 3 |
| 305 | Anonymous 4 |
| 306 | Anonymous 5 |
| 307 | Anonymous 6 |
| 308 | Anonymous 7 |
| 309 | Anonymous 8 |
| 310 | Anonymous 9 |
| 311 | Anonymous 10 |
| 312 | Anonymous 11 |
| 313 | Anonymous 12 |
| 314 | Anonymous 13 |
| 315 | Arnold, Bruce |
| 316 | Ashford, Pauline |
| 317 | Australasian College of Natural Therapies (ACNT) |

(*Continued*)

(Continued)

| *No.* | *Author* |
|---|---|
| 318 | Australasian Society of Clinical and Experimental Pharmacologists and Toxicologists |
| 319 | Australian Acupuncture and Chinese Medicine Association Ltd (AACMA) |
| 320 | Australian Association of Massage Therapies Ltd (AAMT) |
| 321 | Australian Dental Industry Association (ADIA) |
| 322 | Australian Food and Grocery Council (AFGC) |
| 323 | Australian Health & Education Centre |
| 324 | Australian Homoeopathic Association (AHA) |
| 325 | Australian Natural Therapists Association Ltd (ANTA) |
| 326 | Australian Naturopathic Practitioners Association (ANPA) |
| 327 | Australian Register of Naturopaths and Herbalists (ARONAH) |
| 328 | Australian Self-Medication Industry (ASMI) |
| 329 | Australian Skeptics Inc., NSW Branch |
| 330 | Australian Skeptics Inc., Victorian Branch |
| 331 | Australian Subscription Television and Radio Association (ASTRA) |
| 332 | Australian Traditional-Medicine Society (ATMS) |
| 333 | Batagol, Ronald Peter |
| 334 | Berry, Sarah |
| 335 | BioCeuticals Limited |
| 336 | BioMedica Nutraceuticals Pty Ltd |
| 337 | Blackmores Ltd |
| 338 | Boehringer Ingelheim Pty Limited |
| 339 | Centre for Evidence-Based Complementary Medicine (CEBCoM) Pty Ltd |
| 340 | CHOICE |
| 341 | Complaints Resolution Panel (CRP) |
| 342 | Complementary Healthcare Council of Australia |
| 343 | Complementary Medicine Association (CMA) |
| 344 | Consumers Health Forum of Australia (CHF) |
| 345 | Cosmetic Physicians Society of Australia |
| 346 | Dietitians Association of Australia (DAA) |
| 347 | Direct Selling Association of Australia (DSAA) |
| 348 | Ego Pharmaceuticals Pty Ltd (EGO) |
| 349 | Foundation for Advertising Research (FAR) |
| 350 | Free TV Australia Limited |
| 351 | Friends of Science in Medicine (FSM) |
| 352 | Gaibisso, Tracy |
| 353 | Global Therapeutics Pty Ltd |
| 354 | Grimshaw-Jones, Kyle |
| 355 | Health World Limited |
| 356 | Hyams, Jared |

*(Continued)*

(Continued)

| *No.* | *Author* |
|---|---|
| 357 | The International Aromatherapy and Aromatic Medicine Association (IAAMA) |
| 358 | IVD (in vitro diagnostics) Australia Limited |
| 359 | Johnson & Johnson Family of Companies |
| 360 | Korke, Jason |
| 361 | McMullen, Debbie |
| 362 | Medical Technology Association of Australia (MTAA) |
| 363 | Medicines New Zealand |
| 364 | Mordi Skeptics in the Pub |
| 365 | National Herbalists Association of Australia |
| 366 | New Zealand Self Medication Industry (NZSMI) |
| 367 | Mary Osborn |
| 368 | Outdoor Media Association (OMA) |
| 369 | PharmaCare Laboratories Pty Ltd |
| 370 | Pharmaceutical Society of Australia Ltd |
| 371 | Sanofi Consumer Healthcare |
| 372 | Shepheard, Adam |
| 373 | Snell, Beverley |
| 374 | Society of Hospital Pharmacists of Australia (SHPA) |
| 375 | Society of Natural Therapists & Researchers Inc (SNTR) |
| 376 | Soho Flordis International (SFI) |
| 377 | Southern School of Natural Therapies (SSNT) |
| 378 | Stolair Research and Consultancy Services |
| 379 | Stryker South Pacific |
| 380 | Swisse Wellness Pty Ltd |
| 381 | The Communications Council |
| 382 | The Newspaper Works (TNW) |
| 383 | The Pharmacy Guild of Australia (PGA) |
| 384 | The Royal Australian College of General Practitioners (RACGP) |
| 385 | The University of Adelaide |
| 386 | Toyama, Christine |
| 387 | Varnhagen, Julie |
| 388 | Vitry, Agnes |

*Consultation: Mechanisms to maintain the currency of approved Product Information (PI) and Consumer Medicine Information (CMI)* (2013) TGA website, accessed 16 October 2014. https://www.tga.gov.au/submissions-received-mechanisms-maintain-currency-approved-product-information-pi-and-consumer-medicine-information-cmi

| *No.* | *Author* |
|---|---|
| 389 | Advisory Committee on Prescription Medicines (ACPM) |
| 390 | Australian Medical Association (AMA) |

*(Continued)*

(Continued)

| *No.* | *Author* |
|---|---|
| 391 | Australian Medicines Handbook |
| 392 | Australian Self-Medication Industry Inc (ASMI) |
| 393 | Consumers Health Forum of Australia (CHF) |
| 394 | CSL Behring Pty Ltd & bioCSL Pty Ltd |
| 395 | Electronic Distribution Working Group (EDWG) |
| 396 | Faculty of Pharmacy, University of Sydney |
| 397 | Generic Medicines Industry Association (GMiA) |
| 398 | GlaxoSmithKline Australia Pty Ltd |
| 399 | Medicines Australia |
| 400 | Medicines New Zealand |
| 401 | Medicines Information Service, Pharmacy Department, Alfred Hospital |
| 402 | Merck Serono Australia Pty Ltd |
| 403 | MIMS Australia Pty Ltd |
| 404 | Novartis Pharmaceuticals Australia Pty Ltd |
| 405 | Pfizer Australia |
| 406 | Pharmaceutical Society of Australia |
| 407 | Pharmacist (Anonymous) |
| 408 | Society of Hospital Pharmacists of Australia (SHPA) |
| 409 | Sydney Children's Hospital |
| 410 | Various individuals (Anonymous) |
| 411 | Webstercare |

*Consultation: Draft TGA approach to disclosure of commercially confidential information (CCI)* (2013) TGA website, accessed 16 October 2014. https://www.tga.gov.au/submissions-received-draft-tga-approach-disclosure-commercially-confidential-information-cci

| *No.* | *Author* |
|---|---|
| 412 | AbbVie Pty Ltd |
| 413 | Anonymous |
| 414 | Australian Self-Medication Industry Inc |
| 415 | Complementary Healthcare Council of Australia (CHC) |
| 416 | Consumers Health Forum (CHF) of Australia |
| 417 | Dr Agnes Vitry |
| 418 | Generic Medicines Industry Association (GMiA) |
| 419 | GlaxoSmithKline (GSK) Australia |
| 420 | Johnson & Johnson |
| 421 | Medical Technology Association of Australia |
| 422 | Medicines Australia |
| 423 | Novartis Pharmaceuticals Australia Pty Ltd |
| 424 | Pfizer Australia Pty Ltd |

*(Continued)*

(Continued)

*Consultation: TGA guidance on release of supply for medicines manufacturers* (2013) TGA website, accessed 16 October 2014. https://www.tga.gov.au/submissions-received-tga-guidance-release-supply-medicines-manufacturers

| *No.* | *Author* |
|---|---|
| 425 | AbbVie Pty Ltd |
| 426 | Active Pharmaceutical Ingredient Manufacturer's Association of Australia (APIMAA) |
| 427 | Amway of Australia and New Zealand |
| 428 | Australian New Zealand Industrial Gas Association (ANZIGA) |
| 429 | Australian Self Medication Industry Inc. (ASMI) |
| 430 | Biogen Idec Australia Pty Ltd |
| 431 | Bruce Graham Consulting |
| 432 | CMC Regulatory |
| 433 | Complementary Healthcare Council of Australia (CHC) |
| 434 | Consumers Health Forum of Australia (CHF) |
| 435 | Generic Medicines Industry Association (GMiA) |
| 436 | GlaxoSmithKline Pty Ltd |
| 437 | Integria Health Care (Australia) Pty Ltd |
| 438 | Novo Nordisk Pharmaceuticals Pty Ltd |
| 439 | Pfizer Australia Pty Ltd |
| 440 | Sanofi-aventis Australia Pty Ltd |

*Therapeutic Goods Amendment (2013 Measures No. 1) Bill 2013* (2013) Parliament of Australia website, accessed 16 October 2014. http://www.aph.gov.au/Parliamentary_Business/Committees/Senate/Community_Affairs/Completed_inquiries/2010–13/therapeuticgoods/submissions

| *No.* | *Author* |
|---|---|
| 441 | Australian Commission on Safety and Quality in Health Care |
| 442 | Australian Dental Industry Association |
| 443 | Australian Medical Association |
| 444 | Australian Orthopaedic Association |
| 445 | Complementary Healthcare Council of Australia |
| 446 | Department of Health and Ageing |
| 447 | Generic Medicines Industry Association |
| 448 | Dr Doug Kentwell |
| 449 | Medicines Australia |
| 450 | Northern Territory Government |
| 451 | NSW Government |

# References


Abraham J (1995) *Science, politics and the pharmaceutical industry: controversy and bias in drug regulation*, UCL Press, London.

Abraham J and Ballinger R (2012) 'Science, politics, and health in the brave new world of pharmaceutical carcinogenic risk assessment: technical progress or cycle of regulatory capture?', *Social Science & Medicine*, 75:1433–1440.

ACCC (Australian Competition and Consumer Commission) (2017, May) *Therapeutic Goods Administration consultation paper: options for the future regulation of 'low risk' products*, ACCC. https://www.tga.gov.au/submissions-received-options-future-regulation-low-risk-products

Adair RF and Holmgren LR (2005) 'Do drug samples influence resident prescribing behavior? A randomized trial', *The American Journal of Medicine*, 118(8):881–884.

Adams R (2018, 8 November) 'The illusion of transparency: neoliberalism, depoliticisation and information as commodity', *SSRN*, accessed 31 March 2024. https://papers.ssrn.com/sol3/papers.cfm?abstract_id=3281074

Adams R (2020) *Transparency: new trajectories in law*, Routledge, Abingdon and New York.

Adler-Bolton B and Vierkant A (2022) *Health communism: a surplus manifesto*, Verso, London and New York.

Ahmad FB, Cisewski JA and Anderson RN (2024) 'Mortality in the United States: provisional data, 2023', *MMWR Morbidity and Mortality Weekly Report*, 73:677–681. https://doi.org/10.15585/mmwr.mm7331a1

Ahwan L (2020, 23 March) 'Money wasted on vitamins most don't need', *The Daily Telegraph*, accessed 4 October 2024. https://may.idm.oclc.org/login?url=https://www.proquest.com/newspapers/money-wasted-on-vitamins-most-don-t-need/docview/2380666096/se-2?accountid=12309

AIHW (Australian Institute of Health and Welfare) (2018) *Opioid harm in Australia and comparisons between Australia and Canada*, AIHW, accessed 12 September 2024. https://www.aihw.gov.au/reports/illicit-use-of-drugs/opioid-harm-in-australia/summary

Albanese A (2023, 29 November) *National apology to all Australians impacted by the thalidomide tragedy: speech* [media release], Prime Minister of Australia, accessed 29 May 2024. https://www.pm.gov.au/media/national-apology-all-australians-impacted-thalidomide-tragedy

Albert K and Gray G (2023) 'Keeping up with COVID-19 information: capacity issues and knowledge uncertainty early in the pandemic', *Canadian Review of Sociology/Revue Canadienne de Sociologie*, 60(4):594–615.

Alowi M and Kani Y (2018) 'Promotion of prescription drugs and its impact on physician's choice behavior', *Journal of Pharmaceutical Care and Health Systems*, 6:1–7.

Altman D (2020) 'Understanding the US failure on coronavirus: an essay by Drew Altman', *BMJ: British Medical Journal*, 370:1–3.
ANAO (Australian National Audit Office) (1996) *Drug evaluation by the Therapeutic Goods Administration*, Audit Report No. 8 1996–97, ANAO, accessed 8 November 2018. https://www.anao.gov.au/work/performance-audit/drug-evaluation-the-therapeutic-goods-administration
ANAO (2004) *Regulation of non-prescription medicinal products*, Audit Report No. 18 2004–05, ANAO, accessed 8 November 2018. https://www.anao.gov.au/work/performance-audit/regulation-non-prescription-medicinal-products
ANAO (2007) *Administering regulation*, ANAO, accessed 3 July 2016. http://www.anao.gov.au/director/publications/betterpracguides.cfm
ANAO (2011) *Therapeutic goods regulation: complementary medicines*, Audit Report No. 3 2011–12, ANAO, accessed 8 November 2018. https://www.anao.gov.au/work/performance-audit/therapeutic-goods-regulation-complementary-medicines
ANAO (2014) *Administering the code of good manufacturing practice for prescription medicines*, Audit Report No. 30 2013–14, ANAO, accessed 21 May 2018. https://www.anao.gov.au/work/performance-audit/administering-the-code-good-manufacturing-practice-prescription-medicines
Anderson P (1976–1977) 'The antinomies of Antonio Gramsci', *New Left Review*, 100:5–78.
Angell M (2004) *The truth about the drug companies: how they deceive us and what to do about it*, Random House, Toronto.
ARTG (Australian Register of Therapeutic Goods) (2024) *ARTG search visualisation tool*, TGA, accessed 1 October 2024. https://compliance.health.gov.au/artg/
ASMI (Australian Self-Medication Industry) (2015) *ASMI code of practice*, ASMI, accessed 7 November 2016. http://asmi.com.au/about/asmi-code-of-practice/about-the-asmi-code.aspx
ASMI (2012–2013) *Annual report*, ASMI, accessed 8 November 2018. http://asmi.com.au/news-information/annual-reports.aspx
ASMI (2016) *Promotional monitoring panel, PMP*, ASMI, accessed 30 November 2016. http://www.asmi.com.au/advertising/promotional-monitoring-panel.aspx
ASMI (2016–2017) *Annual report*, ASMI, accessed 29 July 2024. http://asmi.com.au/news-information/annual-reports.aspx
*Aspen Pharmacare Australia Pty Ltd and Minister for Health and Ageing* (2012) AATA 362.
*Aspen Pharmacare Australia Pty Ltd and Minister for Health and Ageing* (2012) AATA 376.
*Aspen Pharmacare Australia Pty Ltd and Minister for Health and Ageing* (2013) AATA 197.
*Aspen Pharmacare Australia Pty Ltd and Minister for Health and Ageing* (2013) AATA 649.
Australian Bureau of Statistics (2019, 25 September) *Opioid-induced deaths in Australia*, ABS, accessed 12 September 2024. https://www.abs.gov.au/articles/opioid-induced-deaths-australia
Australian Commission on Safety and Quality in Health Care (2014) *Health literacy: taking action to improve safety and quality*, Australian Commission on Safety and Quality in Health Care, accessed 27 June 2024. https://www.safetyandquality.gov.au/publications-and-resources/resource-library/health-literacy-taking-action-improve-safety-and-quality
*Australian Competition and Consumer Commission v Reckitt Benckiser (Australia) Pty Ltd* (2016) FCAFC 181.
*Australian Competition and Consumer Commission v Reckitt Benckiser (Australia) Pty Ltd (No 7)* (2016) FCA 424.

Australian Government (2016) *Budget 2016–17*, Budget Paper No. 2, Australian Government, accessed 8 November 2018. https://archive.budget.gov.au/2016–17/index.htm

Australian Government (2023) *Australian Government response to the Standing Committee on Health, Aged Care and Sport report: the new frontier—delivering better health to all Australians, inquiry into approval processes for new drugs and novel medical technologies in Australia*, Parliament of Australia, accessed 12 August 2024. https://www.aph.gov.au/Parliamentary_Business/Committees/House/Health_Aged_Care_and_Sport/Newdrugs/Government_Response

Australian House of Representatives (1953) *Parliamentary debates: national health bill 1953, Speech*, 1755–1760 (Sir Earle Page). https://parlinfo.aph.gov.au/parlInfo/search/display/display.w3p;query=Id%3A%22hansard80%2Fhansardr80%2F1953-03-27%2F0040%22

Australian House of Representatives (2005, 17 August) *Therapeutic goods amendment bill 2005, Second reading Speech*, 1–3 (Christopher Pyne).

Australian Senate (1953) *Parliamentary debates: therapeutic substances bill 1953, Second Reading Speech*, 143. https://parlinfo.aph.gov.au/parlInfo/search/display/display.w3p;query=Id%3A%22hansard80%2Fhansards80%2F1953-11-25%2F0050%22

Australian Senate (2000) *Therapeutic goods amendment bill (No. 4) 2000, explanatory memorandum.*

Australian Senate (2005a, 22 June) *Questions on notice: Pan pharmaceuticals*, 156–158. https://parlinfo.aph.gov.au/parlInfo/search/display/display.w3p;query=Id%3A%22chamber%2Fhansards%2F2005-06-22%2F0181%22

Australian Senate (2005b, 9 August) *Questions on notice: Vioxx*, 159–160. https://parlinfo.aph.gov.au/parlInfo/search/display/display.w3p;query=Id%3A%22chamber%2Fhansards%2F2005-08-09%2F0158%22

Australian Senate (2019, 1 August) *Official hansard*, 1471–1472. https://www.aph.gov.au/Parliamentary_Business/Hansard/Hansard_Display?bid=chamber/hansards/0ddd7d01-a5d8-4370-8b5d-bdcd71582383/&sid=0181

Australian Senate Finance and Public Administration Legislation Committee (2013) *Therapeutic goods amendment (pharmaceutical transparency) bill 2013*, accessed 27 July 2024. http://www.aph.gov.au/parliamentary_business/committees/senate_committees?url=fapa_ctte/completed_inquiries/2010–13/therap_goods_amend_bill_2013/report/index.htm

Aykan B and Güvenç-Salgırlı S (2015) 'Responsibilizing individuals, regulating health: debating public spots, risk, and neoliberal governmentality in contemporary Turkey', *New Perspectives on Turkey*, 53(1):71–92.

Ayres I and Braithwaite J (1991) 'Tripartism: regulatory capture and empowerment', *Law & Social Inquiry*, 16(3):435–496.

Ayres I and Braithwaite J (1992) *Responsive regulation: transcending the deregulation debate*, Oxford University Press, New York and Oxford.

Baldwin R and Black J (2008) 'Really responsive regulation', *The Modern Law Review*, 71(1):59–94.

Bandiera R (2021) 'Marx, Foucault, and state–corporate harm: a case study of regulatory failure in Australian non-prescription medicine regulation', *Crime, Law and Social Change*, 76(2):173–193.

Bandiera R and Marmo M (2017) 'Re-framing 'counterfeit from a public health perspective': a case for fraudulent medicine', *Australian & New Zealand Journal of Criminology*, 50(2):195–212.

Barker M (2020,16 April) 'COVID-19: how big pharma and big philanthropy consume the world', *Counterpunch*, accessed 14 September 2024. https://www.counterpunch.org/2020/04/16/covid-19-how-big-pharma-and-big-philanthropy-consume-the-world/

Bashford A (1998) 'Quarantine and the imagining of the Australian nation', *Health*, 2(4):387–402.
Bashford A (2004) *Imperial hygiene: a critical history of colonialism, nationalism and public health*, Palgrave Macmillan, Basingstoke and New York.
Baume PA (1991) *A question of balance: report on the future of drug evaluation in Australia*, Australian Government Publishing Service, Canberra.
Beeson M and Firth A (1998) 'Neoliberalism as a political rationality: Australian public policy since the 1980s', *Journal of Sociology*, 34(3):215–231.
Bensoussan A, Myers SP, Wu SM and O'Connor K (2004) 'Naturopathic and Western herbal medicine practice in Australia: a workforce survey', *Complementary Therapies in Medicine*, 12(1):17–27.
Bernat I and Whyte D (2017) 'State-corporate crime and the process of capital accumulation: mapping a global regime of permission from Galicia to Morecambe Bay', *Critical Criminology*, 25(1):71–86.
Bernstein M (1955) *Regulating business by independent commission*, Princeton University Press, Princeton.
Bhasale A (2021) *Communicating post-market safety risks of medicines with regulatory safety advisories: an international comparison of policy and perceptions* [PhD thesis], University of Sydney, accessed 12 February 2024. https://ses.library.usyd.edu.au/handle/2123/25956
Biggs A (2002) *The Pharmaceutical Benefits Scheme an overview*, Parliament of Australia, accessed 26 May 2024. https://www.aph.gov.au/About_Parliament/Parliamentary_Departments/Parliamentary_Library/Publications_Archive/archive/pbs
Bittle S and Hébert J (2020) 'Controlling corporate crimes in times of de-regulation and re-regulation', in Rorie ML (ed) *The handbook of white-collar crime*, John Wiley & Sons, Hoboken.
Black J and Baldwin R (2010) 'Really responsive risk-based regulation', *Law & Policy*, 32(2):181–213.
Black J and Baldwin R (2012) 'When risk-based regulation aims low: approaches and challenges', *Regulation & Governance*, 6(1):2–22.
*BMA (British Medical Association) v Commonwealth* 1949 79 CLR 201:256.
Braithwaite J (1984) *Corporate crime in the pharmaceutical industry*, Routledge & Kegan Paul, London.
Braithwaite J (2005) *Neoliberalism or regulatory capitalism* (Occasional Paper 5), The Australian National University Open Research Library, accessed 9 July 2021. https://openresearch-repository.anu.edu.au/items/2acd7c1b-300f-4c73-8465-9ed2cca2d7f1
Braithwaite J (2008) *Regulatory capitalism: how it works, ideas for making it work better*, Edward Elgar Publishing, Cheltenham.
Branley A (2019a, 9 July) 'Pharma giant using loophole to falsely promote opioid pain relief products across Australia', *ABC*, accessed 10 September 2024. https://www.abc.net.au/news/2019-07-10/opioid-maker-linked-to-sackler-family-maker-giving-gp-bad-advice/11278416
Branley A (2019b, 23 December) 'Pharmaceutical giant Mundipharma hit with hefty fine over misleading opioid drug information', *ABC*, accessed 10 September 2024. https://www.abc.net.au/news/2019-12-23/mundipharma-hit-by-fine-for-misleading-local-doctors-over-opiods/11823280
Braun LA, Tiralongo E, Wilkinson JM, Poole S, Spitzer O, Bailey M and Dooley M (2010) 'Adverse reactions to complementary medicines: the Australian pharmacy experience', *International Journal of Pharmacy Practice*, 18(4):242–244.
Braun V and Clarke V (2006) 'Using thematic analysis in psychology', *Qualitative Research in Psychology*, 3(2):77–101.
*Broadcasting Act 1942* (Cth).

Brodie M (2019, 4 June) 'Mundi plums up pain portfolio', *Pharma in Focus*, accessed 12 February 2024. https://pharmainfocus.com.au/newsPrint_m.asp?newsid=14992
Brown W (2005) *Edgework: critical essays on knowledge and politics*, Princeton University Press, Princeton.
Buckley NA and Faunce TA (2013) 'Trials and tribulations in the removal of dextropropoxyphene from the Australian Register of Therapeutic Goods', *Medical Journal of Australia*, 199(4):257–260.
Burchell G (1996) 'Liberal government and techniques of the self', in Barry A, Osborne T and Rose N (eds) *Foucault and political reason*, Taylor & Francis Group, London.
Canberra Times (1991a) 'Drug makers call for overhaul of approval system', *Canberra Times*, accessed 11 July 2024. http://nla.gov.au/nla.news-article129098366
Canberra Times (1991b) 'Major changes to drug process soon: Howe', *Canberra Times*, accessed 11 July 2024. https://trove.nla.gov.au/newspaper/article/129093609
Castles I (1988) *Year book Australia 1988*, Australian Bureau of Statistics, Canberra.
Cherla A, Mossialos E, Salcher-Konrad M, Kesselheim AS and Naci H (2022) 'Post-marketing requirements for cancer drugs approved by the European Medicines Agency, 2004–2014', *Clinical Pharmacology & Therapeutics*, 112(4):846–852.
Chinese Medicine Board, AHPRA (Australian Health Practitioner Regulation Agency) (2024) *Registration standards*, AHPRA, accessed 29 July 2024. https://www.chinesemedicineboard.gov.au/Registration-Standards.aspx?_gl=1*1qlh95k*_ga*NjE5NzI0NzA3LjE3MTE2MzEwNzk.*_ga_F1G6LRC%E2%80%A6
Choi CY (1971) *Chinese migration and settlement in Australia, with special reference to the Chinese in Melbourne* [PhD thesis], Australian National University, accessed 6 May 2024. https://openresearch-repository.anu.edu.au/items/9908caf3-297e-4f4e-b1db-803297c7c9cc
CHP Australia (Consumer Healthcare Products Australia) (2021) *2020–21 annual report*, CHP Australia, accessed 1 October 2024. https://www.chpaustralia.com.au/About/Governance/Annual-Reports
CHP Australia (2022) *Terms of agreement for assessment of advertising of therapeutic goods applicant and CHP Australia*, CHP Australia, accessed 27 July 2024. https://www.chpaustralia.com.au/AdCheck/Adcheck-Terms
CHP Australia (2024a) *AdCheck pricing effective 1 June 2024*, CHP Australia, accessed 26 July 2024. https://www.chpaustralia.com.au/AdCheck/About-AdCheck/Application-Fees
CHP Australia (2024b) *Determinations*, CHP Australia, accessed 29 July 2024. https://www.chpaustralia.com.au/About/ASMI-Code-of-Practice/Determinations
CMA (Complementary Medicines Australia) (2013–14) *Annual report*, CMA, accessed 7 December 2016. http://www.cmaustralia.org.au/Annual-Reports
CMA (2015) *CMA marketing & supply code of practice: complementary medicines*, CMA, accessed 7 November 2016. http://www.cmaustralia.org.au/CMA-Codes-of-Practices
Coghlan ML, MakEr G, Crighton E, Haile J, Murray DC, White NE, Byard RW, Bellgard MI, Mullaney I, Trengove R and Allcock RJ (2015) 'Combined DNA, toxicological and heavy metal analyses provides an auditing toolkit to improve pharmacovigilance of traditional Chinese medicine (TCM)', *Scientific Reports*, 5(1):1–9.
Commonwealth of Australia & Others (2010) 'Defence', Submission in *Pharmacare Laboratories Pty Ltd v Commonwealth of Australia*, NSD 1991/2008, 12 May, accessed 8 November 2018. https://www.fedcourt.gov.au/law-and-practice/class-actions/class-actions/documents2/Defence_1.pdf
*Competition and Consumer Act 2010* (Cth).
Costello P (2005, 12 October) *Joint press release: Prime Minister and Treasurer—taskforce on reducing the regulatory burden on business* [media release], The

Treasury, Australian Government, accessed 5 July 2024. http://ministers.treasury.gov.au/DisplayDocs.aspx?doc=pressreleases/2005/087.htm&pageID=003&min=phc&Year=2005&DocType=0
Creswell A (2010, 10 July) 'Untested remedies get TGA tick: Australian register of therapeutic goods', *The Australian*, accessed 16 March 2017. http://www.theaustralian.com.au/news/health-science/untested-remedies-get-tga-tick-australian-register-of-therapeutic-goods/news-story/7b141ba79cf0b130711dcea895cd2042
CRP (Complaints Resolution Panel) (2011) *Complaint 2011-06-001 Nurofen*, CRP, accessed 21 May 2018. https://webarchive.nla.gov.au/awa/20200302084447/http://pandora.nla.gov.au/pan/180786/20200302–1153/www.tgacrp.com.au/complaint-register/indexd4c9.html
CRP (2013) *Complaint 2012/08/010 and 2012/10/024 Nurofen*, CRP, accessed 21 May 2018. https://webarchive.nla.gov.au/awa/20200302084016/http://pandora.nla.gov.au/pan/180786/20200302–1153/www.tgacrp.com.au/complaint-register/index50ec.html
CRP (2014–2015) *Summary of complaints for the financial year 1 July 2014—30 June 2015*, CRP, accessed 7 October 2024 [internet archive]. https://webarchive.nla.gov.au/awa/20200302084643/http://pandora.nla.gov.au/pan/180786/20200302–1153/www.tgacrp.com.au/index.html
CRP (2016–2017) *Summary of complaints for the financial year 1 July 2016—30 June 2017*, CRP, accessed 7 October 2024 [internet archive]. https://webarchive.nla.gov.au/awa/20200302084643/http://pandora.nla.gov.au/pan/180786/20200302–1153/www.tgacrp.com.au/index.html
CRP (2017–2018) *Summary of complaints for the financial year 1 July 2017—30 June 2018*, CRP, accessed 7 October 2024 [internet archive]. https://webarchive.nla.gov.au/awa/20200302084643/http://pandora.nla.gov.au/pan/180786/20200302–1153/www.tgacrp.com.au/index.html
CRP (2020a) *Members of the CRP*, CRP, accessed 7 October 2024 [internet archive]. https://webarchive.nla.gov.au/awa/20200302085205/http://pandora.nla.gov.au/pan/180786/20200302–1153/www.tgacrp.com.au/members-of-the-crp/index.html
CRP (2020b) *Procedures*, CRP, accessed 7 October 2024 [internet archive]. https://webarchive.nla.gov.au/awa/20200302084613/http://pandora.nla.gov.au/pan/180786/20200302–1153/www.tgacrp.com.au/procedures/index.html
Cruikshank B (1999) *The will to empower: democratic citizens and other subjects*, Cornell University Press, New York.
Cumpston JHL (1913) *Quarantine: Australian maritime quarantine and the evolution of international agreements concerning quarantine*, Albert J. Mullet, Government Printer, Melbourne, accessed 27 May 2024. https://catalogue.nla.gov.au/catalog/488903
Cumpston JHL (1914) *The history of small-pox in Australia, 1788–1908*, Albert J. Mullet, Government Printer, Melbourne, accessed 26 May 2024. https://archive.org/details/39002011127157.med.yale.edu
Curthoys A (1973) *Race and ethnicity: a study of the response of British colonists to Aborigines, Chinese and non-British Europeans in New South Wales, 1856–1881* [PhD thesis], Macquarie University, National Library of Australia, accessed 6 May 2024. https://trove.nla.gov.au/work/250661514?keyword=Jacob%20Luck
Dalley H (2003, 4 May) 'Tainted pills' [television transcript], *Sunday* [Channel 9], accessed 14 November 2013. http://sgp1.paddington.ninemsn.com.au/sunday/cover_stories/article_1266.asp?s=1
Darnell M (2004) 'Life and labour for indentured Chinese shepherds in New South Wales, 1847–55', *Journal of Australian Colonial History*, 6:137–158.
Davies J (2011) *Challenging governance theory: from networks to hegemony*, Policy Press, Bristol.

Davis C and Abraham J (2013) *Unhealthy pharmaceutical regulation: innovation, politics and promissory science*, Springer, Basingstoke.
Dean M (1998) 'Risk, calculable and incalculable', *Soziale Welt*, 49(1):25–42.
Dean M (2010) *Governmentality: power and rule in modern society*, Sage, London.
de Haan E and ten Kate A (2023) *Pharma's pandemic profits: pharma profits from COVID-19 vaccines*, Stichting Onderzoek Multinationale Ondernemingen, accessed 14 September 2024. https://www.somo.nl/pharmas-pandemic-profits/
DeJong C, Aguilar T, Tseng CW, Lin GA, Boscardin WJ and Dudley RA (2016) 'Pharmaceutical industry-sponsored meals and physician prescribing patterns for Medicare beneficiaries', *JAMA Internal Medicine*, 176(8):1114–1122.
Department of Community Services and Health (1989) *Annual report 1988–89*, Australian Government Publishing Service, Canberra, accessed 18 June 2024. https://nla.gov.au:443/tarkine/nla.obj-1616164385
Department of Community Services and Health (1990) *Annual report 1989–90*, Australian Government Publishing Service, Canberra, accessed 18 June 2024. https://nla.gov.au/nla.obj-2062463320/view?partId=nla.obj-2068362648
Department of Health (1964) *Annual report by the Director-General of Health for year 1963–64*, AJ Arthur, Commonwealth Government Printer, Canberra, accessed 30 May 2024. https://nla.gov.au:443/tarkine/nla.obj-2772558065
Department of Health (1969) *Annual report by the Director-General of Health for year 1968–69*, Commonwealth Government Printing Office, Canberra, accessed 30 May 2024. https://nla.gov.au:443/tarkine/nla.obj-2771745203
Department of Health (1972) *Director-General of Health: annual report for year 1970–71*, Commonwealth Government Printing Office, Canberra, accessed 30 May 2024. https://nla.gov.au:443/tarkine/nla.obj-2772522617
Department of Health (1973) *Director-General of Health: annual report for year 1971–72*, Commonwealth Government Printing Office, Canberra, accessed 30 May 2024. https://nla.gov.au:443/tarkine/nla.obj-2579191686
Department of Health (1974) *Director-General of Health: annual report for year 1972–73*, The Government Printer of Australia, Canberra, accessed 30 May 2024. https://nla.gov.au:443/tarkine/nla.obj-1745801827
Department of Health (1975) *Director-General of Health: annual report for year 1973–74*, Commonwealth Government Printing Office, Canberra, accessed 30 May 2024. https://nla.gov.au:443/tarkine/nla.obj-1616208285
Department of Health (1976) *Department of Health: annual report of Director-General for year 1974–75*, The Government Printer of Australia, Canberra, accessed 30 May 2024. https://nla.gov.au:443/tarkine/nla.obj-1360702124
Department of Health (1978) *Annual report of the Director-General of Health 1977–78*, Australian Government Publishing Service, Canberra, accessed 30 May 2024. https://nla.gov.au:443/tarkine/nla.obj-1464600858
Department of Health (1979) *Annual report of the Director-General of Health 1978–79*, Australian Government Publishing Service, Canberra, accessed 30 May 2024. https://nla.gov.au:443/tarkine/nla.obj-2656917443
Department of Health (1980) *Annual report of the Director-General of Health 1979–80*, Australian Government Publishing Service, Canberra, accessed 30 May 2024. https://nla.gov.au:443/tarkine/nla.obj-1360667088
Department of Health (1981) *Annual report of the Director-General of Health 1980–81*, Australian Government Publishing Service, Canberra, accessed 30 May 2024. https://nla.gov.au:443/tarkine/nla.obj-1466769597
Department of Health (1984) *Annual report of the Director-General of Health 1983–84*, Australian Government Publishing Service, accessed 30 May 2024. https://nla.gov.au:443/tarkine/nla.obj-1466819007
Department of Health (1985) *Commonwealth Department of Health annual report 1984–85*, Australian Government Publishing Service, accessed 30 May 2024. https://nla.gov.au:443/tarkine/nla.obj-1360663924

Department of Health (2008) *Guidelines for preparing submissions to the Pharmaceutical Benefits Advisory Committee (Version 4.3)*, Department of Health, accessed 25 February 2017. https://pbac.pbs.gov.au/content/information/archived-versions/pbac-guidelines-v4-3-2008.pdf

Department of Health (2011) *Position paper on the promotion of therapeutic goods*, Department of Health, accessed 8 November 2018. https://www.health.gov.au/internet/main/publishing.nsf/Content/Consultation%3A+Position+Paper+on+the+Promotion+of+Therapeutic+Goods

Department of Health (2016a) *Australian Government response to the review of medicines and medical devices regulation*, Department of Health, accessed 20 September 2016. https://www.tga.gov.au/news/news/australian-government-response-review-medicines-and-medical-devices-regulation

Department of Health (2016b) *Australian statistics on medicines 2015*, Department of Health, accessed 2 September 2017. https://m.pbs.gov.au/statistics/asm/asm–2015.html

Department of Health and Aged Care (1999a) *Australian statistics on medicines 1998*, Department of Health and Aged Care, accessed 2 September 2017. https://m.pbs.gov.au/statistics/asm/asm–1998.html

Department of Health and Aged Care (1999b) *National medicines policy*, Department of Health and Aged Care, Canberra.

Department of Health and Aged Care (2023) *National registration and accreditation scheme*, Department of Health and Aged Care, accessed 29 July 2024. https://www.health.gov.au/our-work/national-registration-and-accreditation-scheme

Department of Health and Ageing (2003) *Australian statistics on medicines 1999–2000*, Department of Health and Ageing, accessed 2 September 2017. https://m.pbs.gov.au/statistics/asm/asm-1999–00.html

Department of Health and Ageing (2005) *Australian statistics on medicines 2003*, Department of Health and Ageing, accessed 2 September 2017. https://m.pbs.gov.au/info/statistics/asm/asm–2003.html

Department of Health and Ageing (2011, 8 December) *Government to improve regulation of therapeutic goods* [media release], Department of Health and Ageing, accessed 27 July 2024. https://webarchive.nla.gov.au/awa/20130902003642/http://pandora.nla.gov.au/pan/141595/20130902-0954/www.health.gov.au/internet/ministers/publishing.nsf/Content/mr-yr11-ck-ck05398fc.htm

Department of Health and Ageing (2014, 24 October) *Expert panel to review medicines and medical devices regulation* [media release], Department of Health and Ageing, accessed 27 July 2024. http://www.health.gov.au/internet/ministers/publishing.nsf/Content/C79C3076E4082F48CA257D7A00766E8E/%24File/PD091.pdf

Department of Health and Family Services (1996) *Final report of the alternative medicines summit: Wednesday, 16 October 1996, Old Parliament House, Canberra*, Australian Government, Canberra. https://catalogue.nla.gov.au/catalog/1838954

Devi S (2020) 'US public health budget cuts in the face of COVID-19', *The Lancet*, 20(4):415.

Doran E and Löfgren H (2013) 'Drug promotion in Australia: policy contestation and the tightening of regulation', *Australian Review of Public Affairs*, 11(2):19–41.

Dow A (2018, 3 April) 'Big pharma under fire for spruiking strong painkillers to doctors', *The Sydney Morning Herlad*, accessed 10 September 2024. https://www.smh.com.au/healthcare/big-pharma-under-fire-for-spruiking-strong-painkillers-to-doctors-20180403-p4z7ki.html

Dowden JS (2012) 'Critical appraisal: court in the act', *Australian Prescriber*, 35(2):38–39.

Dowling PJ (1997) *'A great deal of sickness': introduced diseases among the Aboriginal People of colonial Southeast Australia 1788–1900* [PhD thesis], Australian National University, accessed 20 May 2024. https://openresearch-repository.anu.edu.au/items/75a96cfd-3150–4e6b-81a0–28bc06900599

Dukes G, Braithwaite J and Moloney JP (2014) *Pharmaceuticals, corporate crime and public health*, Edward Elgar Publishing, Cheltenham.
Earl N and Smith A (directors) (2013) 'Episode 1' [television program], *The checkout* (season 1, episode 1), ABC Television, Sydney.
*Ego Pharmaceuticals Pty Ltd and Minister for Health and Ageing* (2012) AATA 210.
European Agency for the Evaluation of Medicinal Products (2003) *Mutual recognition agreements between the EU and the respective parties Australia, Canada, New Zealand and Switzerland: guide to the MRAs in operation*, European Agency for the Evaluation of Medicinal Products, accessed 20 March 2017. http://www.emea.europa.eu/Inspections/docs/0002203en.pdf
EUROPOL (European Union Agency for Law Enforcement Cooperation) (2020) *Pandemic profiteering: how criminals exploit the COVID-19 crisis*, EUROPOL, accessed 14 September 2024. https://www.europol.europa.eu/publications-events/publications/pandemic-profiteering-how-criminals-exploit-covid-19-crisis
Fabbri A, Grundy Q, Mintzes B, SwandaRi S, Moynihan R, Walkom E and Bero LA (2017) 'A cross-sectional analysis of pharmaceutical industry-funded events for health professionals in Australia', *BMJ Open*, 7(6):e016701.
Faunce T, Townsend R and McEwan A (2010) 'The Vioxx pharmaceutical scandal: Peterson v Merke Sharpe & Dohme (Aust) Pty Ltd (2010) 184 FCR 1', *Journal of Law and Medicine*, 18(1):38–49.
FDA (Food and Drug Administration) (2024) *Fraudulent Coronavirus disease 2019 (COVID-19) products*, FDA, accessed 13 July 2022. https://www.fda.gov/consumers/health-fraud-scams/fraudulent-coronavirus-disease-2019-covid-19-products
FDA Division of Anti-Inflammatory, Analgesic, and Ophthalmic Drug Products - *HFD-550* (1999) *Medical officer review: Vioxx (rofecoxib), NDA 21–042 (capsules) and NDA 21–052 (oral solution)*, FDA, accessed 6 August 2024. https://www.accessdata.fda.gov/drugsatfda_docs/nda/99/021042_52_vioxx_medr_P1.pdf
Ferguson A and Johnston E (2010, 27 February) 'The other drug war: the politics of big business', *The Sydney Morning Herald*, accessed 25 October 2016. https://www.smh.com.au/business/the-other-drug-war-the-politics-of-big-business-20100226-p8zi.html
Fickweiler F, Fickweiler W and Urbach E (2017) 'Interactions between physicians and the pharmaceutical industry generally and sales representatives specifically and their association with physicians' attitudes and prescribing habits: a systematic review', *BMJ Open*, 7(9):e016408.
Fischer K (2015) 'The influence of neoliberals in Chile before, during, and after Pinochet', in Mirowski P and Plehwe D (eds) *The road from Mont Pèlerin: the making of the neoliberal thought collective*, Harvard University Press, Harvard.
Fitzsimmons C (2003, 25 August) 'I was denied justice, says Pan boss', *The Australian*, accessed 4 July 2024. https://may.idm.oclc.org/login?url=https://www.proquest.com/newspapers/i-wasdenied-justice-says-pan-boss/docview/357656822/se-2?accountid=12309
Ford C (2013) 'Prospects for scalability: relationships and uncertainty in responsive regulation', *Regulation & Governance*, 7(1):14–29.
Foucault M (1977/1995) *Discipline and punish: the birth of the prison* (Sheridan A trans), Random House, New York.
Foucault M (1980) *Power/knowledge: selected interviews & other writings* (Gordon C trans), Pantheon Books, New York.
Foucault M (1982) 'The subject and power' (Sawyer L trans), *Critical Inquiry*, 8(4):777–795.
Foucault M (2000) *Power: essential works of Foucault, 1954–1984*, The New Press, New York.

Foucault M (2004) 'The crisis of medicine or the crisis of antimedicine?' (Knowlton EC, King WJ and O'Farrell C trans), *Foucault Studies*, 1:5–19.
Foucault M (2004/2007) *Security, territory, population: lectures at the Collège de France, 1977–78* (Burchell G trans), Picador, New York.
Foucault M (2008) *The birth of biopolitics: lectures at the Collège de France, 1978–1979* (Burchell G trans), Picador, New York.
Frauley J (2007) 'The expulsion of Foucault from governmentality studies: toward an archaeological-realist retrieval', in Frauley J and Pearce F (eds) *Critical realism and the social sciences: heterodox elaborations*, University of Toronto Press, Toronto.
Frauley J and Pearce F (2007) 'Critical realism and the social sciences: methodological and epistemological preliminaries', in Frauley J and Pearce F (eds) *Critical realism and the social sciences: heterodox elaborations*, University of Toronto Press, Toronto.
*Freedom of Information Act 1982* (Cth).
Friedman M (1951, 17 February) 'Neo-liberalism and its prospects', *Farmland*, 89–93, Hoover Institution Library & Archives, accessed 8 September 2024. https://miltonfriedman.hoover.org/objects/57816/neoliberalism-and-its-prospects?ctx=a71bbb42539de01eadd7a09c27f6a739c42f4966&idx=15
Friedrichs DO and Vegh Weis V (2021) 'COVID-19 and the US health care industry: towards a "critical health criminology" within state crime studies', *State Crime Journal*, 10(1):126–146.
Galligan B (1987) *Politics of the High Court: a study of the judicial branch of government in Australia*, University of Queensland Press, St Lucia.
Galvin R (2002) 'Disturbing notions of chronic illness and individual responsibility: towards a genealogy of morals', *Health: An Interdisciplinary Journal for the Social Study of Health, Illness and Medicine*, 6(2):107–137.
Garattini S and Bertele' V (2007) 'How can we regulate medicines better?', *British Medical Journal*, 335(7624):803–805.
Garside R (2013) 'Addressing social harm: better regulation versus social transformation', *Revista Crítica Penal y Poder*, (5):247–265.
Gide C (1898) 'Has co-operation introduced a new principle into economics?' (Foley CA trans), *The Economic Journal*, 8(32):490–511.
Gilbert JD, Musgrave IF, Hoban C and Byard RW (2014) 'Lethal hepatocellular necrosis associated with herbal polypharmacy in a patient with chronic hepatitis B infection', *Forensic Science International,* 241:138–140
Gill T (2014, 3 December) 'Clinical trials: TGA role' [conference presentation], *Australasian Ethics Network Conference Workshop*, Sydney, accessed 9 March 2024. https://www.tga.gov.au/sites/default/files/presentation-aen-clinical-trials-141203.pdf
Goddard MS (2014) 'How the pharmaceutical benefits scheme began', *Medical Journal of Australia*, 201(S1):S23–S25.
Goldacre B (2012) *Bad pharma: how drug companies mislead doctors and harm patients*, Fourth Estate, London.
Gordon N and Green P (2021) 'State crime, structural violence and Covid-19', *State Crime Journal*, 10(1):4–15.
Gøtzsche P (2013) *Deadly medicines and organised crime: how big pharma has corrupted healthcare*, Radcliffe Publishing, London.
Grabosky P (2017) 'Meta-regulation', in Drahos P (ed) *Regulatory theory: foundations and applications*, Australian National University Press, Canberra.
Gramsci A (1971/1992) *Selections from the prison notebooks* (Hoare Q and Nowell Smith G trans), International Publishers, New York.
Gramsci A (1975/1992) *Prison notebooks, Volume 1* (Buttigieg JA trans), Columbia University Press, New York.

Gray G and van Rooij B (2021) 'Regulatory disempowerment: how enabling and controlling forms of power obstruct citizen-based regulation', *Regulation & Governance*, 15(3):800–821.

Gunningham N (2011) 'Enforcing environmental regulation', *Journal of Environmental Law*, 23(2):169–201.

Haggan M (2018, 16 February) 'Ad pre-approvals for therapeutics stay. . . for now', *Australian Journal of Pharmacy*, accessed 21 February 2018. https://ajp.com.au/news/ad-pre-approvals-therapeutics-stay-now/

Haines F (2011) *The paradox of regulation: what regulation can achieve and what it cannot*, Edward Elgar Publishing, Cheltenham and Northampton.

Haines F (2016) 'Taming business? Understanding effectiveness in the control of corporate and white-collar crime', in Matthews R (ed) *What is to be done about crime and punishment? Towards a 'public criminology'*, Palgrave Macmillan, London.

Hales G (2024, 23 July) 'Decolonising global health' [podcast], *The Big Decolonisation Dialogue*, accessed 1 October 2024. https://open.spotify.com/episode/7aVMfpECOAbohpDuMYacSE?si=826e0302a42343d4

Hall L (2011, 26 March) 'Pan debacle yields further $67.5m payout', *The Sydney Morning Herald*, accessed 24 May 2018. https://www.smh.com.au/business/pan-debacle-yields-further-67–5m-payout-20110325–1c9vo.html

Hampton P (2005) *Reducing administrative burdens: effective inspection and enforcement*, HM Treasury, United Kingdom Government, accessed 21 April 2024. https://www.regulation.org.uk/library/2005_hampton_report.pdf

Hanrahan C, Elvery S, McGhee A and Liddy M (2017) 'Political donations: new data maps industries' web of influence', *ABC*, accessed 8 November 2018. http://www.abc.net.au/news/2017-02-09/political-donations-industry-dataset/8229192

Hansen J (2019, 13 January) 'The rise of big Suppla', *The Daily Telegraph*, accessed 11 November 2020. https://may.idm.oclc.org/login?url=https://www.proquest.com/newspapers/rise-big-suppla/docview/2166578767/se-2?accountid=12309

*Harrington, United States Trustee, Region 2 v. Purdue Pharma L. P. et al.*, 23–124 (2nd Cir, 2023). https://www.supremecourt.gov/search.aspx?filename=/docket/docketfiles/html/public/23–124.html

Harvey K and Dwyer J (2021, 14 June) *TGA lists first AUST L (A) herbal product, but where's the evidence?*, InSight+, MJA, accessed 26 July 2024. https://insightplus.mja.com.au/2021/21/tga-lists-first-aust-la-herbal-product-but-wheres-the-evidence/

Harvey K, Vickers M and Arnold BB (2021) 'Complementary medicines advertising policy Part II: unethical conduct in the Australian market after July 2018', *Australian Health Review*, 45(1):84–89.

Hayward CR (1998) 'De-facing power', *Polity*, 31(1):1–22.

*Health World Limited and Minister for Health and Ageing* (2013) AATA 388.

Hillyard P and Tombs S (2004) 'Beyond criminology?', in Hillyard P, Pantazis C, Tombs S and Gordon D (eds) *Beyond criminology: taking harm seriously*, Pluto Books, London.

Hobday L (reporter) (2012, 30 May) 'Diet pill avoids sanctions by changing its name' [radio transcript], *PM*, ABC Radio National, accessed 2 March 2017. http://www.abc.net.au/pm/content/2012/s3514707.htm

Holmes J (2005, 11 April) 'Total recall' [television transcript], *Four Corners*, accessed 16 October 2014. http://www.abc.net.au/4corners/content/2005/s1343195.htm

Horwitz RB (1986) 'Understanding deregulation', *Theory and Society*, 15:139–174.

Hughes WM (1921, 3 March) 'Creation of department of health', *Commonwealth of Australia Gazette*, No. 20, National Library of Australia, accessed 19 May 2024. https://trove.nla.gov.au/newspaper/article/232182037?searchTerm=%22Creation%20of%20Department%20of%20Health%22

Humphrys E (2019) *How labour built neoliberalism: Australia's accord, the labour movement and the neoliberal project*, Brill, Leiden and Boston.

Hutter BM (2006) *The role of non-state actors in regulation*, London School of Economics and Political Science, Centre for Analysis of Risk and Regulation (CARR), Discussion Paper No. 37, pp. 1–19.
*Immigration Restriction Act 1901* (Cth).
Industries Assistance Commission (1976) *Pharmaceutical and veterinary products: industries assistance commission report*, Commonwealth Government Printer, Canberra, accessed 8 July 2024. https://nla.gov.au:443/tarkine/nla.obj-2587288177
Industries Assistance Commission (1978) *Annual report 1977–78*, Australian Government Publishing Service, accessed 11 July 2024. https://nla.gov.au:443/tarkine/nla.obj-2720249077
Industries Assistance Commission (1986) *Pharmaceutical products*, Australian Government Publishing Service, Canberra, accessed 11 July 2024. https://nla.gov.au:443/tarkine/nla.obj-1746228494
Industry Commission (1996) *The pharmaceutical industry*, Australian Government Publishing Service, Canberra.
Institute for Safe Medication Practices (2015, 28 January) *A critique of a key drug safety reporting system*, Institute for Safe Medication Practices, accessed 14 January 2017. https://www.ismp.org/quarterwatch/drug-safety-reporting-system
INTERPOL (International Criminal Police Organization) (2020, 19 March) *Global operation sees a rise in fake medical products related to COVID-19* [media release], INTERPOL, accessed 15 September 2024. https://www.interpol.int/en/News-and-Events/News/2020/Global-operation-sees-a-rise-in-fake-medical-products-related-to-COVID-19
Ivec M, Braithwaite V, Wood C and Job J (2015) *Applications of responsive regulatory theory in Australia and overseas: update*, RegNet Occasional Paper 23, RegNet Research Paper No. 2015/72, Regulatory Institutions Network, Australian National University, SSRN, accessed 29 June 2016. https://papers.ssrn.com/sol3/papers.cfm?abstract_id=2586888
Jackson L (2001) 'Paying the price: has the pharmaceutical industry broken the scheme which delivers Australians cheap medicines?' [television transcript], *Four Corners*, ABC Television, accessed 18 February 2024. http://www.abc.net.au/4corners/stories/s248583.htm
Jessop B (1983) 'Accumulation, state, & hegemonic projects', *Kapitalistate*, 10/11:89–112.
Jessop B (1990) *State theory: putting the capitalist state in its place*, Polity Press, Cambridge.
Jessop B (2002) 'Liberalism, neoliberalism, and urban governance: a state-theoretical perspective', *Antipode*, 34(3):452–472.
Jessop B (2007) 'From micro-powers to governmentality: Foucault's work on statehood, state formation, statecraft and state power', *Political Geography*, 26(1):34–40.
Jessop B (2008) *State power: a strategic-relational approach*, Polity Press, Cambridge.
Jessop B (2010) 'Redesigning the state, reorienting state power, and rethinking the state', in Leicht KT and Jenkins JC (eds) *Handbook of politics: state and society in global perspective*, Springer, New York.
Jessop B (2012) 'Marxist approaches to power', in Amenta E, Nash K and Scott A (eds) *The Wiley-Blackwell companion to political sociology*, Blackwell Publishing, Chichester.
Jessop B and Sum NL (2006) 'Toward a cultural international political economy: poststructuralism and the Italian School', in de Goede M (ed) *International political economy and poststructural politics*, Palgrave Macmillan, Basingstoke.
Jordana J and Levi-Faur D (2004) *The politics of regulation: examining regulatory institutions and instruments in the governance age*, Edward Elgar, Cheltenham.
Joseph J (2002) *Hegemony: a realist analysis*, Routledge, London and New York.

Joseph J (2003) 'Re-stating hegemonic theory', *Journal of Critical Realism*, 2(1):127–137.
Joseph J (2004) 'Foucault and reality', *Capital & Class*, 28(1):143–165.
Joseph J (2006) 'Marxism, the dialectic of freedom and emancipation', in Dean K, Joseph J, Roberts JM and Wight C (eds) *Realism, philosophy and social science*, Palgrave Macmillan, Basingstoke and New York.
Joseph J (2010) 'The limits of governmentality: social theory and the international', *European Journal of International Relations*, 16(2):233–246.
Joseph J (2014) 'Combining hegemony and governmentality to explain global governance', *Spectrum: Journal of Global Studies*, 6(1):1–15.
Joseph J (2016) 'Governing through failure and denial: the new resilience agenda', *Millennium*, 44(3):370–390.
Joseph J (2017) 'The hegemony of governmentality: towards a research agenda', *All Azimuth: A Journal of Foreign Policy and Peace*, 6(2):5–18.
Joseph J (2018) 'Responsibilising through failure and denial: governmentality as double failure', in Ulbert C, Finkenbusch P, Sondermann E and Debiel T (eds) *Moral agency and the politics of responsibility*, Routledge, Abingdon and New York.
Joseph J (2024) 'Gramsci, post-Marxism and critical realism', in Carrol WK (ed) *The Elgar companion to Antonio Gramsci*, Edward Elgar Publishing, Cheltenham.
Jüni P, Nartey L, Reichenbach S, SteRchi R, Dieppe PA and Egger M (2004) 'Risk of cardiovascular events and rofecoxib: cumulative meta-analysis', *The Lancet*, 364(9450):2021–2029.
Katz D, Caplan AL and Merz JF (2010) 'All gifts large and small: toward an understanding of the ethics of pharmaceutical industry gift-giving', *The American Journal of Bioethics*, 10(10):11–17.
Kelly M, Kaye KI, Davis SR and Shenfield GM (2004) 'Factors influencing adverse drug reaction reporting in New South Wales teaching hospitals', *Journal of Pharmacy Practice and Research*, 34(1):32–35.
Khoury S (2018) 'Pesticideland: Brazil's poison market', in Bittle S, Snider L, Tombs S and Whyte D (eds) *Revisiting the crimes of the powerful: Marxism, crime and deviance*, Routledge, Abingdon and New York.
KPMG (1997) *Review of Therapeutic Goods Administration on behalf of the Department of Health & Family Services*, KPMG Management Consulting, Sydney. https://catalogue.nla.gov.au/catalog/1817021
Kramer R and Michalowski R (2006) 'The invasion of Iraq', in Michalowski R and Kramer R (eds) *State-corporate crime: wrongdoing at the intersection of business and government*, Rutgers, New Brunswick.
Kramer RC, Michalowski RJ and Kauzlarich D (2002) 'The origins and development of the concept and theory of state-corporate crime', *Crime & Delinquency*, 48(2):263–282.
Krumholz HM, Ross JS, Presler AH and Egilman DS (2007) 'What have we learnt from Vioxx?', *British Medical Journal*, 334(7585):120–123.
Lasslett K (2010a) 'Crime or social harm? A dialectical perspective', *Crime, Law and Social Change*, 54:1–19.
Lasslett K (2010b) 'Scientific method and the crimes of the powerful', *Critical Criminology*, 18(3):211–228.
Lasslett K (2015) 'The state at the heart of capitalism: Marxist theory and Foucault's lectures on governmentality', *Critical Sociology*, 41(4–5):641–658.
Law J (2006) *Big pharma: how the world's biggest drug companies control illness*, Constable & Robinson, London.
Legislative Council of Tasmania (1881) *Intercolonial Conference: minutes of proceedings of the Intercolonial Conference Held at Sydney, January 18, 1881*, Parliament of Tasmania, accessed 6 May 2024. https://www.parliament.tas.gov.au/resources/about-parliament/ppweb/pp1881

Leighton P and Wyatt T (2021) 'The case for studying social harm', in Davies P, Leighton PS and Wyatt T (eds) *The Palgrave handbook of social harm*, Palgrave Macmillan, Cham.

Lemke T (2001) 'The birth of bio-politics: Michel Foucault's lecture at the Collège de France on neo-liberal governmentality', *Economy and Society*, 30(2):190–207.

Lemke T (2002) 'Foucault, governmentality, and critique', *Rethinking Marxism*, 14(3):49–64.

Lemke T (2007) 'An indigestible meal? Foucault, governmentality and state theory', *Distinktion: Scandinavian Journal of Social Theory*, 8(2):43–64.

Lenz W (1962) 'Thalidomide and congenital abnormalities', *The Lancet*, 279(7219):45–46.

Leonardo Alves T, Martins de Freitas AF, Van Eijk ME and Mantel-Teeuwisse AK (2014) 'Compliance of disease awareness campaigns in printed Dutch media with national and international regulatory guidelines', *PLoS One*, 9(9):e106599.

Levi-Faur D (2005) 'The global diffusion of regulatory capitalism', *The Annals of the American Academy of Political and Social Science*, 598(1):12–32.

Lewandowsky S, Ecker UK, Seifert CM, Schwarz N and Cook J (2012) 'Misinformation and its correction: continued influence and successful debiasing', *Psychological Science in the Public Interest*, 13(3):106–131.

Lexchin J (1984) *The real pushers: a critical analysis of the Canadian drug industry*, New Star Books, Vancouver.

Lexchin J (2006) 'Relationship between pharmaceutical company user fees and drug approvals in Canada and Australia: a hypothesis-generating study', *Annals of Pharmacotherapy*, 40(12):2216–2222.

Li R, Curtis K, Zaidi ST, Van C and Castelino R (2020), 'Effect of the black triangle scheme and its online educational campaign on the quantity and quality of adverse drug event reporting in Australia: a time series analysis', *Expert Opinion on Drug Safety*, 19(6):747–753.

Lieb K and Scheurich A (2014) 'Contact between doctors and the pharmaceutical industry, their perceptions, and the effects on prescribing habits', *PLoS One*, 9(10):1–8.

Lloyd C (2012) 'Settler economies and Indigenous encounters: the dialectics of conquest, hybridisation and production regimes', in Fijn N, Keen I, Lloyd C and Pickering M (eds) *Indigenous participation in Australian economies II: historical engagements and current enterprises*, Australian National University E Press, Canberra.

Loder E, Godlee F, Barbour V and Winker M (2013) 'Restoring the integrity of the clinical trial evidence base', *British Medical Journal*, 364:1–2.

Löfgren H and de Boer R (2004) 'Pharmaceuticals in Australia: developments in regulation and governance', *Social Science & Medicine*, 58(12):2397–2407.

Low J, Hattingh L and Forrester K (2010) *Australian pharmacy law and practice*, Elsevier, Sydney.

Lundh A, Lexchin J, Mintzes B, Schroll JB and Bero L (2017) 'Industry sponsorship and research outcome', *Cochrane Database of Systematic Reviews*, art. no. MR000033. https://doi.org/10.1002/14651858.MR000033.pub3

MA (Medicines Australia) (2003) *Code of conduct 2003*, MA, accessed 24 September 2024. http://www.medicinesaustralia.com.au/public/annual_reports/Medicines%20Australia%202003%20Code%20of%20Conduct%20Report.pdf

MA (2006) *Code of conduct*, 15th edn, MA, accessed 1 March 2017. http://medicinesaustralia.com.au/pages/page16.asp

MA (2008) *Code of conduct annual report 2007–2008*, MA, accessed 24 September 2024. https://medicinesaustralia.com.au/code-of-conduct/code-of-conduct-reports/

MA (2009) *Code of conduct annual report 2008–2009*, MA, accessed 1 October 2024. http://medicinesaustralia.com.au/code-of-conduct/code-of-conduct-reports/annual-reports/

MA (2010) *Code of conduct complaints relating to activities directed at the general public January—March 2010*, MA, accessed 1 March 2017. https://medicinesaustralia.com.au/code-of-conduct/code-of-conduct-reports/quarterly-reports/

MA (2014) *Code of conduct annual report 2013–2014*, MA, accessed 24 September 2024. https://medicinesaustralia.com.au/code-of-conduct/code-of-conduct-reports/annual-reports/

MA (2015) *Code of conduct*, 18th edn, MA, accessed 7 November 2016. https://medicinesaustralia.com.au/code-of-conduct/code-of-conduct-current-edition/

MA (2016) *Annual report 2015–2016*, MA, accessed 1 October 2024. https://www.medicinesaustralia.com.au/publications/annual-reports/

MA (2018) *Code of conduct: annual report 2017–2018*, MA, accessed 24 September 2024. https://www.medicinesaustralia.com.au/code/lodging-responding-to-a-code-of-conduct-complaint/outcomes-of-complaints/

MA (2019) *Code of conduct*, 19th edn (Version 2), MA, accessed 28 July 2024. https://www.medicinesaustralia.com.au/code/about-the-code/code-of-conduct-current-edition/

MA (2020, 15 September) *Vale William Delaat AM* [media release], MA, accessed 27 July 2024. https://www.medicinesaustralia.com.au/media-release/vale-william-delaat-am/#:~:text=Mr%20Delaat%20served%20on%20the,of%20the%20Pharmaxis%20Audit%20Committee

MA (2024a) *Member company reports*, MA, 1 April—30 September 2015, accessed 28 July 2024 [internet archive]. https://web.archive.org/web/20160328082805/https://medicinesaustralia.com.au/code-of-conduct/education-events-reports/educational-event-reports/member-company-reports/

MA (2024b) *Healthcare professional consultant reports*, MA, 1 January 2015—30 September 2015, accessed 28 July 2024 [internet archive]. https://web.archive.org/web/20160330191518/https://medicinesaustralia.com.au/code-of-conduct/education-events-reports/healthcare-professional-consultant-reports/member-company-reports/

Ma P, Marinovic I and Karaca-Mandic P (2015) 'Drug manufacturers' delayed disclosure of serious and unexpected adverse events to the US Food and Drug Administration', *JAMA Internal Medicine*, 175(9):1565–1566.

Ma Y (2019, 15 July) 'Mundi said "no, no, no" to MA', *Pharma in Focus*, accessed 12 February 2024. https://pharmainfocus.com.au/newsPrint_m.asp?newsid=15164

Mackee N (2012, 4 June) 'Testosterone marketing "disease mongering" ', *MJA InSight*, accessed 26 March 2017. https://www.doctorportal.com.au/mjainsight/2012/21/testosterone-marketing-disease-mongering/

Mahon R (1979) 'Regulatory agencies: captive agents or hegemonic apparatuses', *Studies in Political Economy*, 1(1):162–200.

Makkai T and Braithwaite J (1994) 'Reintegrative shaming and compliance with regulatory standards', *Criminology*, 32(3):361–385.

Martin EA (2007) *Concise medical dictionary*, 7th edn, Oxford University Press, New York.

Marsden R (1999) *The nature of capital: Marx after Foucault*, Routledge, London and New York.

Mascini P (2013) 'Why was the enforcement pyramid so influential? And what price was paid?', *Regulation & Governance*, 7(1):48–60.

Mascini P and Van Wijk E (2009) 'Responsive regulation at the Dutch Food and Consumer Product Safety Authority: an empirical assessment of assumptions underlying the theory', *Regulation & Governance*, 3(1):27–47.

Matheson A (2016) 'Ghostwriting: the importance of definition and its place in contemporary drug marketing', *British Medical Journal*, 354:1–7.
McBride WG (1961) 'Thalidomide and congenital abnormalities', *The Lancet*, 278(7216):1358.
McDonald F, Duckett S and Campbell E (2023) 'Commonwealth power to improve access, quality, and efficiency of medical care: does section 51 (xxiiiA) of the Constitution limit politically feasible health policy options today?', *Federal Law Review*, 51(2):232–256.
McEwen J (2007) *A history of the therapeutic goods regulation in Australia*, TGA, Canberra.
McSwane JD (2022) *Pandemic, Inc.: chasing the capitalists and thieves who got rich while we got sick*, Simon & Schuster, New York.
Médecins Sans Frontières (2020, 27 March) *MSF calls for no patents or profiteering on COVID-19 drugs, tests, and vaccines in pandemic* [media release], Médecins Sans Frontières, accessed 14 September 2024. https://msfaccess.org/msf-calls-no-patents-or-profiteering-covid-19-drugs-tests-and-vaccines-pandemic
Meloni M (2023) 'An unproblematized truth: Foucault, biopolitics, and the making of a sociological canon', *Social Theory & Health*, 21(2):99–118.
Mendes P (1998) 'From Keynes to Hayek: the social welfare philosophy of the Liberal Party of Australia, 1983–1997', *Policy and Society*, 15(1):65–87.
Mignolo WD (2021) *The politics of decolonial investigations*, Duke University Press, Durham and London.
Mignolo WD and Walsh CE (2018) *On decoloniality: concepts, analytics, praxis*, Duke University Press, Durham and London.
Moore S, HiLl EM, Dyson L, Tildesley MJ and Keeling MJ (2022) 'Retrospectively modeling the effects of increased global vaccine sharing on the COVID-19 pandemic', *Nature Medicine*, 28(11):2416–2423.
Moran S (2008, 20 August) 'Drug body's bitter pill', *The Australian*, accessed 29 July 2016. https://www.theaustralian.com.au/news/health-science/drug-bodys-bitter-pill/news-story/c8cebb8baae0efcbd667536a232ea551?sv=14cc9098d8401fe73e7a36e5f4fc387
Morgan B and Yeung K (2007) *An introduction to law and regulation*, Cambridge University Press, New York.
Morgan MA, Dana J, Loewenstein G, Zinberg S and Schulkin J (2006) 'Interactions of doctors with the pharmaceutical industry', *Journal of Medical Ethics*, 32(10):559–563.
Moynihan R (2001, 23 February) 'Drug industry celebrates a win in the battle for benefits', *Australian Financial Review*, accessed 18 February 2024. https://www.afr.com/policy/health-and-education/drug-industry-celebrates-a-win-in-the-battle-for-benefits-20010223-j875l
NAA (National Archives of Australia) (2024) *Agency details for: CA 17*, NAA, accessed 19 May 2024. https://recordsearch.naa.gov.au/SearchNRetrieve/Interface/DetailsReports/AgencyDetail.aspx?reg_no=CA
National Academies of Sciences, Engineering, and Medicine (2020) *Decarcerating correctional facilities during COVID-19: advancing health, equity, and safety*, National Academies of Sciences, Engineering, and Medicine, accessed 8 July 2024. https://nap.nationalacademies.org/catalog/25945/decarcerating-correctional-facilities-during-covid-19-advancing-health-equity-and
*National Health Act (No. 72) 1959* (Cth).
*National Health (Medicines for Pensioners) Regulations* 1951.
National Organization of Social Security Claimants' Representatives (2024, 15 May) *Disability recipients nearly 7 times more likely to die of COVID-19, according to SSA data*, National Organization of Social Security Claimants' Representatives, accessed

13 September 2024. https://nosscr.org/disability-recipients-nearly-7-times-more-likely-to-die-of-covid-19-according-to-ssa-data/

Newman C and Kellam J (2004) 'Panic and pandemonium and the largest recall in the world: the Australian pan pharmaceuticals crisis', *Australian Product Liability Reporter*, 15(1):1–7.

Nicholas K (2003, 30 April) 'PM defends recall as drug boss claims witch-hunt', *Financial Review*, accessed 4 July 2024. https://www.afr.com/policy/health-and-education/pm-defends-recall-as-drugs-boss-claims-witch-hunt-20030430-jun2x

Nielsen VL and Parker C (2009) 'Testing responsive regulation in regulatory enforcement', *Regulation & Governance*, 3(4):376–399.

Nik-Khah E (2014) 'Neoliberal pharmaceutical science and the Chicago School of Economics', *Social Studies of Science*, 44(4):489–517.

Nita Y, Batty KT and Plumridge RJ (2005) 'Adverse drug reaction reporting: attitudes of Australian hospital pharmacists and doctors', *Journal of Pharmacy Practice and Research*, 35(1):9–14.

Offe C and Keane J (1984) *Contradictions of the welfare state*, Hutchinson, London.

O'Malley P (2016) 'Governmentality and the analysis of risk', in Burgess A, Alemanno A and Zinn J (eds) *Routledge handbook of risk studies*, Routledge, London.

Open letter, The People's Vaccine (2023) 'Never again', accessed 14 September 2024. https://app.box.com/s/016uv7schj901mdchxm64gt9ckli81w9

O'Reilly B (2016, 3 October) 'Advertising reform: watering down consumer protection', *MJA InSight*, accessed 20 December 2016. http://www.doctorportal.com.au/mjainsight/2016/38/advertising-reform-watering-down-consumer-protection/

Ostwald D, Cramer M and Albu N (2020) 'The global economic impact of the pharmaceutical industry', *WifOR Institute*, accessed 15 September 2024. https://www.wifor.com/en/download/the-global-economic-impact-of-the-pharmaceutical-industry-3/

Owoh K (1996) 'Fragmenting health care: the World Bank prescription for Africa', *Alternatives*, 21(2):211–235.

Oxfam International (2020) *Pandemic profits exposed*, Oxfam International, accessed 14 September 2024. https://www.oxfam.org/en/press-releases/pandemic-profiteers-exposed-report

Paolucci P (2003) 'Foucault's encounter with Marxism', *Current Perspectives in Social Theory*, 22:3–58.

Parella A, Braunack-Mayer A, Gold M, MarsHall H and Baghurst P (2013) 'Healthcare providers' knowledge, experience and challenges of reporting adverse events following immunisation: a qualitative study', *BMC Health Services Research*, 13(313):1–12.

Parker C (2006) 'The "compliance" trap: the moral message in responsive regulatory enforcement', *Law & Society Review*, 40(3):591–622.

Parker L, Karanges EA and Bero L (2019) 'Changes in the type and amount of spending disclosed by Australian pharmaceutical companies: an observational study', *BMJ Open*, 9(2):e024928.

Parliament of Australia (2013) *Code of conduct advisory group: members*, Parliament of Australia, accessed 29 July 2024. https://www.aph.gov.au/DocumentStore.ashx?id=6db900d9-d144–43b6-ae27-d67fd3570581

Pash C (2014, 6 March) '10 ex–Howard government ministers who moved into the lobbying industry', *Business Insider Australia*, accessed 1 April 2017. https://www.businessinsider.com.au/10-former-howard-government-politicians-who-moved-into-the-lobbying-industry-2014–3

Paul R (2017) 'Risk: new issue or new tool in regulation and governance research?', in Paul R, Mölders M, Bora A, Huber M and Münte P (eds) *Society, regulation and governance: new modes of shaping social change?*, Edward Elgar, Cheltenham.

PBS (Pharmaceutical Benefits Scheme) (2024) *Pharmaceutical benefits: fees, patient contributions and safety net thresholds*, PBS, accessed 8 July 2024. https://m.pbs.gov.au/healthpro/explanatory-notes/front/fee.html

Pearce F (2007) 'Bhaskar's critical realism: an appreciative introduction and a friendly critique', in Frauley J and Pearce F (eds) *Critical realism and the social sciences: heterodox elaborations*, University of Toronto Press, Toronto.

Pearce F and Tombs S (1990) 'Ideology, hegemony, and empiricism: compliance theories of regulation', *British Journal of Criminology*, 30(4):423–443.

Pearce F and Tombs S (1997) 'Hazards, law and class: contextualizing the regulation of corporate crime', *Social & Legal Studies*, 6(1):79–107.

Pearce F and Woodiwiss T (2001) 'Reading Foucault as a realist', in Lopez J and Potter G (eds) *After postmodernism: an introduction to critical realism*, The Athlone Press, London and New York.

Pemberton S (2015) *Harmful societies: understanding social harm*, Policy Press, Bristol.

Petersen A (1997) 'Risk, governance and the new public health', in Petersen A and Bunton R (eds) *Foucault, health and medicine*, Routledge, London.

*Peterson v Merck Sharpe & Dohme (Aust) Pty Ltd* (2010) FCR 180.

Pfizer (2010) 'Taking multiple medications for your heart?', *Agribusiness*, 10(1):21. https://issuu.com/executivemedia/docs/agribusiness

Pharm-a-Care Laboratories (2010, 12 May) 'Further amended statement of claim', Submission in *Pharmacare Laboratories Pty Ltd v Commonwealth of Australia*, NSD 1991/2008, accessed 8 November 2018. https://www.fedcourt.gov.au/law-and-practice/class-actions/class-actions/documents2/Further_Amended_StatementOfClaim.pdf

*Pharmaceutical Benefits Act 1944* (Cth).

*Pharmaceutical Benefits Act 1947* (Cth).

PIC/S (Pharmaceutical Inspection Convention and the Pharmaceutical Inspection Cooperation Scheme) (2009) *Guide to good manufacturing practice for medicinal products*, PIC/S, accessed 1 October 2024. http://tga.gov.au/industry/manuf-pics-gmp-medicines.htm#intro

Plehwe D (2015) 'Introduction', in Mirowski P and Plehwe D (eds) *The road from Mont Pèlerin: the making of the neoliberal thought collective*, Harvard University Press, Harvard.

Pons-Hernández M (2022) 'Power(ful) connections: exploring the revolving doors phenomenon as a form of state-corporate crime', *Critical Criminology*, 30(2):305–320.

Poor People's Campaign (2022) *A poor people's pandemic report: mapping the intersections of poverty, race and COVID-19*, Poor People's Campaign, accessed 18 July 2024. https://www.poorpeoplescampaign.org/pandemic-report/

Poulantzas N (1973) *Political power and social classes*, NLB, London.

Pradelle A, Mainbourg S, ProvEncher S, Massy E, Grenet G and Lega JC (2024) 'Deaths induced by compassionate use of hydroxychloroquine during the first COVID-19 wave: an estimate', *Biomedicine & Pharmacotherapy*, 171:116055. https://doi.org/10.1016/j.biopha.2023.116055

*Quarantine Act 1908* (Cth).

*R v Jain* (Unreported, District Court of New South Wales, Walmsley SC, 2 September 2005).

*R v Pan Pharmaceuticals Pty Ltd* (2008) NSWDC 221.

Rawlinson P (2017a) 'Immunity and impunity: corruption in the state-pharma nexus', *International Journal for Crime, Justice and Social Democracy*, 6(4):86–99.

Rawlinson P (2017b) 'Pharmatechnologies and the ills of medical progress', in McGuire MR and Holt TJ (eds) *The Routledge handbook of technology, crime and justice*, Routledge, Abingdon and New York.

Raymen T (2022) *The enigma of social harm: the problem of liberalism*, Routledge, Abingdon.

Reserve Bank of Australia (2024) *Recession*, Reserve Bank of Australia, accessed 7 July 2024. https://www.rba.gov.au/education/resources/explainers/

recession.html#:~:text=For%20instance%2C%20in%20Australia%20GDP,underemployment%20rate%20also%20increased%20sharply
Robertson J and Newby DA (2013) 'Low awareness of adverse drug reaction reporting systems: a consumer survey', *The Medical Journal of Australia*, 199(10):684–686.
Robinson R (2004, 17 April) 'The Pan pain', *The Herald Sun*, accessed 4 July 2024. https://may.idm.oclc.org/login?url=https://www.proquest.com/newspapers/panpain/docview/360521541/se-2?accountid=12309
Rodriguez LJ (2009) 'Regulatory decision making: structure and agency in the development of the organizational sentencing guidelines', *Crime, Law and Social Change*, 51(1):109–125.
Roe M (1976) 'The establishment of the Australian Department of Health: its background and significance', *Historical Studies*, 17(67):176–192.
Roknuzzaman AS, Sarker R, Nazmunnahar, Shahriar M, MosharRAfa RA and Islam MR (2024, 22 January) 'The WHO has declared COVID-19 is no longer a pandemic-level threat: a perspective evaluating potential public health impacts', *Clinical Pathology*. https://journals.sagepub.com/doi/full/10.1177/2632010X241228053.
Rose N and Miller P (1992) 'Political power beyond the state: problematics of government', *British Journal of Sociology*, 43(2):173–205.
Ross JS, Gross CP and Krumholz HM (2012) 'Pharmaceutical-industry sponsored research: promoting transparency', *American Journal of Public Health*, 102(1):72–80.
Rutledge P, Crookes D, McKinstry B and Maxwell SRJ (2003) 'Do doctors rely on pharmaceutical industry funding to attend conferences and do they perceive that this creates a bias in their drug selection? Results from a questionnaire survey', *Pharmacoepidemiology and Drug Safety*, 12(8):663–667.
Sah S and Fugh-Berman A (2013) 'Physicians under the influence: social psychology and industry marketing strategies', *Journal of Law, Medicine & Ethics*, 41(3):665–672.
Sansom L, Delaat W and Horvath J (2015) *Review of medicines and medical devices regulation: stage 2—report to the Minister for Health on the regulatory frameworks for complementary medicines and the advertising of therapeutic goods*, Department of Health, accessed 20 November 2015. http://www.health.gov.au/internet/main/publishing.nsf/Content/Expert-Review-of-Medicines-and-Medical-Devices-Regulation
Schwarcz D (2014) 'Preventing capture through consumer empowerment programs: some evidence from insurance regulation', in Carpenter D and Moss DA (eds) *Preventing regulatory capture: special interest influence and how to limit it*, Cambridge University Press, New York.
Scott C (2004) 'Regulation in the age of governance: the rise of the post-regulatory state', in Jordana J and Levi-Faur D (eds) *The politics of regulation: institutions and regulatory reforms for the age of governance*, Edward Elgar Publishing, Cheltenham.
Scott C (2017) 'The regulatory state and beyond', in Drahos P (ed) *Regulatory theory: foundations and applications*, Australian National University Press, Canberra.
Shirlow E and Faunce T (2009) 'Medical law reporter: recent legal developments and the authority of the Australian Therapeutic Goods Administration', *Journal of Law and Medicine*, 16(5):764–769.
Silk BJ, Scobie HM, Duck WM, Palmer T, Ahmad FB, Binder AM, Cisewski JA, Kroop S, Soetebier K, Park M, Kite-Powell A, Cool A, ConnElly E, Dietz S, Kirby AE, Hartnett K, Johnston J, Khan D, Stokley S, Paden CR, Sheppard M, Sutton P, RazzagHi H, Anderson RN, ThorNburg N, Meyer S, WomaCk C, Weakland AP, McMorrow M, Broeker LR, Winn A, Hall AJ, Jackson B, Mahon BE, and Ritchey MD (2023, 12 May) 'COVID-19 surveillance after expiration of the public health emergency declaration: United States, May 11, 2023', *MMWR Morbidity and Mortality Weekly Report*, 72:523–528. https://doi.org/10.15585/mmwr.mm7219e1

Sim J and Tombs S (2021, 27 January) 'The failings behind the UK's abysmal death toll', *The Guardian*, accessed 18 July 2024. https://www.theguardian.com/world/2021/jan/27/the-failings-behind-the-uks-abysmal-death-toll

Simoes EJ and Jackson-Thompson J (2023) 'The United States public health services failure to control the coronavirus epidemic', *Preventive Medicine Reports*, 31:1–5. https://doi.org/10.1016/j.pmedr.2022.102090

Simon WH (2010) 'Optimization and its discontents in regulatory design: bank regulation as an example', *Regulation & Governance,* 4(1):3–21.

Skerritt J (2019, 28 June) 'Regulatory requirements: clinical trials, access to unapproved medicines and the TGA registration process' [conference presentation], *University of Melbourne Research Forum*, Victoria, accessed 9 March 2024. https://arts.unimelb.edu.au/__data/assets/pdf_file/0012/3183789/John-Skerritt.pdf

Smith RJ, Bertilone C and Robertson AG (2016) 'Fulminant liver failure and transplantation after use of dietary supplements', *Medical Journal of Australia,* 204(1):30–32.

The Sydney Morning Herald (2003, 30 April) 'Tainted pills scandal explodes', *The Sydney Morning Herald*, accessed 4 July 2024. https://www.smh.com.au/national/tainted-pills-scandal-explodes-20030430-gdgok3.html

TGA (Therapeutic Goods Administration) (2000) *Submission to the Productivity Commission review of cost recovery by Commonwealth agencies*, Productivity Commission, accessed 21 May 2024. https://www.pc.gov.au/inquiries/completed/cost-recovery/submissions

TGA (2003, 21 January) *Travacalm original tablets blister pack: medicine recall*, TGA, accessed 3 July 2024. https://www.tga.gov.au/news/product-recalls/travacalm-original-tablets-blister-pack

TGA (2004) *Australian regulatory guidelines for prescription medicines*, TGA, accessed 8 November 2018. http://www.tga.gov.au/pmeds/argpm.htm

TGA (2006) *The Australian clinical trial handbook: a simple, practical guide to the conduct of clinical trials to international standards of Good Clinical Practice (GCP) in the Australian context*, TGA, accessed 9 March 2024. https://www.tga.gov.au/sites/default/files/clinical-trials-handbook.pdf

TGA (2008) *Commonwealth government settlement with Pan Pharmaceuticals and its former chief executive* [media release], TGA, accessed 26 June 2013. https://www.tga.gov.au/media-release/commonwealth-government-settlement-pan-pharmaceuticals-and-its-former-chief-executive

TGA (2010a) *Australian Public Assessment Report (AusPAR) for prescription medicines: guidance document*, TGA, accessed 19 August 2024. https://web.archive.org/web/20140702134810/http://tga.gov.au/industry/pm-auspar-guidance.htm#.U7QNonbP1qY

TGA (2010b, 8 October) *Sibutramine (Reductil) withdrawal in Australia*, TGA, accessed 12 April 2017. https://www.tga.gov.au/alert/sibutramine-reductil-withdrawal-australia

TGA (2010c, 10 December) *Thelin (sitaxentan): worldwide withdrawal*, TGA, accessed 12 April 2017. https://www.tga.gov.au/alert/thelin-sitaxentan-worldwide-withdrawal

TGA (2011a) *Regulation of therapeutic goods advertising in Australia*, TGA, accessed 8 July 2014. http://www.tga.gov.au/industry/advertising-regulation.htm

TGA (2011b, 2 December) *TGA to cancel four prescription pain-killers from 1 March 2012* [media release], TGA, accessed 19 August 2024. https://www.tga.gov.au/news/media-releases/tga-cancel-four-prescription-pain-killers-1-march-2012#:~:text=The

TGA (2011c) *TGA reforms: a blueprint for TGA's future*, TGA, accessed 8 November 2018. http://tga.gov.au/about/tga-reforms-blueprint.htm

TGA (2011d) *The Therapeutic Goods Administration's risk management approach to the regulation of therapeutic goods*, TGA, accessed 15 July 2014. http://tga.gov.au/industry/basics-regulation-risk-management.htm

TGA (2012a) *Advertising regulatory framework: options for reform*, TGA, accessed 6 June 2016. https://www.tga.gov.au/sites/default/files/advertising-framework-120529.pdf

TGA (2012b) *Evidence required to support indications for listed medicines (excluding sunscreens and disinfectants)* [consultation 1], TGA, accessed 23 February 2018. http://www.tga.gov.au/newsroom/consult-cm-evidence-listed-medicines-120423.htm

TGA (2012c) *Evidence required to support indications for listed medicines (excluding sunscreens and disinfectants)* [consultation 2], TGA, accessed 23 February 2018.

TGA (2012d) *Information about weight loss product 'Undoit'*, TGA, accessed 21 May 2018. https://www.tga.gov.au/information-about-weight-loss-product-undoit

TGA (2012e) *Nurofen: Reckitt Benckiser (Australia) Pty Ltd—Complaint no. 2011/06/001*, TGA, accessed 21 May 2018. https://www.tga.gov.au/advert-complaint/nurofen-reckitt-benckiser-australia-pty-ltd-complaint-no-201106001

TGA (2012f) *Risk management plans for prescription medicines*, TGA, accessed 26 June 2024. https://www.tga.gov.au/risk-management-plans-prescription-medicines

TGA (2012g) *TGA business plan 2012–2013*, TGA, accessed 27 May 2018. https://www.tga.gov.au/about-tga/corporate-information/tga-plans-and-reports/tga-business-plans

TGA (2012h) *The TGA regulatory framework*, TGA, accessed 8 July 2014. https://www.tga.gov.au/tga-regulatory-framework

TGA (2013a) *Consultation regulation impact statement: regulating the advertising of therapeutic goods to the general public*, TGA, accessed 8 November 2018. https://www.tga.gov.au/consultation/consultation-regulation-impact-statement-regulating-advertising-therapeutic-goods-general-public

TGA (2013b) *Guidance 8: product information*, TGA, accessed 15 February 2017. https://www.tga.gov.au/guidance-8-product-information

TGA (2013c) *Guidance on licensing/certification inspections*, TGA, accessed 13 July 2014. https://www.tga.gov.au/publication/guidance-licensingcertification-inspections

TGA (2013d) *Listed medicines: the role of Australia's medicines regulator*, TGA, accessed 20 November 2016. http://www.tga.gov.au/community-qa/listed-medicines-role-australias-medicines-regulator

TGA (2013e, 29 April) *Manufacturer inspections: a risk-based approach to frequency*, TGA, accessed 21 June 2016. https://www.tga.gov.au/manufacturerinspections riskbasedapproachfrequency

TGA (2013f) *Mechanisms to maintain the currency of approved product information (PI) and consumer medicine information (CMI): public consultation paper*, TGA, accessed 14 March 2017. http://tga.gov.au/newsroom/consult-opr-currency-pi-cmi-130513.htm

TGA (2013g) *Minor variations to registered prescription medicines: chemical entities*, TGA, accessed 11 April 2017. http://tga.gov.au/industry/pm-minor-variations-chemical.htm

TGA (2014a) *Australian requirements and recommendations for pharmacovigilance responsibilities of medicines*, TGA, accessed 24 November 2016. https://www.tga.gov.au/australian-requirements-and-recommendations-pharmacovigilance-responsibilities-sponsors-medicines

TGA (2014b) *Dextropropoxyphene: questions and answers*, TGA, accessed 19 August 2024. https://www.tga.gov.au/dextropropoxyphene-questions-and-answers

TGA (2014c) *Half-yearly performance report: January to June 2014*, TGA, accessed 2 August 2022. https://www.tga.gov.au/resources/publication/publications/half-yearly-performance-reports#y2014

TGA (2014d) *Half-yearly performance report: July to December 2014*, TGA, accessed 2 August 2022. https://www.tga.gov.au/resources/publication/publications/half-yearly-performance-reports#y2014

TGA (2014e) *Nurofen: Reckitt Benckiser (Australia) Pty Ltd—Complaints no. 2012-08-010 and 2012-10-024*, TGA, accessed 21 May 2018. https://www.tga.gov.au/advert-complaint/nurofen-reckitt-benckiser-australia-pty-ltd-complaints-no-2012-08-010-and-2012-10-024
TGA (2014f) *Submissions received: consultation regulation impact statement—regulating the advertising of therapeutic goods to the general public*, TGA, accessed 16 October 2014. https://www.tga.gov.au/submissions-received-consultation-regulation-impact-statement-regulating-advertising-therapeutic-goods-general-public
TGA (2014g) *Summary of fees and charges: at 1 July 2014*, TGA, accessed 9 July 2014. http://www.tga.gov.au/schedule-fees-and-charges
TGA (2014h) *TGA approach to disclosure of commercially confidential information (CCI)*, TGA, accessed 10 April 2017. https://www.tga.gov.au/resources/publication/publications/tga-approach-disclosure-commercially-confidential-information-cci
TGA (2014i) *TGA business plan 2014–2015*, TGA, accessed 21 February 2018. https://www.tga.gov.au/about-tga/corporate-information/tga-plans-and-reports/tga-business-plans
TGA (2015a, 15 April) *Australian Therapeutic Goods Advisory Council* [media release], TGA, accessed 22 September 2024. http://www.tga.gov.au/committee/australian-therapeutic-goods-advisory-council
TGA (2015b) *Half-yearly performance report: January to June 2015*, TGA, accessed 1 June 2016. https://www.tga.gov.au/half-yearly-performance-reports
TGA (2015c) *Mandatory requirements for an effective application: applicable for applications lodged from 1 July 2015*, TGA, accessed 26 June 2024. https://www.tga.gov.au/sites/default/files/mandatory-requirements–150701.pdf
TGA (2016a) *Australian regulatory guidelines for complementary medicines (ARGCM)*, TGA, accessed 8 November 2018. http://www.tga.gov.au/publication/australian-regulatory-guidelines-complementary-medicines-argcm
TGA (2016b) *Consultation: the regulatory framework for advertising therapeutic goods*, TGA, accessed 5 June 2017. https://www.tga.gov.au/sites/default/files/consultation-regulatory-framework-advertising-therapeutic-goods-november–2016.pdf
TGA (2016c, 30 September) *Manufacturer inspections: a risk-based approach to frequency*, TGA, accessed 29 November 2016. https://www.tga.gov.au/manufacturer-inspections-risk-based-approach-frequency
TGA (2016d) *Medicines and vaccines post-market vigilance: statistics for 2015*, TGA, accessed 24 November 2016. https://www.tga.gov.au/sites/default/files/medicines-and-vaccines-post-market-vigilance-statistics–2015.pdf
TGA (2016e) *Performance statistics report: July 2015 to June 2016*, TGA, accessed 2 August 2022. http://www.tga.gov.au/performance-statistics-report-july-2015-june-2016
TGA (2016f) *Reporting adverse events*, TGA, accessed 24 November 2016. https://www.tga.gov.au/reporting-adverse-events
TGA (2017a) *Annual performance statistics report: July 2016 to June 2017*, TGA, accessed 8 February 2018. https://www.tga.gov.au/annual-performance-statistics-report-july-2016-june-2017
TGA (2017b) *Cancellations*, TGA, accessed 21 June 2017. https://www.tga.gov.au/cancellations
TGA (2017c) *Consultation: strengthening monitoring of medicines in Australia—enhanced medicines vigilance*, TGA, accessed 21 March 2017. http://www.tga.gov.au/consultation/consultation-strengthening-monitoring-medicines-australia
TGA (2017d) *Pharmacovigilance responsibilities of medicine sponsors: Australian recommendations and requirements*, TGA, accessed 6 February 2018. https://www.tga.gov.au/publication/pharmacovigilance-responsibilities-medicine-sponsors

TGA (2018a) *Annual performance statistics report: July 2017 to June 2018*, TGA, accessed 2 August 2022. https://www.tga.gov.au/resources/publication/publications/annual-performance-statistics-report-july-2017-june-2018
TGA (2018b) *Cancellations requested by the sponsor: regulatory actions*, TGA, accessed 4 May 2018. https://www.tga.gov.au/ws-sc-index
TGA (2018c) *Compliance undertaking*, TGA, accessed 8 November 2018. http://www.tga.gov.au/compliance-undertaking
TGA (2018d) *Decisions in relation to complaints about advertisements (sorted by date)*, TGA, accessed 8 November 2018. https://www.tga.gov.au/decisions-relation-complaints-about-advertisements-sorted-date
TGA (2018e) *Listed complementary medicines*, TGA, accessed 26 June 2024. https://www.tga.gov.au/listed-complementary-medicines
TGA (2019a) *Annual performance statistics report: July 2018 to June 2019*, TGA, accessed 2 August 2022. https://www.tga.gov.au/resources/publication/publications/annual-performance-statistics-report-july-2018-june-2019
TGA (2019b, 20 December) *Mundipharma fined for misleading advertising of opioids to health professionals* [media release], TGA, accessed 10 August 2024. https://www.tga.gov.au/news/media-releases/mundipharma-fined-misleading-advertising-opioids-health-professionals#:~:text=Mundipharma
TGA (2019c) *Risk management plans for medicines and biologicals*, TGA, accessed 26 June 2024. https://www.tga.gov.au/publication/risk-management-plans-medicines-and-biologicals
TGA (2019d) *Therapeutic goods advertising compliance 2018–19 annual report*, TGA, accessed 27 July 2024. https://www.tga.gov.au/resources/publication/publications/therapeutic-goods-advertising-compliance-2018–19-annual-report#:~:text=The%20advertising%20requirements%20are%20specified,the%20advertising%20of%20therapeutic%20goods
TGA (2020a) *Annual performance statistics reports: 2019–20*, TGA, accessed 2 August 2022. https://www.tga.gov.au/resources/publication/publications/annual-performance-statistics-report-july-2019-june-2020
TGA (2020b) *Australian regulation of prescription medical products*, TGA, accessed 26 June 2024. https://www.tga.gov.au/australian-regulation-prescription-medical-products
TGA (2020c) *TGA regulatory framework*, TGA, accessed 1 October 2024. https://www.tga.gov.au/tga-regulatory-framework
TGA (2020d) *Restricted representations*, TGA, accessed 16 September 2024. https://www.tga.gov.au/how-we-regulate/advertising/restricted-and-prohibited-representations-advertising/restricted-and-prohibited-representations/restricted-representations
TGA (2021a) *Advertising to health professionals*, TGA, accessed 29 July 2024. https://www.tga.gov.au/resources/resource/guidance/advertising-health-professionals
TGA (2021b) *Australian clinical trial handbook: guidance on conducting clinical trials in Australia using 'unapproved' therapeutic goods*, TGA, accessed 9 March 2024. https://www.tga.gov.au/sites/default/files/australian-clinical-trial-handbook.pdf
TGA (2021c) *Performance statistics report: 2020–21*, TGA, accessed 2 August 2022. https://www.tga.gov.au/resources/publication/publications/annual-performance-statistics-report-july-2020-june-2021
TGA (2021d) *Therapeutic goods advertising compliance: annual report 2020–21*, TGA, accessed 16 September 2024. https://www.tga.gov.au/resources/publication/publications/therapeutic-goods-advertising-compliance-2022–23-annual-report
TGA (2022a) *Black triangle scheme information for sponsors*, TGA, accessed 13 August 2024. https://www.tga.gov.au/resources/resource/guidance/black-triangle-scheme-information-sponsors

TGA (2022b) *Compliance actions and outcomes*, TGA, accessed 4 September 2024. https://www.tga.gov.au/how-we-regulate/compliance-and-enforcement-hub/compliance-actions-and-outcomes#:~:text=In

TGA (2022c) *Compliance management*, TGA, accessed 22 August 2024. https://www.tga.gov.au/how-we-regulate/compliance-and-enforcement-hub/compliance-management

TGA (2022d) *Performance report 2021–22*, TGA, accessed 15 August 2024. https://www.tga.gov.au/resources/publication/publications/regulator-performance-report-july-2021-june-2022

TGA (2022e) *Therapeutic goods advertising compliance 2021–22 annual report*, TGA, accessed 27 July 2024. https://www.tga.gov.au/resources/publication/publications/therapeutic-goods-advertising-compliance-2021–22-annual-report

TGA (2023a) *Cost recovery implementation statement 2023–2024*, TGA, accessed 1 August 2024. https://www.tga.gov.au/sites/default/files/2023–12/cost-recovery-implementation-statement-2023–2024.pdf

TGA (2023b) *Performance report 2022–23*, TGA, accessed 9 August 2024. https://www.tga.gov.au/resources/publication/publications/therapeutic-goods-administration-performance-report-2022–23

TGA (2023c) *Therapeutic goods advertising compliance 2022–23 annual report*, TGA, accessed 27 July 2024. https://www.tga.gov.au/resources/publication/publications/therapeutic-goods-advertising-compliance-2022–23-annual-report

TGA (2024a, 13 March) *Caruso's Natural Health Pty Ltd fined for alleged offences relating to regulatory requirements* [media release], TGA, accessed 1 October 2024. https://www.tga.gov.au/news/media-releases/carusos-natural-health-pty-ltd-fined-alleged-offences-relating-regulatory-requirements

TGA (2024b) *The black triangle scheme*, TGA, accessed 13 August 2024. https://www.tga.gov.au/how-we-regulate/monitoring-safety-and-shortages/report-adverse-event-or-incident/report-adverse-events-medicines-and-biologicals/black-triangle-scheme#:~:text=they%20are%20identified.-,How%20the%20Black%20Triangle%20Scheme%20works,Product%20Information%20(PI)%20documents

TGA (2024c) *Database of adverse event notifications (DAEN): medicines*, TGA, accessed 2 August 2024. https://daen.tga.gov.au/medicines-search/

TGA (2024d) *Fees and charges: summary*, TGA, accessed 1 October 2024. https://www.tga.gov.au/how-we-regulate/fees-and-payments/summary-fees-and-charges/summary-fees-and-charges-applications-submitted-tga

TGA (2024e) *Infringement notices*, TGA, accessed 1 August 2024. https://www.tga.gov.au/how-we-regulate/compliance-and-enforcement-hub/compliance-actions-and-outcomes/infringement-notices

TGA (2024f) *Australian prescription medicine decision summaries*, TGA, accessed 1 October 2024. https://www.tga.gov.au/resources/auspmd

TGA (2024g) *Prescription medicines under evaluation*, TGA, accessed 1 October 2024. https://www.tga.gov.au/resources/prescription-medicines-under-evaluation

TGA (2024h) *Reformatting product information: frequently asked questions*, TGA, accessed 13 August 2024. https://www.tga.gov.au/resources/resource/guidance/reformatting-product-information-frequently-asked-questions

TGA (2024i) *Sponsors*, TGA, accessed 9 August 2024. https://www.tga.gov.au/resources/sponsor

TGA (2024j) *TARGIN oxycodone hydrochloride/naloxone hydrochloride 5/2.5 mg modified release tablets blister pack (156067)*, ARTG, TGA, accessed 10 September 2024. https://www.tga.gov.au/resources/artg/156067

TGA (2024k) *Undoit Plus (cancelled under 30(2)(ba), (c) and (e))*, TGA, accessed 19 August 2024. https://www.tga.gov.au/resources/cancellations-suspensions/undoit-plus-cancelled-under-302ba-c-and-e

TGA Expert Committee on Complementary Medicines in the Health System (2003) *Report to the parliamentary secretary to the Minister for Health and Ageing*, TGA, accessed 19 August 2024. http://www.tga.gov.au/docs/html/cmreport1.htm
The Thalidomide Trust (2017) *About thalidomide*, The Thalidomide Trust, accessed 9 May 2018. https://www.thalidomidetrust.org/about-us/about-thalidomide/
*Therapeutic Goods (Permissible Indications) Determination (No. 1)* 2021.
*Therapeutic Goods (Therapeutic Goods Advertising Code) Instrument* 2021.
*Therapeutic Goods Act 1966* (Cth).
*Therapeutic Goods Act 1989* (Cth).
*Therapeutic Goods Advertising Code 2015* (Cth).
*Therapeutic Goods Amendment (2016 Measures No. 1) Act 2017* (Cth).
*Therapeutic Goods Amendment (2017 Measures No. 1) Act 2018* (Cth).
*Therapeutic Goods Amendment (Pharmaceutical Transparency) Bill* 2013.
*Therapeutic Goods and Other Legislation Amendment (Vaping Reforms) Act 2024* (Cth).
*Therapeutic Goods Regulations 1990* (Cth).
*Therapeutic Substances Act 1953* (Cth).
*Therapeutic Substances Act 1959* (Cth).
*Therapeutic Substances Regulations* 1956.
Thomas DP (2004) 'The upsurge of interest in Indigenous health in the 1950s and 1960s', *Medical Journal of Australia*, 180(10):521–523.
Thynne T and Gabb GM (2016) 'Therapeutic drug safety for Indigenous Australians: how do we close the gap?', *The Medical Journal of Australia*, 204(1):16–17.
Tombs S (2012) 'State-corporate symbiosis in the production of crime and harm', *State Crime Journal*, 1(2):170–195.
Tombs S (2016) *Social protection after the crisis: regulation without enforcement*, Policy Press, Bristol.
Tombs S and Whyte D (2015) *The corporate criminal: why corporations must be abolished,* Routledge, Abingdon.
Toogoolawa Consulting Pty Ltd (2002) *Report of a review of advertising therapeutic products in Australia and New Zealand*, Toogoolawa Consulting, accessed 27 June 2024. https://www.tga.gov.au/sites/default/files/review-advertising-0211.pdf
Trading Economics (2024) *Australia government budget*, Trading Economics, accessed 10 July 2024. https://tradingeconomics.com/australia/government-budget#:~:text=source%3A
University of Sydney (2014) *Professor Emeritus Lloyd Sansom AO*, University of Sydney, accessed 27 July 2024. https://www.sydney.edu.au/content/dam/corporate/documents/university-archives/honorary-awards/s/professor-emeritus-lloyd-sansom-ao.pdf
US Centers for Medicare & Medicaid Services (2024, 9 October) *Historical*, US Centers for Medicare & Medicaid Services, accessed 14 September 2024. https://www.cms.gov/data-research/statistics-trends-and-reports/national-health-expenditure-data/historical
Vickers M and Harvey K (2021) 'Complementary medicines advertising policy Part I: unethical conduct in the Australian market before July 2018', *Australian Health Review*, 45(1):77–83.
Vitry A, Lexchin J and Mansfield PR (2007) 'Is Australia's national medicines policy failing? The case of COX-2 inhibitors', *International Journal of Health Services*, 37(4):735–744.
Vox (2021, 28 April) 'How rich countries are making the pandemic last longer' [video], *YouTube*, accessed 22 July 2024. https://www.youtube.com/watch?v=2ty2J0s2W0c
Walpen B (2004) *Die offenen feinde und ihre gesellschaft: eine hegemonietheoretische studie zur Mont Pèlerin Society*, VSA-Verlag, Hamburg.

Watego C, Singh D and Macoun A (2021) *Partnership for justice in health: scoping paper on race, racism and the Australian health system*, The Lowitja Institute Melbourne, accessed 1 October 2024. https://search.informit.org/doi/pdf/10.3316/informit.9781921889769

Watego C and Whop LJ (2022, 15 February) 'Racism is a public health crisis: but Black death tolls aren't the answer', *The Conversation*, accessed 1 October 2024. https://theconversation.com/racism-is-a-public-health-crisis-but-black-death-tolls-arent-the-answer-176453

Watson I (2017) 'Aboriginal laws and colonial foundation', *Griffith Law Review*, 26(4):469–479.

Watson I (2018) 'First nations, indigenous peoples: our laws have always been here', in Watson I (ed) *Indigenous peoples as subjects of international law*, Routledge, Abingdon & New York.

Wazana A (2000) 'Physicians and the pharmaceutical industry: is a gift ever just a gift?', *Journal of the American Medical Association*, 283(3):373–380.

Weaver DA (2024) 'The mortality experience of disabled persons in the United States during the COVID-19 pandemic', *Health Affairs Scholar*, 2(1):1–9.

WHO (World Health Organization) Regional Office for Europe (1978) *Declaration of Alma-Ata*. https://iris.who.int/handle/10665/347879

WHO (2024) *WHO COVID-19 dashboard*, WHO, accessed 18 July 2024. https://data.who.int/dashboards/covid19/deaths?n=c

Wong E (2001) *Regulation of medicines in Australia*, Legislative Council Secretariat, Government of Hong Kong, Hong Kong, accessed 7 December 2016. https://app7.legco.gov.hk/rpdb/en/uploads/2000–2001/RP/RP15_00–01_20010824_en.pdf

Woolhandler S, HimmelStein DU, Ahmed S, Bailey Z, Bassett MT, Bird M, Bor J, Bor D, Carrasquillo O, Chowkwanyun M, Dickman SL, FiSher S, GAffney A, Galea S, Gottfried RN, Grumbach K, Guyatt G, Hansen H, Landrigan PJ, Lighty M, McKee M, McCormick D, McGregor A, MiRza R, Morris JE, Mukherjee JS, Nestle M, Prine L, SAaDi A, Schiff D, Shapiro M, Tesema L and Venkataramani A (2021) 'Public policy and health in the Trump era', *The Lancet*, 397(10275):705–753.

World Health Assembly, 21 (1968) *Pharmaceutical advertising*, World Health Organization. https://iris.who.int/handle/10665/91190

Wright EJ (2023) 'Decolonizing zemiology: outlining and remedying the blindness to (post) colonialism within the study of social harm', *Critical Criminology*, 31(1):127–144.

W't Jong G, Stricker BHC and Sturkenboom MC (2004) 'Marketing in the lay media and prescriptions of terbinafine in primary care: Dutch cohort study', *British Medical Journal*, 328(7445):931.

Yeung K (2004) *Securing compliance: a principled approach*, Hart Publishing, Oxford.

Yuan HC (2020) *Optimising written medicine information for prescription medicines* [PhD thesis], University of Sydney, accessed 13 August 2024. https://ses.library.usyd.edu.au/handle/2123/23676

# Index

Page numbers in *italic* indicate a figure, and page numbers in **bold** indicate a table on the corresponding page. Numbers followed by n refer to a note.

FSC
www.fsc.org
MIX
Papier | Fördert
gute Waldnutzung
FSC® C083411

Kolibri 360 GmbH
Ferdinand-Jühlke-Straße 7
99095 Erfurt, Deutschland
produktsicherheit@kolibri360.de